IDEA MAGAZINE FOR TEACHERS®

The MAILBOX®

2014–2015 YEARBOOK

The Education Center, LLC
Greensboro, North Carolina

The Mailbox® 2014–2015 Preschool Yearbook

Managing Editor, *The Mailbox* Magazine: Kimberly A. Brugger

Editorial Team: Becky S. Andrews, Diane Badden, Kimberley Bruck,
Karen A. Brudnak, Pam Crane, Chris Curry,
Tazmen Fisher Hansen, Marsha Heim, Lori Z. Henry,
Troy Lawrence, Tina Petersen, Gary Phillips (COVER ARTIST), Mark Rainey,
Rebecca Saunders, Sharon M. Tresino

ISBN 978-1-61276-527-3
ISSN 1088-5536

©2015 The Education Center, LLC, PO Box 9753, Greensboro, NC 27429-0753

Printed in the United States of America.

The Mailbox® Yearbook
PO Box 6189
Harlan, IA 51593-1689

Look for *The Mailbox® 2015–2016 Preschool Yearbook* in the summer of 2016. The Education Center, LLC, is the publisher of *The Mailbox*®, *Teacher's Helper*®, and *Learning*® magazines, as well as other fine products. Look for these wherever quality teacher materials are sold, call 866.477.4273, or visit TheMailbox.com.

HPS260603

Contents

Departments

Features

Book Units

Center Units

Literacy Units

Math Units

Teacher Resource Units

Thematic Units

Index

Arts & Crafts for Little Hands

Arts & Crafts
for Little Hands

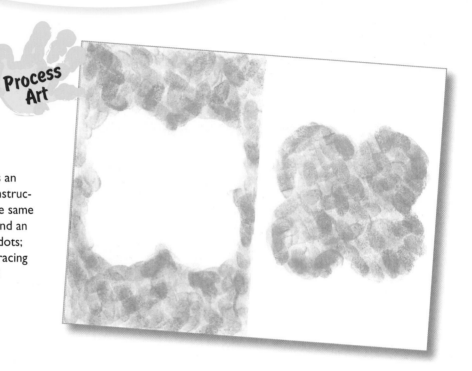

Process Art

Pointer Pointillism

All you need for this dotted artwork is an ink pad and your fingertip! Fold white construction paper in half card-style; then trace the same stencil on each half. Using your fingertip and an ink pad, fill the inside of one tracing with dots; then fill the space around the remaining tracing with dots. Simply beautiful, inside and out!

Janet Boyce
Tomball, TX

Process Art

Apple Art

Making this super apple craft reinforces the concept of circles! Dip one end of a cardboard tube in red paint and press it repeatedly on a sheet of construction paper. When the paint is dry, cut an apple shape from the paper. Next, cut a slit in the apple and tape a worm cutout so it's peeking through the slit.

Suzanne Moore
Tucson, AZ

Arts & Crafts
for Little Hands

Stained Glass Leaves

To make one of these fabulous leaf projects, cut a leaf pattern from card stock. Then attach a piece of clear Con-Tact paper to one side. Press colorful leaves onto the Con-Tact paper and then place a second piece over the leaves. These projects look great displayed in a window!

Angela Stup
Four Seasons Learning Center
Hampstead, MD

This keepsake tree
Will remind you of fall
And of me as well
When I'm no longer small!

A Keepsake Tree

Crumple colorful tissue paper squares and glue them to a twig. Press air-drying clay into a small clay or plastic pot. Then push the twig into the clay. To complete the project, attach a copy of the poem shown to the pot. What a lovely fall gift!

Adrieana Olabi
Salam Nursery
Dubai, United Arab Emirates

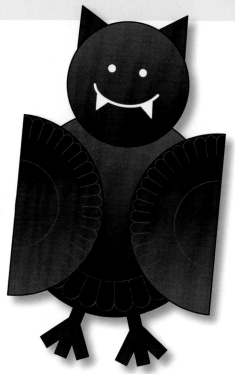

Circle Bat

This cute little bat is made from three circles! To make one, paint two paper plates black. Cut one plate in half and then glue the halves to the whole plate to make wings. Next, use a white crayon or gel pen to draw eyes and a mouth with fangs on a black construction paper circle (head). Attach black construction paper triangles (ears) to the top of the head. Then glue the head to the project. If desired, attach black paper strip legs and feet as well.

Mary Robles
Portland, OR

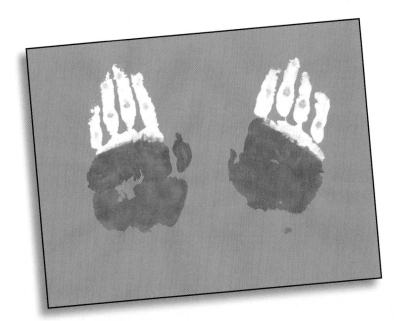

Handy Corn

Before making this project, study a piece of candy corn and note that it has yellow, orange, and white stripes. Next, paint a hand with yellow, orange, and white stripes so it resembles a piece of candy corn. Press it on a sheet of paper. Then wash your hand and repeat the process with the second hand.

Rose M. Russell
The Bluffs School
Jupiter, FL

Process Art

Guess the Print!

Gather fall items that have a variety of textures, such as hay, gourds, leaves, corn, and pinecones. Take a photo of each object. Prepare several shallow containers of paint. Have each child choose an object, dip it in the paint, and then press, drag, and tap it on a sheet of paper. (Hint: jot down the name of the item chosen on the backside of each project.) When the projects are dry, attach a printout of the corresponding photo to the back of each paper. Then bind the papers together to make a book! Students guess the fall object used to make the print. Then they check their answer by flipping the page and looking at the photo.

Danielle Lockwood
Colchester, CT

Cooperative Artwork

Musical Chairs Painting

This unique and fun project will be a hit with your little ones! Place a few sheets of paper at a table and provide a variety of paints and painting tools. Have each child write his name on his paper; this will be the paper he takes home. Play music and have little ones walk around the table. Stop the music and then prompt each child to stand in front of a sheet. Have him use one of the utensils to add to a friend's painting. After a few moments, start the music again. Continue for several rounds until each child has a masterpiece to take home!

Kristen Peterson
Butterfly Hill Nature Preschool
Alexandria, MN

Arts & Crafts
for Little Hands

Process Art

Hanukkah Candles

These candles look lovely on a wall display with a Hanukkah-themed border! To make one, get a strip of white paper and make two flame-shaped Con-Tact covering cutouts. Rub a white candle on the paper. Then watercolor over the rubbings, noticing how the wax resists the paint. Set the paper aside. Next, remove the backing from one of the flame cutouts. Then press red and orange tissue paper pieces onto the sticky surface. Remove the backing from the second cutout and place it over the first one, sandwiching the tissue paper between them. Trim the flame as needed. Finally, attach the flame to the candle.

Missy Goldenberg
Beth Shalom Nursery School
Overland Park, KS

Shiny Snowflakes

The forecast calls for flurries of flakes when you try this art project! Give each child a piece of aluminum foil and have him lay it shiny side up. Have the child dip the end of a thread spool (resembling a wagon wheel) into white paint. Then have him press the spool onto the foil to make prints. Have him repeat the process, making prints with blue and purple paint too. What a gorgeous snowfall!

Barb Stefaniuk
Kerrobert Tiny Tots Playschool
Kerrobert, Saskatchewan, Canada

Santa Binoculars

These handy binoculars are the perfect thing to use when looking for signs of Santa! To make one, paint two small cardboard tubes red. Press the tubes together and put a line of glue where they meet. Then hold them in place with a spring-style clothespin. Next, squeeze a square of white glue in the middle of a black paper strip and sprinkle glitter over the glue. Allow the paint and glue to dry. Then glue cotton batting around one end of the tubes and the black strip around the other end.

For extra fun, place holiday ribbon, tinsel, and pieces of wrapping paper on trees and bushes near your school. Then take little ones outside for a walk with their binoculars and help them find the signs of Santa! Collect the clues as you go.

Judy Legendre, Learning Express, Lakehurst, NJ

Angel Cutout Craft

fold

Materials:
9" x 12" sheet of white construction paper
3" flesh-tone construction paper circle (head)
white construction paper (for handprints)
small star cutout (or wooden star)
half a gold pipe cleaner
yarn

shallow pan of yellow paint
gold glitter
crayons
tape
glue

Setup:
Fold the 9" x 12" paper in half lengthwise. Then use the guide shown to make a body cutout.

Steps:
1. Draw a face on the head and then glue on yarn hair.
2. Shape the pipe cleaner half so it resembles a halo. Then tape the halo to the back of the head.
3. Glue the head to the body.
4. Attach the star to one end of a piece of yarn. Then attach it to the back of the project so that the star shows in the opening.
5. Make yellow handprints (wings) on the white construction paper. Then sprinkle glitter over the wet paint. When the paint is dry, cut out the wings and attach them to the project.

Mary Ann Craven
Fallbrook United Methodist Preschool and Kindergarten
Fallbrook, CA

Rudolph's Bright Nose

To make a reindeer, arrange three 1" x 9" strips of brown construction paper on a sheet of green construction paper as shown. Attach two sticky dots for Rudolph's eyes. Add pupils with a black marker. Squeeze a blob of white glue where Rudolph's nose should be and then sprinkle on red glitter. Shake off the excess and allow the glue to dry.

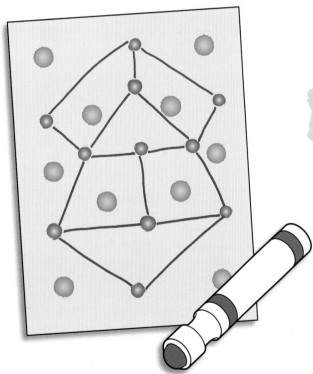

Process Art

Dot-to-Dot Design

Dabble in dot-to-dot art with this bingo dauber activity. Make dots on the paper with several bingo daubers. Use a marker to connect the dots. Use crayons to add details as desired.

Candy Cane

Shake, Rattle, and Roll!

Roll out this painting technique, and you'll have a group of grinning preschoolers on your hands! You'll also have an assortment of seasonal project possibilities. All you need is tempera paint, a golf ball, a nonbreakable transparent container with a flat bottom and a snug-fitting lid, and white construction paper cut to fit inside the container. Lay the paper inside the container, spoon about three dollops of tempera paint (same or different colors) onto the paper, drop in the golf ball, and snap on the lid. Then grasp the container with both hands and steer the golf ball through the paint by carefully tilting, shaking, and swaying the container. When a desired effect is achieved, remove the artwork from the container and set it aside to dry. This is so much fun!

Nancy Goldberg—3-Year-Olds
B'nai Israel Schilit Nursery School
Rockville, MD

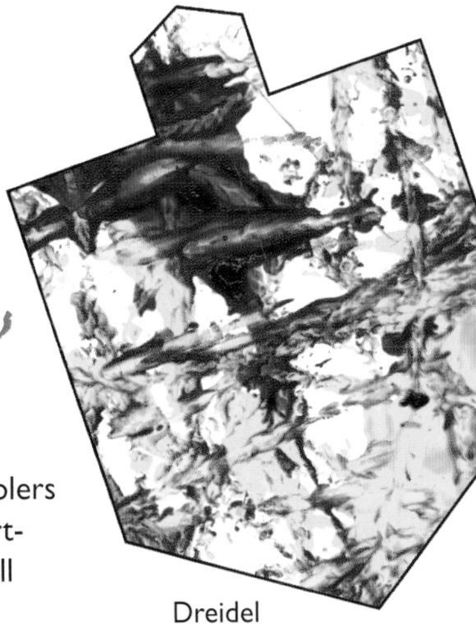

Dreidel

Wreath

Unity Cup

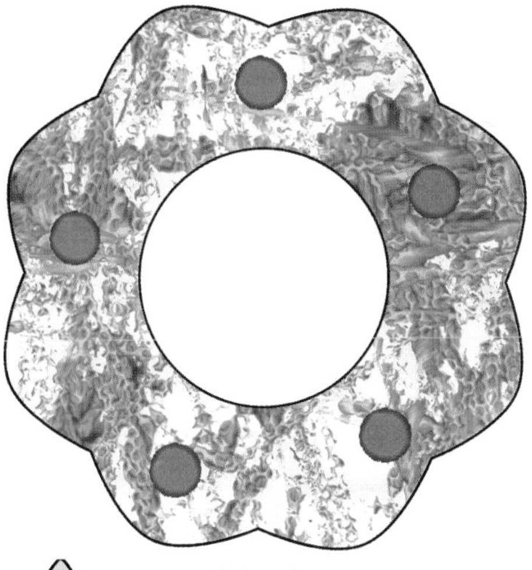

Star of David

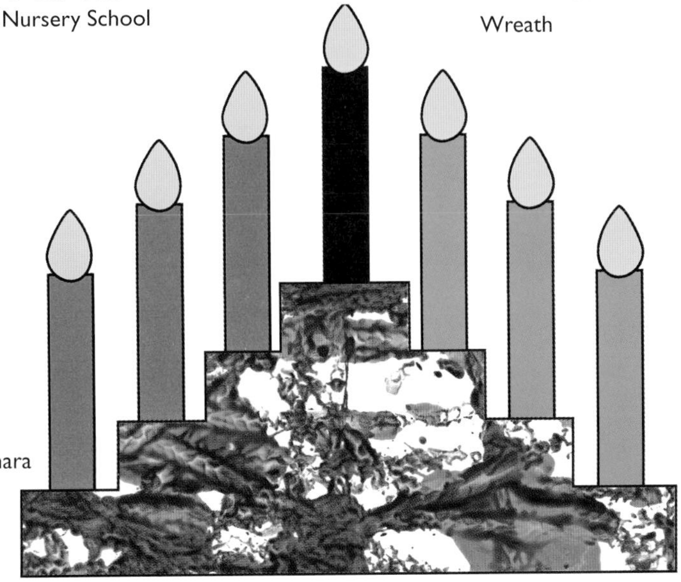

Kinara

Balloon Print Snowman

Place white paint in a tray. Blow up three balloons, making them different sizes. Press the large balloon into the paint and then make a print on a blue sheet of paper. Repeat the process with the medium balloon and the small balloon so the prints resemble a snowman. Next, cut or tear pieces of construction paper to make a hat, eyes, buttons, and any other desired features or accessories. Then glue the pieces to the snowman. After the project, dispose of the balloons properly.

Lysette Cukar
Our Lady of Angels Preschool
Burlingame, CA

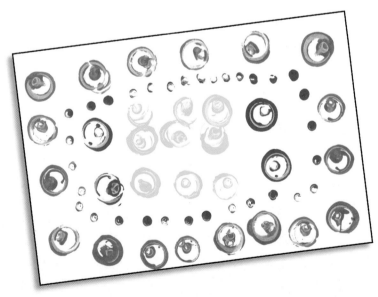

Baby Bottle Painting

Baby bottles make easy painting tools for little hands, and the end result is unique! Gather baby bottles (with nipples attached). For each bottle, set out a different color of paint in a shallow container. Dip a bottle (nipple end) into a dish of paint. Then press the nipple onto the paper. (Depending on how hard you press, you can vary the design that results.)

Lisa Toler
Stillwater Academy
Logansport, IN

Arts & Crafts
for Little Hands

Handsome Penguins

This simple craft is perfect for wintertime! Make a black oval cutout (body), a smaller white oval cutout (belly), two white circle cutouts (eyes), and an orange triangle cutout (beak). Add pupils to the eyes and then glue the parts together as shown. Next, make orange handprints on a sheet of paper. When the paint is dry, cut out the handprints and attach them to the penguin so they resemble feet. What a cute little craft!

Megan Taylor
Glenn Heights, TX

Process Art

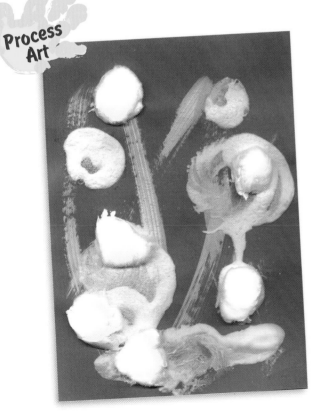

So Snowy!

To make this winter masterpiece, brush diluted white paint over a large sheet of construction paper using sweeping motions. Next, use cotton balls to dab and spread a mixture of equal parts nonmentholated shaving cream and white glue onto the paper. Leave the cotton balls attached to the paper. Finally, sprinkle sea salt over the artwork.

Jane Mandia
Little Friends Preschool
Marlboro, NY

My Mailbox

This lovely mailbox is perfect for holding valentines at a class party! To make one, line up a paper plate and plate half so the insides are together as shown. Then punch holes along the plate half's edge, going through both plates. Next, decorate the inside of the full plate and the outside of the half plate with markers, crayons, or paint as desired. Write your name on the plate half. Then line the pieces up again so the insides are together and lace them in place with yarn. Finally, punch a hole at the top of the project and add a yarn hanger.

Janet Boyce
Hinojosa Early Childhood and Pre-Kindergarten Center
Houston, TX

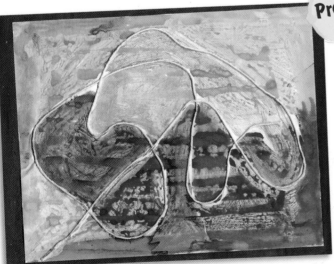

Process Art

String Squiggle Thing

Apply a thick layer of glue stick to a sheet of white copy paper. Then press a length of string onto the glue, overlapping the string as desired. Allow the glue to dry. Then brush watercolors in the spaces created by the string. If desired, mount the finished painting on a 9" x 12" sheet of black construction paper.

Janet Boyce

Arts & Crafts
for Little Hands

Lucky Foam

Process Art

This St. Patrick's Day activity is big on foamy fun! Mix equal parts of white glue and shaving cream. Then gently mix a few drops of green food coloring into the mixture. Spread some of the mixture on a piece of green tagboard and then press shamrock cutouts and St. Patrick's Day confetti into the foam. Finally, sprinkle gold glitter over the project. Allow several days for the lucky foam to dry.

C. Welwood
Learning Experience
Calgary, Alberta, Canada

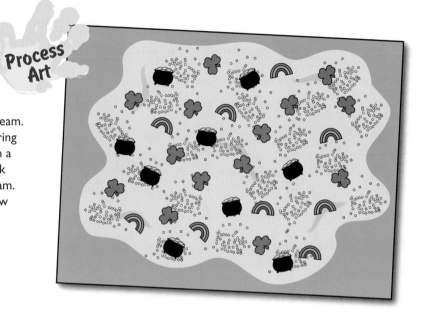

Process Art

Rainbow Splash!

This simple process art uses supplies from the kitchen! To make this masterpiece, brush a layer of corn syrup over a sheet of paper. Then squeeze drops of food coloring onto the corn syrup. The colorful bursts will look lovely! Allow a few days for the project to dry.

Darlene Taig
Willow Creek Cooperative Preschool
Westland, MI

Sticky Flowers

To make this lovely flower garden, attach a variety of colorful sticky dots and hole reinforcers to a light green sheet of paper. Then use markers to add petals, stems, and leaves to transform the page into a flower garden! What a simple and fun craft!

Janet Boyce
Hinojosa Early Childhood and Pre-Kindergarten Center
Houston, TX

"Egg-cellent" Eggs!

The patterns on this egg are made from bulletin board border! Make a copy of the egg pattern on page 23. Then place a piece of bulletin board border on the egg and trace it. Do this several times. Then color in the spaces between the lines with chalk. If desired, spray the chalk with a fixative to prevent smearing. (The fixative is for teacher use only.) Then cut out the egg and glue it to a sheet of black construction paper.

Janet Boyce

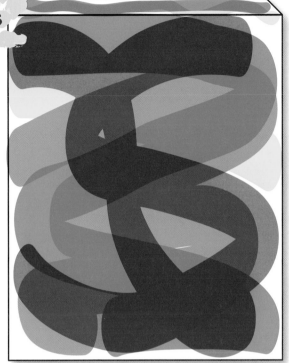

Process Art

From Box to Canvas

Spotlight Earth Day with this project that transforms trash into three-dimensional art! Get an empty cereal box and paint it white. (The white paint will help subsequent layers of paint stand out more.) When the white paint is completely dry, put several blobs of colorful paint on the box. Then use a plastic card to drag and spread the paint all over the box.

Heather A. Eades
Sunnycrest Christian Academy
Golden, CO

Process Art

Paint and Roll

In advance, wrap Bubble Wrap cushioning material around a large cardboard tube and then secure it in place with staples or tape. Next, paint a design on the Bubble Wrap. Then roll the tube over a sheet of construction paper. If desired, add more paint to the Bubble Wrap and repeat the process. The result is a colorful process art masterpiece!

Suzanne Moore
Tucson, AZ

Arts & Crafts
for Little Hands

Honey Drizzle

To make this easy process art, tint clear gel glue yellow so it resembles honey. Then drizzle the honey on a sheet of yellow paper. (If desired, put the honey in a small disposable cup and then use a craft stick to drizzle it.) When a desired effect is achieved, set the painting aside to dry. Once dry, attach small bee stickers to the page (or draw small bees).

Janet Boyce
Hinojosa Early Childhood and Pre-Kindergarten Center
Houston, TX

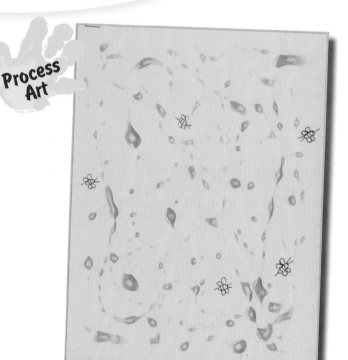

Process Art

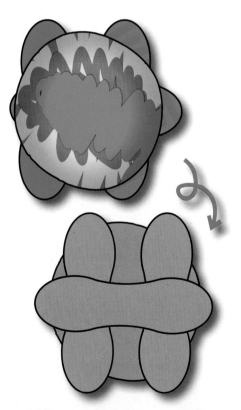

Rock Turtle

Get a small smooth rock. Then glue wooden ice cream spoons to the rock so it resembles a turtle with a head, four legs, and a tail. Let the glue dry. Then paint the turtle as desired. This cute little project makes a nice gift!

Cindy Laskowsky
New Adventures Child Development Center
Prescott, AZ

Streamer Shimmers

Process Art

Materials for one:
aluminum foil
pieces of crepe paper streamer
wide foam brush
diluted glue

Art process:
1. Brush glue on the foil.
2. Lay a piece of streamer on the glue and press it in place.
3. Repeat Steps 1 and 2 as desired.

Filling Father's Shoes

Lace up this special magnetic picture frame to fill fathers' hearts with joy!

No one could ever fill Dad's shoes!

Love, Addie

Supplies:
poster board shoe (pattern on page 24)
small photograph of the child
self-adhesive magnetic tape
12" length of yarn
hole puncher
tape
markers
scissors

Setup:
Tape each end of the yarn to make a shoelace. Hole-punch six holes in the shoe cutout. Program the shoe with the message shown. Cut an opening sized to fit the photograph.

Steps:
1. Thread the yarn through the holes. *(Tie a bow.)*
2. Write your name on the shoe cutout.
3. Decorate the shoe as desired.
4. Tape your photograph to the back of the shoe so it shows through the opening.
5. Attach magnetic tape to the back of the shoe.

Art Journaling With Your Little Ones!

Paint and Print

Materials:

tray or cookie sheet
piece of Bubble Wrap cushioning material
paper

paint
large paintbrush
fine-tip permanent marker

Steps:

1. Paint on the tray, quickly applying the paint.
2. Ball up the Bubble Wrap cushioning material and press it randomly on the paint to add texture.
3. Press the paper on the paint and rub it with your hand. Remove the paper and allow it to dry.
4. Write (or dictate) about something that happened that day or your current feelings.

Stencil and Spritz

Materials:

stencils
paint
spray bottle with diluted paint

sponge
paper

Steps:

1. Place a stencil on your paper. Use a sponge to dab paint on the stencil. Remove the stencil.
2. Repeat the process with a second stencil and a different color of paint.
3. Spritz the paper with paint. Allow the paint to dry.
4. Write (or dictate) about something that happened that day or your current feelings.

Consider making several pieces of journaled process art with your little ones. Then bind the artwork together into a completed journal!

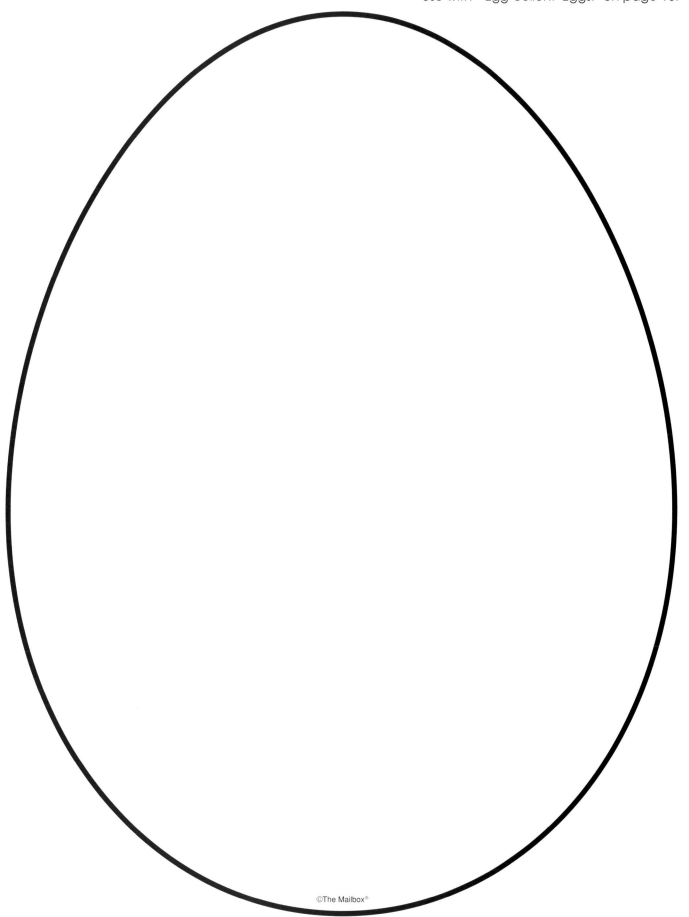

Egg Pattern
Use with "'Egg-cellent' Eggs!" on page 18.

©The Mailbox®

Shoe Pattern
Use with "Filling Father's Shoes" on page 21.

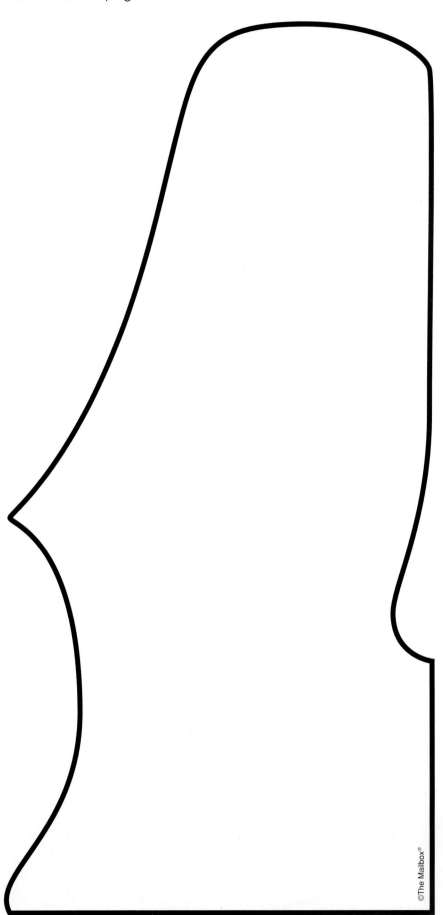

©The Mailbox®

BUSY KIDS®

Busy Kids®

Fine- and Gross-Motor Activities for Developing Little Muscles and Big Muscles

Fine motor

Bath Mat Fun!

Purchase an inexpensive bath mat with suction cups on the bottom. Place the bath mat so that the suction cup side is up and set play dough nearby. A child pinches off a piece of play dough and rolls it in his hands to form a small ball. Then he sets the ball on a suction cup. He continues as time permits.

Elytta Durkee
Peace Lutheran Preschool
Sun Prairie, WI

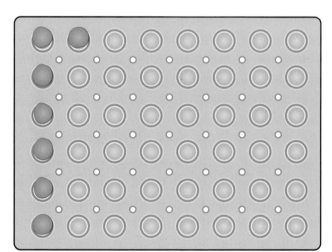

Gross motor

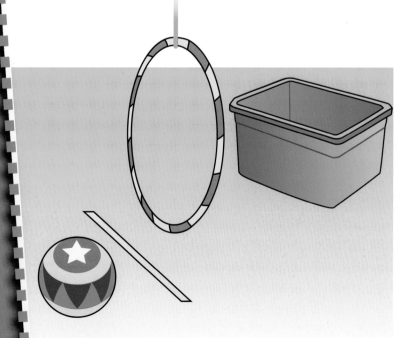

Through the Hoop

Suspend a large plastic hoop. Attach a length of tape close to the hoop and provide a beach ball. On the other side of the hoop, place a large tub. A child stands on the line and gently tosses the ball through the hoop and into the tub. He retrieves the ball and repeats the activity.

Marie E. Cecchini
West Dundee, IL

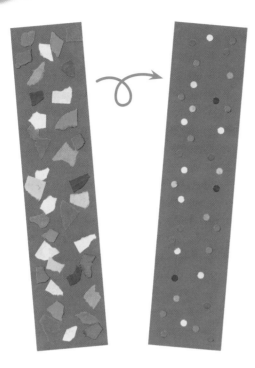

Punched Designs

Set out paper strips, scrap paper, hole punchers, and glue sticks. A child punches holes in a paper strip. Then she tears paper scraps into small pieces so that she has a piece of paper to cover each hole. To complete the activity, she glues each piece over a hole. The flip side will reveal a wonderful piece of dot art!

Janet Boyce
Tomball, TX

From Basket to Basket

Gather two large baskets and a collection of small stuffed toys. Set the baskets on the floor so that there are a couple of feet between them. Place the toys in one basket. A child stands between the baskets with his back to the empty basket. He picks up a toy, holds it behind his head and then drops it, trying to get the toy in the basket. He continues with the remaining toys.

Karen Eiben, The Learning House Preschool, La Salle, IL

Pom-Pom Drop

Fold a piece of cardboard so it stands up. Then glue a cardboard tube to it as shown. Place an empty bowl directly below the tube and set a bowl of pom-poms nearby. A child picks up each pom-pom, drops it into the top of the tube, and watches it fall into the bowl.

Norma Loera
A. S. Children's Center
Northridge, CA

Going the Distance

Take students to a large open room, such as a gym. If the floor is not lined, attach a long length of masking tape. Give each youngster a small foam ball and have him stand on the line. Then, at your signal, direct each child to throw his ball. After all the balls have stopped moving, guide youngsters to determine which ball was thrown the farthest. Invite them to retrieve the balls and then repeat the activity using actions such as tossing, rolling, and kicking.

Lida Mills
Hodgkins Park District
Hodgkins, IL

Busy Kids®

Fine- and Gross-Motor Activities for Developing Little Muscles and Big Muscles

Fine motor

Popcorn Ball

Set out yellow paper plates and yellow tissue paper. A child tears pieces from the tissue paper. Then she crumples each piece and glues it to the plate. The finished result looks like a buttery popcorn ball!

Janet Boyce
Hinojosa Early Childhood and Pre-Kindergarten Center
Houston, TX

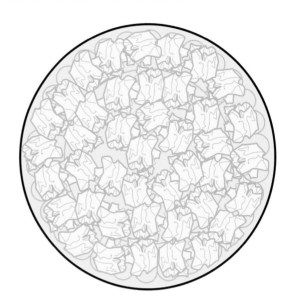

Gross motor

Shake and Roll!

Get a maraca and a ball. Invite youngsters to sit in a circle. Then roll the ball to a child. Have the child roll the ball to a classmate. Encourage students to continue the game until you shake the maraca, prompting them to freeze. Play another round of the game, inviting a child to shake the maraca!

Deborah J. Ryan, Newberg, OR

Colorful Towers

Push uncooked spaghetti noodles into a chunk of clay and place a bowl of colorful ringed cereal nearby. A child slides the cereal pieces onto the noodles as desired. **To incorporate math skills,** encourage youngsters to sort the cereal by color onto separate noodles or make a different pattern on each noodle.

Robin Saxe
Kiddie Campus
Utica, NY

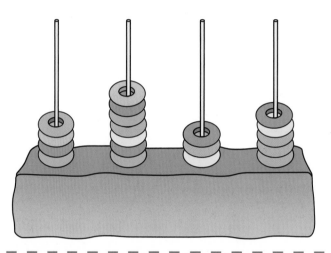

Pepperoni Pizza, Please!

Decorate a supersize circle cutout so it resembles a cheese pizza. Label a class supply of jumbo red paper circles (pepperoni slices) with a few different numbers. Place the pizza in a large open area and scatter the pepperoni slices around the room. Invite youngsters to move around the room as you lead them in singing the song shown. At the end of the song, each child hops onto a pepperoni slice. Announce a number. All youngsters standing on pepperoni slices with that number place their slices on the pizza and then sit down. Continue until all the slices are on the pizza. Then scatter the pepperoni slices around the room again and play another round!

(sung to the tune of "Pop! Goes the Weasel")

All around the pizza shop,
The children move so quietly.
They tiptoe all around the room
And hop on pepperoni.

Jan Volpe, Little Friends of Grace, Westminster, MD

Kitty Prints

Cover a table with a length of orange bulletin board paper. Set a washable black ink pad nearby. To make a cat's pawprint, a child presses her thumb on the ink pad and then makes a print on the paper. Next, she uses her pinkie finger to make four prints around the top of the thumbprint. She continues making pawprints as time allows.

Janet Boyce, Hinojosa Early Childhood and Pre-Kindergarten Center, Houston, TX

A Bed for Winter

After teaching students about animals that hibernate when the weather turns cold, set up a small pop-up tent or large cardboard box (cave). Scatter artificial leaves across the room from the cave. Then provide a large foam die near the cave. Have a child roll the die, count the dots, and run to the leaves and count that amount. Then have her run back to the cave and toss the leaves inside. Continue with other children until there is a nice cozy bed in the cave.

Karen Smith
Little Tid-Bits
Fresno, CA

Busy Kids®

Fine- and Gross-Motor Activities for Developing Little Muscles and Big Muscles

Fine motor

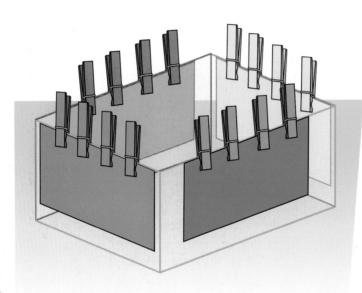

Clip by Color

Get a lidded container and plastic spring-style clothespins in four different colors. Label the sides of the container to match the colors of the clothespins and then place the clothespins in the container. A child removes the lid and dumps out the clothespins. Then she clips the clothespins around the top of the container, matching the clothespins to the labels.

Vivian Boccia
Simonsdale Presbyterian Preschool
Portsmouth, VA

Fine motor

Candy Cane Creation

Place an oversize poster board candy cane drawing with stripe outlines at a table along with glue and red-tinted wagon wheel pasta. Each child visits the center and glues on pasta wheels to fill in the candy cane stripes.

Wintry Walk

To get little ones ready for an imaginary walk in the snow, have them pretend to put on their coats, hats, scarves, and snow boots. Then lead students around the room on a pretend walk through the snow, having them take big steps, tiptoe, shuffle their feet, and slide.

Fine motor

Splendid Sewing

In advance, remove the front panels from used holiday cards; then hole-punch the edges. Attach a length of curling ribbon to a hole in each panel and place the panels in a container. A child chooses a panel and then laces the curling ribbon through the holes. When he is finished, he attaches it to a designated wall. Other children repeat the process as desired and add their lacing projects to the wall to make a holiday quilt display.

Busy Kids®

Fine- and Gross-Motor Activities for Developing Little Muscles and Big Muscles

Fine motor

Bedazzled Dough

Set out play dough with sequins mixed into the dough. Provide plastic knives. A youngster searches for sequins in a lump of dough, pinching and pulling it apart as he works. He uses a plastic knife to cut the dough and help dig out the sequins. When he's finished, he presses the sequins back into the dough and then kneads it to conceal the sequins.

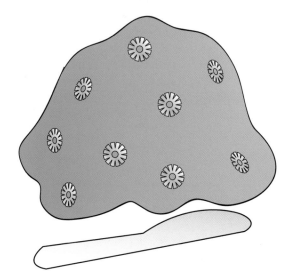

Gross motor

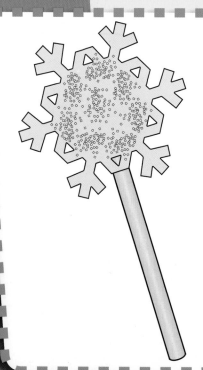

Freeze!

To make a wand, decorate a snowflake cutout and tape it to a dowel rod. Then write a different letter on each of several large circles and attach them to the floor. Play a recording of lively music and invite youngsters to dance around the circles. Stop the music and have youngsters freeze. Move around the circle and tap a child with the snowflake wand. Direct him to name the letter on the circle closest to him. Tap a couple more students and have them name the letters near them. Restart the music to play another round.

Rose Cox
York-ES J Consortium Head Start
Bristol, IN

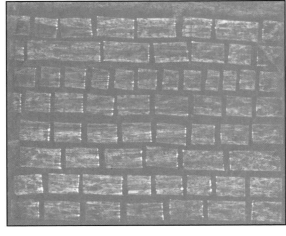

Ice Blocks

Set out sheets of blue construction paper, tape, and white crayons with the wrappers removed. A child tears off pieces of tape and sticks them to her paper in rows so they resemble ice blocks. (You may want to draw lines on the paper to help youngsters with tape placement.) Then she rubs a white crayon over the ice blocks.

Janet Boyce, Hinojosa Early Childhood and Pre-Kindergarten Center, Houston, TX

Snowball Targets

Attach a vinyl tablecloth that has large pictures on it to a fence or other structure in your outdoor play area. During outdoor play, invite youngsters to make snowballs and throw them at the images on the tablecloth. This snowball throwing is both safe and fun!

Teomi Cole, Village Green Preschool, Sterling, MA

Jumping Beans

Have youngsters sit in a circle. Choose a child to be the jumping bean and direct her to stand in the center of the circle. Then lead the seated students in singing the song below. As you sing, the jumping bean jumps up and down and from side to side. At the end of the song, she chooses another youngster to be the jumping bean.

(sung to the tune of "Mary Had a Little Lamb")

[Jenny] is a jumping bean,
Jumping bean, jumping bean.
[Jenny] is a jumping bean
Who jumps from here to there.

Rocio Casillas
Magallanes Family Daycare
Long Beach, CA

All Covered Up!

Set a bowl of wrapped chocolate candy hearts and a pair of tongs near a big heart cutout. A child uses the tongs to pick up a candy heart and place it on the cutout. She continues in this manner until the entire heart cutout is covered. After the child completes the center, help her count the heart candies and then give her one for a special treat!

Busy Kids®

Fine- and Gross-Motor Activities for Developing Little Muscles and Big Muscles

Gross motor

Gathering Gold

Purchase several small mesh bags of gold-wrapped chocolate coins. Set a black pot in the center of a large open area and scatter the bags around the pot. A child walks around the area, picks up each bag, and tosses it into the pot.

Nancy Morgan
Care-A-Lot In-home Daycare and Preschool
Bremerton, WA

Fine motor

Potato Pals

Set out large baking potatoes and a supply of colorful golf tees. A child pushes the tees into a potato to make a person or an animal. Youngsters will love to make more than one potato pal!

Janet Boyce
Hinojosa Early Childhood and Pre-Kindergarten Center
Houston, TX

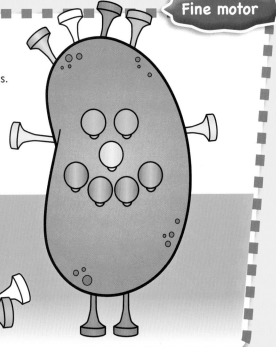

Looking for Letters

This gross-motor activity also reinforces letter matching! Give each child in a small group a different letter card or manipulative. Direct each youngster to visually find the matching letter in your classroom alphabet display. Then have him march to the display and hold the manipulative beneath the matching letter. Repeat the activity with different youngsters and gross-motor movements, such as galloping, jumping, or crawling.

Angela Arndt, Rowan University, Glassboro, NJ

Clip and Pass

Give each child a spring-type clothespin and have the children sit in a circle with you. Place a large white pom-pom (bunny tail) in your hand and pass it to the child to your right. Have her use her clothespin to take it from your hand. She passes the bunny tail to the child to her right, and he uses his clothespin to take it. Youngsters continue passing the bunny tail as described until it goes all the way around the circle. To challenge youngsters, pass several bunny tails around the circle at once!

Janet Boyce
Hinojosa Early Childhood and Pre-Kindergarten Center
Houston, TX

Fast or Slow?

Youngsters will love this twist on Duck, Duck, Goose! Read a favorite version of *The Tortoise and the Hare*. Then have youngsters sit in a circle and invite a child to walk around the circle, gently tapping each classmate on the shoulder until he gets to the child he wants to choose. When he gets to this child, he taps her on the shoulder and says either "Hare!" or "Tortoise!" Then both youngsters move around the circle like the chosen character. The first child sits back down, and the child who was tapped becomes the next tapper.

Deborah J. Ryan
Newberg, OR

Hare!

Soup Scoop

Stir together different types of pasta (soup) in a large pot and put a ladle in the pot. Set the pot on a table along with a muffin tin and bowl. A child ladles soup into the bowl. Then she sorts the pasta by placing each type in a different section of the muffin tin.

Janet Boyce
Hinojosa Early Childhood and Pre-Kindergarten Center
Houston, TX

Busy Kids®

Fine- and Gross-Motor Activities for Developing Little Muscles and Big Muscles

Seed, Seed, Sprout

Please your little sprouts with this game! In a large open area, seat youngsters in a circle. Assign one child to be the gardener and give her an empty plastic watering can to hold. To play, the gardener walks around the circle gently tapping each classmate's shoulder with her hand while saying the word *seed*. Then the gardener pretends to water a student's head while saying the word *sprout*. The chosen student acts like a sprouting seed by slowly standing up. Then the two students switch places and the sprout becomes the gardener for another round of play.

Colorful Words

Punch holes in color word cards and place the cards near pipe cleaners in matching colors. A youngster chooses a pipe cleaner and finds the matching card. Then he inserts the pipe cleaner into a hole in the card and twists it in place.

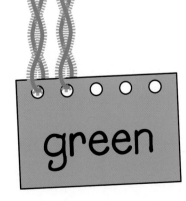

A Beautiful Basket

Set an open-weave laundry basket near a supply of artificial flowers and lengths of ribbon. A child weaves the ribbons through the holes in the basket. Then he adds the flowers to the basket by sticking them in the holes or weaving the stems into the basket.

Janet Boyce
Cokato, MN

Volcanoes and Dinosaurs

Gather students in a large open area and then divide them into two groups. Give each child in one group a strip of red fabric. Then tell students in that group that they are volcanoes and the fabric strip is hot lava. Tell students in the other group that they are dinosaurs. The dinosaurs move around the area like dinosaurs while the volcanoes try to touch them with the lava. After a dinosaur is touched, she stops moving. After all the dinosaurs have stopped moving, the groups switch roles and play again.

Julie Christensen
Parker, CO

Cozy Caterpillars

Set out rotini pasta (caterpillars) and colorful lengths of yarn. A child makes a cocoon around each caterpillar by wrapping a piece of yarn around it. After all the caterpillars are in their cocoons, he unwraps them to ready the area for the next visitor.

Janet Boyce
Cokato, MN

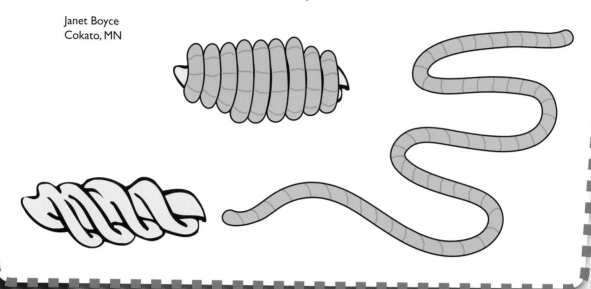

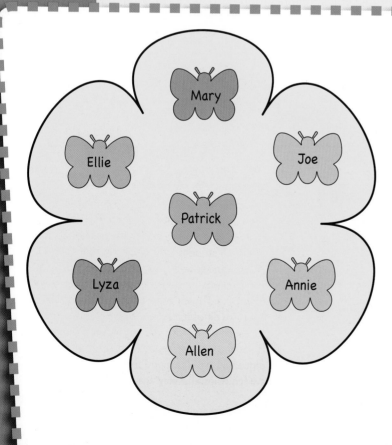

Flower to Flower

Personalize a butterfly cutout for each child. Place two jumbo flower cutouts several feet apart in a large open area. Arrange the butterflies on one of the flowers and have youngsters stand in a line behind it. At your signal, the first child picks up his butterfly, "flutters" to the other flower, puts the butterfly on it, and sits down. Play continues until all the butterflies have been moved.

Clare Cox
Homer Davis Elementary
Tucson, AZ

Apple in the Grass
Fine-motor skills

How to use: Give each child a copy of this page and have her trace and color the apple and the worm. Then have her fold the paper on the solid line and color the back of the folded portion green. Next, have her unfold the paper and cut on the dotted lines, being sure to stop at the fold. Finally, have her refold the paper.

Fall Is a Hoot!

Note to the teacher: Give each child a copy of this page, fall-colored paper scraps, crayons, and glue. Have him color the picture. Then direct him to tear the paper scraps and glue the pieces to the page so they resemble leaves.

Sweet Fellow

Finish the gingerbread man.

Note to the teacher: If desired, copy the page onto brown paper. After students have finished their drawings, have them drizzle white paint on their gingerbread men so it resembles frosting.

A Fancy Flake

Note to the teacher: Have each child use a blue crayon to trace the dotted lines of the snowflake. Then invite him to squeeze dots of glue on his paper and sprinkle silver or iridescent glitter over the glue.

Off We Go!

Note to the teacher: Give each child a copy of this page. Have her color each kite and trace each kite tail. Then invite her to make bows on the kite strings by gluing dyed bow tie pasta to the lines.

Cut, Glue, and Trace!

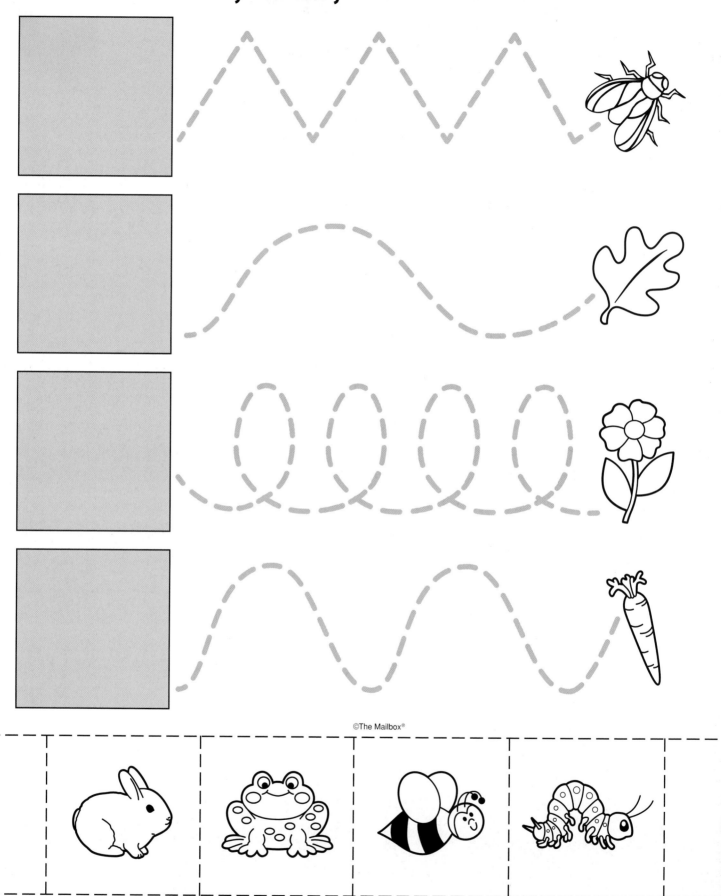

©The Mailbox®

Note to the teacher: Give each child a copy of this page. Have her color and cut out the picture cards. Then invite her to match each critter with the correct picture and glue the card in the appropriate box. Finally, have her use a crayon to trace each dotted line.

CIRCLE TIME

Circle Time

This is my friend Mia!

Circle of Classmates

Youngsters introduce their classmates with this fun game! Arrange a class supply of chairs in a circle facing inward; then place a photo of a different child under each chair. Play music and have youngsters walk around inside the circle of chairs. Stop the music and prompt each child to sit in a chair and remove the photo from under the seat. (If a child gets her own photo, have her exchange photos with a neighbor.) Then prompt each child to show the photo and say, "This is my friend [child's name]!" After each photo has been shown, have students place them back under the chairs. Then restart the music and play another round. *Participating in a game, oral language*

Billiejean Martin
Nora Stewart Early Learning Center
Columbia, MO

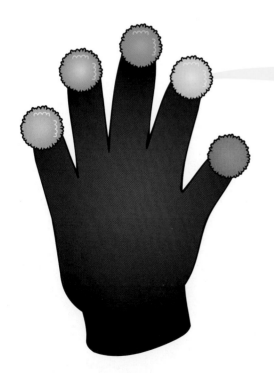

Where Is...?

Reinforce color names with this sing-along activity! Hot-glue colorful pom-poms to the fingers of a glove. To begin, put on the glove and help little ones identify the colors of the pom-poms. Then put your hand behind your back and lead students in singing the song shown, bringing out your hand and holding up the appropriate finger during the second line. Place your hand behind your back during the last line. Sing the song four more times, substituting a different color each time. *Identifying colors*

(sung to the tune of "Where Is Thumbkin?")

Where is [color]? Where is [color]?
Here I am. Here I am.
Hello, [color]. How are you?
Very well—I thank you!
Time to go. Time to go.

Susan Cargill, Berryhill Elementary, Tulsa, OK

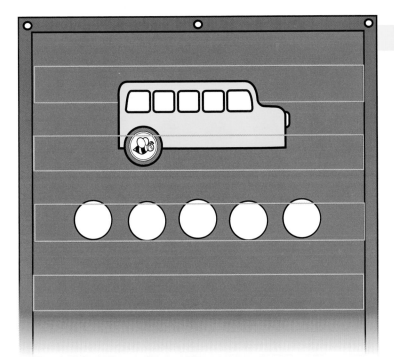

The Wheels on the Bus

Cut out a copy of the wheel patterns on page 64. Also cut out a simple school bus shape. Display the bus and one wheel in a pocket chart as shown. Place the remaining wheels below the bus facing away. Have students identify the picture on the wheel. Then lead little ones in singing the song shown. At the end of the song, invite a child to take a wheel from below the bus and identify the picture. If the pictures on the two wheels match, help him place his wheel in the chart to complete the bus. Then invite each youngster to pretend to drive a bus. If the pictures do not match, set the card aside and continue with other children until a match is found. Repeat until all the wheels are matched. *Visual discrimination, matching*

(sung to the tune of "The Wheels on the Bus")

The bus needs a wheel so it can go,
It can go, it can go.
The bus needs a wheel so it can go
Driving to and fro!

Jackie Wright, Summerhill Children's House, Enid, OK

Let's Talk Hair

Set a chair in front of your group-time area. Then invite a volunteer to sit in the chair. Have students recite the chant shown. Then encourage the youngster to name the color of her hair. Continue with several other little ones. If desired, finish the activity by prompting youngsters to help you sort them by hair color! *Speaking*

[Child's name], [child's name], in the chair,
Tell us what color is your hair:
Brown or blond or black or red?
Or is it purple upon your head?

Keely Saunders, Bonney Lake Early Childhood Education Assistance Program, Bonney Lake, WA

My hair is brown!

Circle Time

Mystery Shapes

Attach circle, square, and triangle cutouts to index cards. Place the cards in a pocket chart with the shapes facing away. Also cut out a class supply of circles, squares, and triangles. To begin, give each child a shape. Then lead youngsters in saying the chant shown, flipping one of the cards at the end to reveal the shape. Have students identify the shape and then ask each child with a matching shape to hold it in the air. Scan the shapes for accuracy; then help youngsters arrange the shapes side by side in the chart. Continue in the same manner, having students place each set of shapes in a different row. **Identifying shapes, matching shapes**

The hidden shapes are a mystery.
Flip one over and show it to me!

Tricia Kylene Brown
Bowling Green, KY

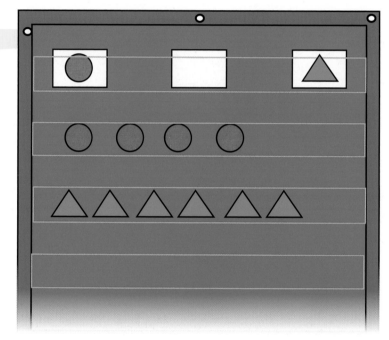

Show and Spell

Gather a name card for each child. Then walk around the outside of the circle as you sing the song shown. At the end of the song, drop a child's own name card in his lap. Then ask him to display the card and say his name. Say the letters in his name. Then repeat the activity! **Speaking, reinforcing letter names**

(sung to the tune of "The Farmer in the Dell")

You have a special name.
You have a special name.
When I give you your name card,
Let's show and spell your name!

adapted from an idea by Keely Peasner
Midland's Kiddie Korral
Tacoma, WA

Circle Time

Who Lives Here?

To review youngsters' addresses, write each child's address on a separate envelope. Place the envelopes in a tote bag. Pretend to be a mail carrier. Take an envelope from the bag, show it to students, and ask, "Who lives at [address]?" Have the child who lives at that address raise his hand and then deliver the envelope to him. Continue until all the envelopes have been delivered.

Hollie Parker
First Presbyterian Preschool
Dunedin, FL

Falling Leaves

Personalize a leaf cutout for each child and place the leaves on a parachute (or bedsheet). Gather youngsters around the parachute. As you lead them in singing the song shown, have students lift the parachute to toss the leaves. At the end of the song, encourage each child to find her leaf.

(sung to the tune of "London Bridge")

All the leaves are falling down,
Falling down, falling down.
All the leaves are falling down
To the ground.

Look around and find your leaf,
Find your leaf, find your leaf.
Look around and find your leaf
On the ground.

Katie Backhaus
Kensington School
Lagrange, IL

How Many Eyes?

Draw two silly monsters on the board, varying the number of body parts on each monster. Name a body part and lead youngsters in counting and comparing to determine which monster has more of that part. Continue in the same manner with different body parts.

Amy Brinton
Garden Heights Preschool
Madison, WI

Who's at the Door?

This giggle-inducing Halloween ditty is sure to delight little ones. Cut apart a copy of the cards on page 65 and place them in a plastic pumpkin. Sing the first verse of the song below. Then invite a child to take a card from the pumpkin and show it to the group. Lead students in singing the second verse, inserting the appropriate picture name, and encourage them to knock on a hard surface when indicated. Continue with each remaining card.

(sung to the tune of "Ten Little Indians")

Halloween, Halloween—who will come a-knocking?
Halloween, Halloween—who will come a-knocking?
Halloween, Halloween—who will come a-knocking?
Who will you see at your door?

Knock, knock, knock—it's a [picture name] that's a-knocking.
Knock, knock, knock—it's a [picture name] that's a-knocking.
Knock, knock, knock—it's a [picture name] that's a-knocking.
That's who you see at your door!

Colleen Dabney
Williamsburg, VA

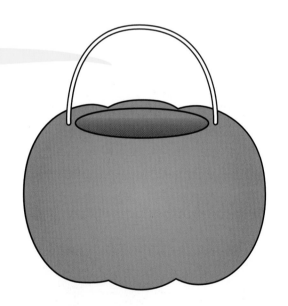

Jelly in the Bowl

Get little ones up and wiggling with a delightful gross-motor activity! Have students stand in a circle. Then lead them in singing the song as they jiggle like jelly. Next, have the boys stand in the center of the circle and jiggle as you sing the song again, replacing the word *jelly* with *boys*. Then direct the boys and girls to switch places and repeat the song. If desired, continue singing verses using colors of clothing, substituting the color word for the word *jelly*.

(sung to the tune of "The Farmer in the Dell")

Jelly in the bowl,
Jelly in the bowl.
Wiggle, woggle,
Wiggle, woggle.
Jelly in the bowl.

Betty Silkunas
Fernandina Beach, FL

Turkey Feathers

Youngsters are sure to enjoy this Thanksgiving-themed version of "Who Stole the Cookie From the Cookie Jar?" Place colorful craft feathers around a simple turkey cutout. Then invite each child to take a feather from the turkey's tail and hide it behind her back. Lead youngsters in saying the call-and-response chant shown until each child has been named. At the end, prompt everyone to reveal their feathers and toss them in the air as they say, "We all took the feathers from the turkey's tail!"

Class: Who took a feather from the turkey's tail?
Teacher: [Ella] took a feather from the turkey's tail.
[Ella]: Who, me?
Teacher: Yes, you.
[Ella]: Couldn't be!
Class: Then who?

Kathleen Reynolds
Middlebury, VT

Circle Time

Edible Coins

Youngsters estimate and count with this idea! Place chocolate Hanukkah gelt in a plastic jar. Pass the jar around the circle and have each child guess the number of coins it contains; write each child's name and guess on a sheet of chart paper. Lead the class in counting the coins aloud as you remove them from the jar. After youngsters evaluate their estimates, give each student a coin to unwrap and eat!

Ellen Farina, Hebrew Academy
Margate, FL

Sarah	10
Jon	8
Morgan	22
Lee	10
Jana	18

Color Sticks

Gather paint in green, blue, red, pink, and black. Then paint a class supply of craft sticks, making sure to make a few of each color. (Don't worry about covering the entire stick with paint. A portion of the stick will do.) Have the children sit in a circle and give a stick to each child. Then say the first direction below, prompting the children with green sticks to stand and jump as if they're on a trampoline. After a few seconds, have them sit down. Then continue with each remaining direction. To play another round, collect and then redistribute the sticks.

Directions:
If you're holding green, bounce on a trampoline.
If you're holding blue, play peekaboo.
If you're holding red, put your hands on your head.
If you're holding pink, let's see you wink.
If you're holding black, stand up and quack.

Joann Cannatella
Brooklyn, NY

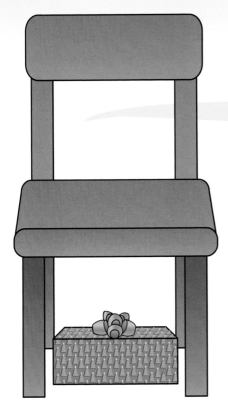

Ho, Ho, Ho!

Little ones pretend to be Santa with this jolly activity! In advance, place a class treat in a box and wrap it like a present. To begin, ask a volunteer to sit in a chair and close her eyes. Then invite a second volunteer to play Santa. Santa picks up the present and quietly places it under the chair. When he sits back down, all of the children shout, "Ho, ho, ho!" The youngster in the chair opens her eyes and has three chances to guess Santa's identity. When Santa is revealed, choose two new youngsters for the next round. When each youngster has had a chance to play, share the present's contents with your little ones!

Anna Katrina Enverga
Alphabits Learning Center
Manchester, NH

Whose Art Is This?

Display student artwork on a wall. Then write each student's name on an index card and attach it near the corresponding artwork facing away from the viewers. Direct students' attention to one of the pieces of artwork. Help youngsters discuss what they see. Then have little ones guess whose artwork it is. After several guesses, reveal the name and prompt youngsters to applaud. Continue with the remaining pieces of artwork.

Carole Watkins
Timothy Ball Elementary
Crown Point, IN

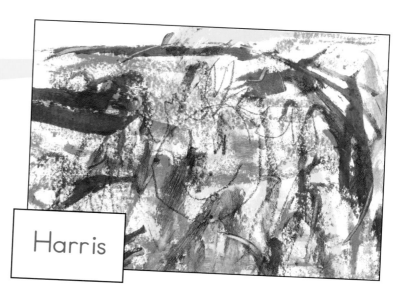

Harris

Circle Time

The Snowflake Shake

Cut out several copies of the snowflakes on page 66. Then label each one with a different number. Place them in a gift bag along with a variety of other shape cutouts. Have a child choose a cutout. If it's a shape, have her name the shape. If it's a snowflake, have her say, "Snowflake shake!" and then identify the number. Encourage all youngsters to stand and shake while you count to the number. *Identifying numbers, counting, identifying shapes*

adapted from an idea by Carissa Dwyer
Discovery Kids Preschool
Maple Plain, MN

Fur Fun

Discuss polar bears with your little ones, explaining that the fur on the polar bear appears to be white but is actually clear! Then sing this cute little song with your students, prompting them to answer the question at the end of the song. Continue with grizzly bear *(brown)*, panda bear *(black and white)*, koala *(gray)*, black bear *(black)*, and teddy bear *(any color)*. *Investigating living things*

(sung to the tune of "The Farmer in the Dell")

What color is its fur?
What color is its fur?
A [polar bear], a [polar bear]—
What color is its fur?

Donna Obrien, Orange Park, FL

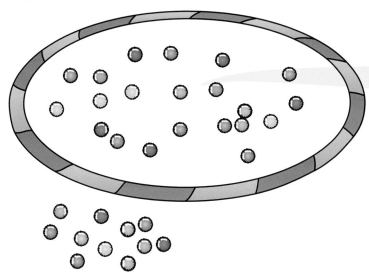

Pom-Poms Begone!

Counting, understanding the concept of zero

Place a plastic hoop on the floor and scatter pom-poms within the hoop. Name a number (or show a number card) and have a child remove that number of pom-poms from the hoop. Continue with different numbers and youngsters until no pom-poms remain. Then reinforce that there are zero pom-poms in the hoop and zero means "none."

Suzanne Moore
Tucson, AZ

Ten Little Hearts

Understand the last number named tells the number of objects counted

Make ten heart cutouts and give each heart to a different child. Have youngsters kneel in a row. Then lead students in singing the song shown. As you sing the first verse, point to each child from left to right and have them stand. Then, as you sing the second verse, have each youngster sit. Repeat the activity until all children have a chance to hold a heart.

(sung to the tune of "Ten Little Indians")

One little, two little, three little valentines;
Four little, five little, six little valentines;
Seven little, eight little, nine little valentines;
Ten little valentine hearts!

Ten little, nine little, eight little valentines;
Seven little, six little, five little valentines;
Four little, three little, two little valentines;
One little valentine heart!

Doria Owen
William Paca Old Post Road Elementary
Abingdon, MD

Circle Time

Baa or Roar?

Letter-sound association, participating in a group game

Cut out a copy of the cards on page 67 and place them in a bag. Then give the bag to a child and have her draw a card. Prompt her to "read" the card and then place it back in the bag. If it says "Baa!" have her curl up in a ball in the middle of the circle like a sweet little sheep. If it says "Roar!" encourage her to run around the outside of the circle like a rambunctious lion and then return to her own seat. Continue until the bag makes it all the way around the circle. Then have the youngsters in the middle of the circle go back to their seats and begin another round!

Randi Austin Nelson
Fairview Elementary
Carthage, MO

Meet Those Feet!

Listening to a read-aloud, counting

Read aloud *The Foot Book* by Dr. Seuss. Then have students sit in a circle with their legs crossed. Have one child straighten his legs. Prompt students to count his feet. Then have the classmate next to him straighten her legs. Have little ones count the feet on both students. Continue until all youngsters have straightened their legs and you have counted how many feet you meet in your classroom!

Janet Boyce
Hinojosa Early Childhood and Pre-Kindergarten Center
Houston, TX

Circle Time

The mystery student is a girl.

Guess Who!

Critical thinking

With this engaging game, students use clues to figure out the identity of the mystery student. Direct youngsters to stand. Give a clue, such as "The mystery student has brown hair." Everyone who has brown hair remains standing, and those who don't sit down. After each clue is given, invite two youngsters to guess the mystery student. Continue as described until the mystery student is named.

Jennifer Gemar
Tripp-Delmont School District
Tripp, SD

Chicks in Eggs

Identifying colors, participating in a class game

Gather a class supply of plastic eggs. Place identical pom-poms (chicks) in all the eggs except one. Place a different-color pom-pom in the final egg. While the students are out of the room, hide the eggs. At circle time, invite each child to find an egg and then return to the circle-time area. Ask each child to open his egg and name the color of his chick. Give the youngster with the chick of a different color a basket and have him collect the eggs. Invite him to help you quickly rehide the eggs while his classmates cover their eyes.

Carole Watkins
Timothy Ball Elementary
Crown Point, IN

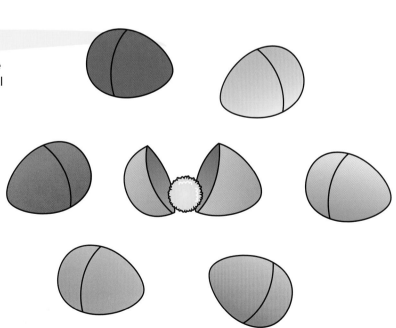

Circle Time

Colorful Cookies

Test students' observation skills with this simple game. Make circle cutouts (cookies) in different colors and place them on a cookie sheet. Gather youngsters around the cookie sheet. Hold up each cookie and have them name the color. Then direct them to cover their eyes as you remove a cookie from the sheet. Have them uncover their eyes and invite a volunteer to name the missing cookie. Continue for several more rounds.

Deborah J. Ryan
Newberg, OR

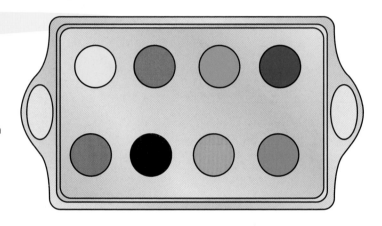

Flower Fun

Reinforce listening skills and positional words with this springtime activity. Give each child an artificial flower or a flower cutout (patterns on page 68). Announce a direction such as "jump over your flower" or "put your flower on your head." After giving several directions, invite volunteers to give directions.

Keely Hallin
Bonney Lake Early Childhood Education Assistance Program
Bonney Lake, WA

A Unique Garden

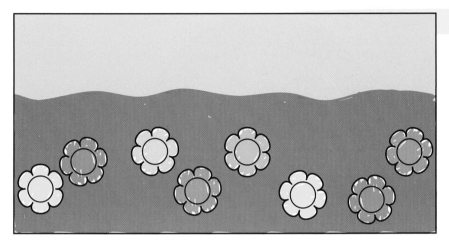

Create a one-of-a-kind garden with this version of pin the tail on the donkey. Draw a garden scene minus the flowers on a length of bulletin board paper. Then give each child a cutout copy of a flower pattern from page 68 and have her color it. Place a loop of tape on the back of a child's flower. Then have her close her eyes (or have her wear a sleep mask), walk toward the garden (with guidance if needed), and attach her flower to the garden. After each child has added a flower to the garden, invite students to stand back and look at their colorful creation. *Spatial relationships, visual memory*

Clare Cox, Homer Davis Elementary, Tucson, AZ

Frogs on a Log

Place a length of brown bulletin board paper (log) on the floor. Have youngsters stand behind the log and pretend to be frogs. Name a word and then, in turn, invite each little frog to name a real or nonsense word that rhymes with your word. After a child names a rhyming word, he jumps on the log. After all the frogs are on the log, have them jump off the log. Then play another round with new frogs! *Rhyming, gross-motor skills*

adapted from an idea by Cindy Hoying
Centerville, OH

Wheel Picture Cards
Use with "The Wheels on the Bus" on page 51.

©The Mailbox®

©The Mailbox®

©The Mailbox®

©The Mailbox®

©The Mailbox®

©The Mailbox®

©The Mailbox®

©The Mailbox®

©The Mailbox®

©The Mailbox®

©The Mailbox®

©The Mailbox®

©The Mailbox®

©The Mailbox®

Snowflake Patterns

Use with "The Snowflake Shake" on page 58.

©The Mailbox®

©The Mailbox®

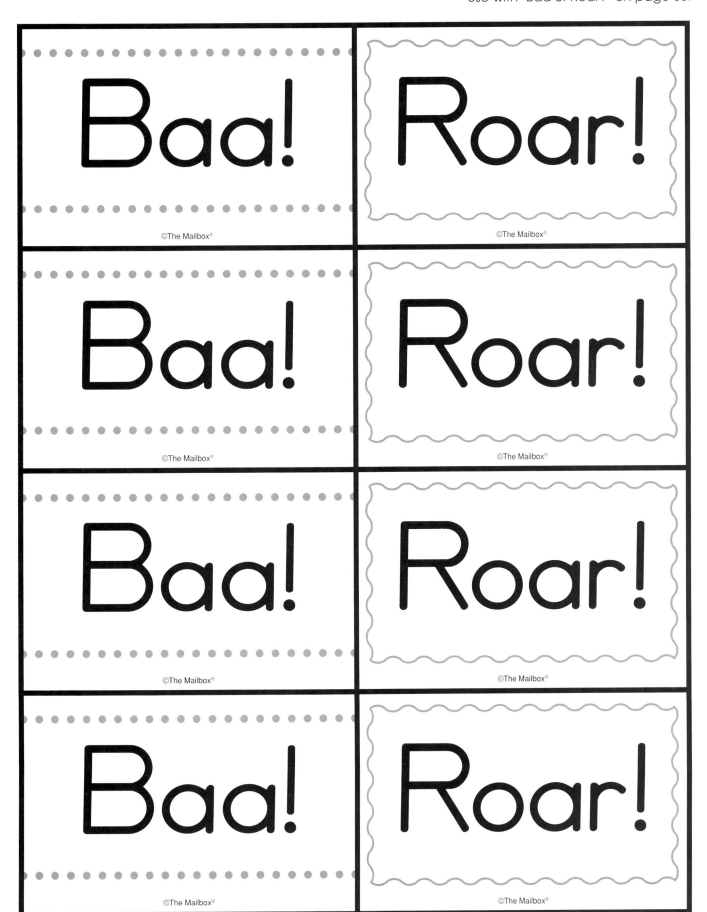

Baa!
©The Mailbox®

Roar!
©The Mailbox®

Baa!
©The Mailbox®

Roar!
©The Mailbox®

Baa!
©The Mailbox®

Roar!
©The Mailbox®

Baa!
©The Mailbox®

Roar!
©The Mailbox®

Flower Patterns
Use with "Flower Fun" on page 62 and "A Unique Garden" on page 63.

©The Mailbox®

©The Mailbox®

CLASSROOM DISPLAYS

The Letter Bus!

idea contributed by Jeanne-Marie Peterson
Crozet, VA

Make the Display

Make a large school bus cutout from yellow bulletin board paper and attach it to a wall. Make sure the bus has several large windows. If desired, add other details, such as a road and sun, to the display.

Use the Display

1. Give each child a letter cutout and encourage her to decorate it with markers, crayons, and a variety of collage items. Attach the decorated letters to the windows of the bus so it appears as if the letters are going for a ride.

2. Print out pictures of animals or objects that begin with the letter your little ones are currently studying. (An Internet image search will turn up plenty of options.) Attach the pictures to the bus.

3. Have students sing the song shown, inserting the name and sound of the letter on your display. Then encourage them to point to and name the pictures, having them focus on the beginning sound of each name.

(sung to the tune of "The Wheels on the Bus")

The [Ms] on the bus go [/m/, /m/, /m/].
[/m/, /m/, /m/, /m/, /m/, /m/].
The [Ms] on the bus go [/m/, /m/, /m/]
All through the town!

> When you have a few extra minutes to fill, lead students in singing the song to review letter sounds they've already learned.

Take a photo of each child sitting cross-legged. Then print a copy of each photo. Have each child brush diluted glue onto a tagboard pumpkin shape. Then have her press orange tissue paper squares on the glue. When the project is dry, trim away any tissue paper hanging off the edges. If the tagboard has curled, press it beneath a stack of heavy books. Finally, display the pumpkins and trimmed photos on a board decorated as shown.

Sharon Berkley, Son Shine Christian Preschool, Pasadena, TX

Turkey and All the Snippings!

Gather paper scraps in fall colors and place them in a tub along with pairs of scissors. Encourage students to snip the papers into little pieces in the tub. Next, have each child color a copy of the turkey on page 76. Then encourage her to spread glue over the turkey's feathers. Prompt her to sprinkle the paper snips over the glue. Then display these fun and simple projects.

Jacqueline K. Darienzo
Uxbridge Early Learning Center
Uxbridge, MA

CLASSROOM DISPLAYS

Get in Shape   For the Holidays!

Make a large triangular tree cutout. Have little ones decorate the tree with circle cutouts (ornaments). Then mount the tree and a brown rectangle cutout (stump) on a bulletin board or wall. Help each child make either a square gift craft or a star-shaped Santa craft. Then attach the gifts and Santas around the tree. Finally, add the fun title shown!

Nicole Hoesel
Sanford Child Development Center
Fargo, ND

Ms. Peasner's Holiday Stars

This starry bulletin board twinkles and shines! Have each child use watercolors to paint a personalized copy of the Star of David pattern on page 77. After the paint is dry, invite her to add glitter glue to the star. Cut out the stars and attach them to a board along with a title similar to the one shown.

CLASSROOM DISPLAYS

Tiptoe Through the Snow!

Paint snow on a length of dark bulletin board paper. Then help each child press a bare foot on a tray of white paint and then onto the paper. Also have each child make a few fingerprints (snowflakes). When the paint is dry, use markers to add stick arms, eyes, a nose, and buttons. Display the paper as shown.

Carol Reineking, Head Start Preschool, Sheboygan Falls, WI

Friends Make Life Sweeter

Have each child glue a photo of himself to a heart cutout. Then have him tape a paint stir stick to the back of the heart. Help him gather pink cellophane around the heart and secure it with ribbon or yarn. Mount the projects on a wall with the title shown.

adapted from an idea by Carolyn Jones
St. Athanasius SAFE Program
Louisville, KY

CLASSROOM DISPLAYS

Would You Try Green Eggs and Ham?

Combine literacy and math skills with this display! After a read-aloud of *Green Eggs and Ham* by Dr. Seuss, ask little ones if they would try green eggs and ham. Then have each child use light green paint and green pom-poms to make two fried eggs on a construction paper frying pan cutout. Next, have him attach a green ham cutout. Have him orient the ham to make a smile if he would try it and a frown if he wouldn't. Display the projects.

Pamela Todd, South Shore Christian Academy, Weymouth, MA

This simple display is terrific for Earth Day! Make a copy of the trash can on page 78 for each child. Then have her color the trash can and glue pieces of a clean food wrapper to the can. Mount the cans on a board or wall with the title shown.

Teresa Wensil, Tiny Tears Daycare, Albemarle, NC

CLASSROOM DISPLAYS

Put Your Frog on a Log

Alexis
Trevon

Shalin
Becca

Jacob

Enhance this spring attendance display with the cattail project on page 306.

Change up your attendance display for spring with this cute idea! Make a class supply of colorful frog die-cuts and personalize each one. Cut log shapes from brown construction paper and add details as desired. Then mount the logs on a sheet of blue poster board programmed as shown. Attach Velcro fasteners to the logs and frogs. Then display the poster board on a wall or place it on a table. Scatter the frogs nearby. When youngsters arrive, they each pick up their frog and attach it to a log.

Amy Rain Monahan
Alton, IL

Sail Into Summer!

To make this summer display, post a large sun and sailboat on a sheet of blue bulletin board paper. Add wave details. Then attach brown paper to the bottom of the display so it resembles sand. Have youngsters make sand pail, sea star, and sand dollar crafts. Then attach them to the sand. It's almost summertime!

Kim Dessel, Pixie Preschool and Kindergarten, Spotswood, NJ

Turkey Pattern

Use with "Turkey and All the Snippings!" on page 71.

©The Mailbox®

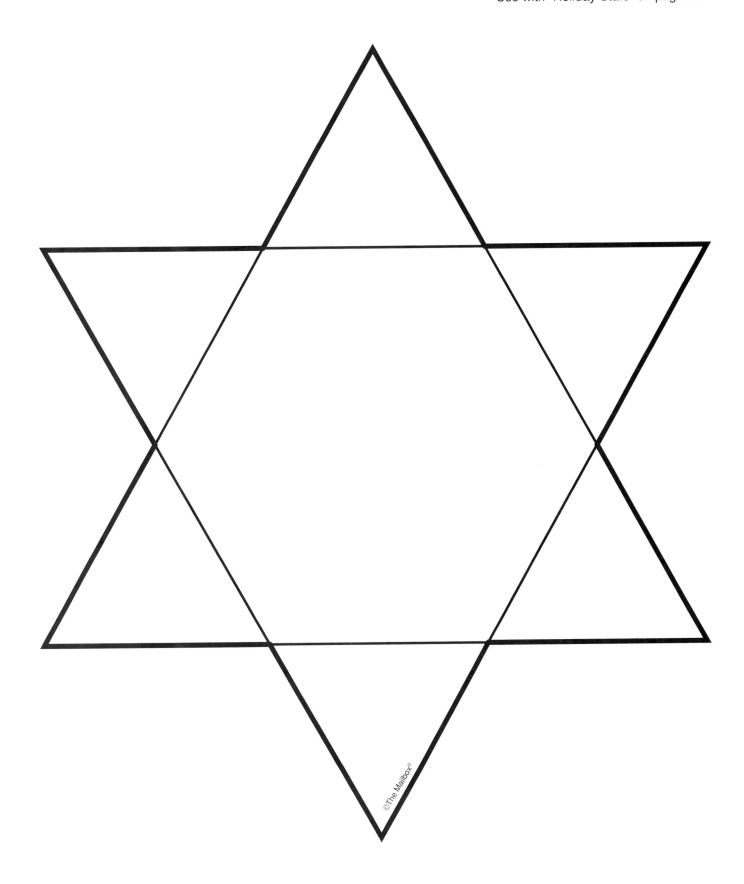

©The Mailbox®

Trash Can Pattern

Use with "Put Litter Where It Belongs!" on page 74.

©The Mailbox®

HOLIDAYS & SEASONAL CELEBRATIONS®

Six Little Monsters

Counting, gross-motor skills

Have little ones recite this adorable action rhyme. Follow up the rhyme with some monster counting practice! Have little ones stomp six times, peekaboo six times, and stir pretend monster stew six times. What fun!

One little monster stomps around.	*Stomp.*
Two little monsters don't make a sound.	*Whisper.*
Three little monsters playing peekaboo.	*Play peekaboo with hands over eyes.*
Four little monsters make monster stew!	*Pretend to stir stew.*
Five little monsters just have some fun.	*Dance in place.*
Six little monsters—and now we're done!	*Clap to the beat on the final four words.*

adapted from an idea by Tricia Kylene Brown
Bowling Green, KY

Turkey Trot

Reinforcing number names

Help youngsters name some turkey-related actions, such as gobbling, pecking, flapping, and scratching. Next, hold up a number card. Help a child identify the number. Then name an action and encourage youngsters to repeat the action the corresponding number of times. Gobble, gobble, gobble!
Tricia Kylene Brown

Falling Foliage

Rhyming

Gather scrap construction paper in fall colors. To begin, call on a child and name a word. If the word rhymes with *fall*, have the child choose a piece of paper and tear a small piece from it. Continue until each child has torn a piece of paper. Then have everyone toss their papers into the air and watch them fall. They look just like falling leaves!
Tricia Kylene Brown

Crows in the Cornfield

Developing gross-motor skills, playing a group game

In a large open space, divide your class into two separate groups—crows and scarecrows. Have the scarecrows stand in random locations with their arms outstretched. Tell the scarecrows that they can move their arms but they can't move their legs. Gather the crows on one side of the room. On your signal, encourage the crows to "fly" through the field of scarecrows, weaving and moving so they don't get touched. When the crows make it to the other side of the room, have students switch roles. *Keely Saunders, Bonney Lake Early Childhood Education Assistance Program, Bonney Lake, WA*

Holidays
& Seasonal Celebrations®

Holiday Bingo!

Gather a supply of rubber stamps, making sure that nine of them are related to the winter holidays. Place all the stamps in a basket or box and provide an ink pad. Gather youngsters and give each child a copy of the grid on page 86. Have a child reach into the basket and remove a stamp. If it's a holiday-related stamp, she stamps it in one of the spaces on her grid and then places it back in the basket. If it isn't a holiday stamp, she just places it back in the basket. Youngsters continue, taking turns, until all the boxes have been filled with different images. *Carole Watkins, Timothy Ball Elementary, Crown Point, IN*

Beautiful Bows

Get a bag of holiday bows and place them at a center. Have little ones visit the center and make patterns with the bows. If your youngsters need extra assistance, make patterns ahead of time and take photos of them. Print the photos and place the printouts at the center for little ones to use as a reference when they're making patterns. *Hilda Cline, St. Petal, MS*

Toss It In!

Give a beanbag toss a seasonal twist with a Santa hat! Gather a small group of youngsters and give each child a beanbag. Hold the Santa hat upside down and have each child toss his bean-bag into the hat. When students are comfortable with this activity, have children take turns holding the hat while the remaining youngsters toss the beanbags. *Nancy Jandreau, Kids Corner Day Care, Potsdam, NY*

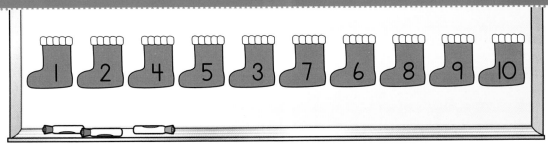

Stockings in a Row

Number each of ten stocking cutouts from 1 to 10. Display the stockings out of sequence in a row. Lead students in reading the row of numbers and guide them to notice that the numbers are not in order. Enlist volunteers to help you rearrange the stockings so they are in the correct order. *Colleen Higgins, Children's Garden, St. Davids, PA*

Jingle Rings

Make some merry music with these simple instruments. For each child, slip two or three medium to large jingle bells on a two-inch binder ring (available at office supply stores). Snap the ring closed, and you're ready to shake, shake, shake to some holiday tunes! *Shelley Hoster, PreK, Jack and Jill Early Learning Center, Norcross, GA*

Magic Reindeer Chow

Help little ones mix up a batch of Magic Reindeer Chow to leave for Santa's reindeer! Mix together a canister of oatmeal and a small container of brightly colored sugar crystals. Have each child take a turn stirring the mixture; then help him scoop some into a snack-size plastic bag. Attach a note to the bag telling moms and dads to sprinkle the chow on their lawns on Christmas Eve! *Kendi Morris, Beale Elementary School, Gallipolis Ferry, WV*

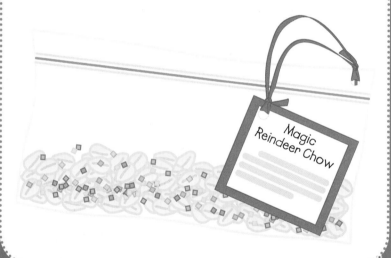

Kwanzaa Fruit

Families who celebrate Kwanzaa often display a basket of fruit among other Kwanzaa symbols. Present a basket of fruit. Explain that the fruit reminds people of the importance of hard work. Growing fruit is hard work, but the tasty fruit is a reward at the end. Have students explore and identify the fruit. Then give each youngster a snack of mixed fruit to celebrate hard work! *Deborah Garmon, Groton, CT*

New Year Practice Party

Explain that a whole new year will begin very soon and the year will change from 2014 to 2015. Next, have each youngster share something new he wants to try in the new year, such as a new food or activity. If desired, record students' responses on a sheet of chart paper. Then serve little ones sparkling grape juice and cookies. Finally, have them count backward from ten to one and then yell "Happy New Year!" *Christine Vohs, College Church Preschool, Olathe, KS*

Holidays & Seasonal Celebrations®

Pass the Snowman

Have little ones sit in a circle. Give a child a snowman cutout. (An Internet image search will turn up plenty of options.) Then have youngsters pass the snowman around the circle as quickly as they can as you lead them in singing the song shown. When the song is finished, have the child with the snowman pretend to melt to the floor just like the snowman would! Then play another round of this fun game!

Kristen Crust, Becky Seaman, and Jennifer Wilson,
Wonder Years Child Care, Jersey Shore, PA

(sung to the tune of "Clementine")

Pass the snowman, pass the snowman,
Pass the snowman—don't delay!
Pass it quickly.
Make it zippy!
Or he'll melt and go away.

In the new year, I will have a princess birthday party.

Alli

New Year's Predictions

Your preschoolers are sure to have some big ideas for the coming year! Give each child a copy of page 87. Write her prediction for the coming year as she dictates for you. Then ask her to illustrate her idea. Bind all the pages to make a class book. If desired, decorate the cover with confetti and glitter glue. Share the resulting book during a group time and place it in your classroom library for continued student enjoyment.

A Handful of Sweets

Candies won't melt in these hands! Trace two hands on a sheet of paper. Get wrapped chocolate Valentine's Day candies and a die. Gather two children. Have one child roll the die, count the dots, and place the corresponding number of candies on a hand. Have a second child repeat the process, placing the candies on the other hand. Then help little ones count the sets together. Continue for several rounds. If desired, give each child a candy when finished. ***Combining sets, counting***

Melissa Voorhees, Rainbow Station, Fremont, OH

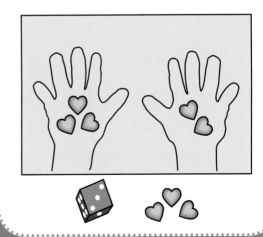

Holidays & Seasonal Celebrations®

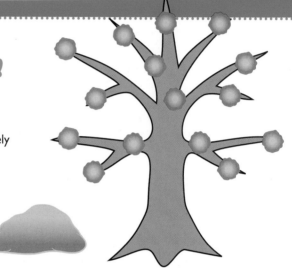

Scented Cherry Blossoms!

Exploring the sense of smell

Add a package of unsweetened cherry-flavored drink mix to your favorite play dough recipe. Place the dough on a table along with an oversize tree cutout. A youngster smells the lovely scented dough as she creates blossoms and places them on the tree.

Janet Boyce
Hinojosa Early Childhood and Pre-Kindergarten Center
Houston, TX

Stuff the Eggs!

Developing fine-motor skills

Place Easter grass in your sensory table (or a plastic tub). Separate plastic eggs and scatter them in the grass. Also scatter items that will fit in the eggs, such as pom-poms, plastic bugs, and craft foam shapes. Encourage youngsters to visit the center and then stuff and unstuff the eggs as desired!

Megan Taylor
Rowlett, TX

Jelly Bean Fun

Matching colors, reinforcing the names of body parts, gross-motor skills

For this active game, make a copy of the cards on page 88 and color each jelly bean a different color. Place the jelly bean cards and body part cards in separate gift bags. Next, make large jelly bean cutouts in colors that match the cards. Scatter the cutouts on the floor. To play, have a child choose a jelly bean card and a body part card. Then have her touch that body part to the corresponding jelly bean cutout! For an extra challenge, have her use a certain movement, such as marching or crawling, to get to that jelly bean!

Amy Jandebeur
Frogs to Fairy Dust
Yukon, OK

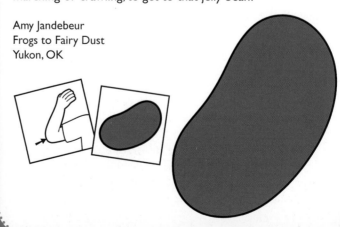

Holidays
& Seasonal Celebrations®

Wormy Pickup

Developing fine-motor skills

Get plastic worms (available at your local sporting goods store) and place them in a sensory table full of crinkled brown paper shreds. Provide tweezers and encourage little ones to use them to pick out the worms!

Dawn Mitten
Cumberland County Learning Center
Carlisle, PA

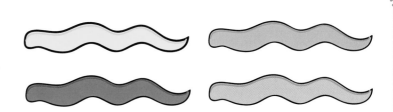

Let's Take a Hike

Participating in a song

The weather is warmer out, so it's a lovely time to take a walk! Lead youngsters in singing this engaging song about being outdoors!

(sung to the tune of "The Farmer in the Dell")

I like to take a hike.
I like to take a hike.
[Up the hills and down the hills],
I like to take a hike.

Continue with the following:
Hiking here and hiking there
Squishing through the sticky mud
Swishing through the tickly grass

Cindy Hoying
Centerville, OH

Dear Mama,

You are sweet like a strawberry;
Yes, it's true!
Here are some reasons
Why I love you:

You give me hugs.
You read me books.
You tuck me in.

Love,
Carter

A Berry for Mom

Dictating information to be written down

This personalized note holder is not only pleasing to look at but it smells great too! Mix one envelope of unsweetened, strawberry-flavored drink mix with two tablespoons of white glue. To make a strawberry note holder, paint a jumbo pasta shell with the glue mixture. While the glue is still wet, attach green tissue paper leaves and sprinkle red glitter on the shell. After the shell is dry, hot-glue (for teacher use only) it to a wooden spring-type clothespin. Next, attach a strip of magnetic tape to the back of the clothespin. Complete a tagboard copy of one of the Mother's Day cards on page 89, and clip it to the note holder.

©The Mailbox® • TEC41076 • Dec. 2014

In the new year, I will

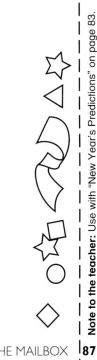

©The Mailbox® • TEC41077 • Jan./Feb. 2015

Note to the teacher: Use with "New Year's Predictions" on page 83.

Game Cards

Use with "Jelly Bean Fun" on page 84.

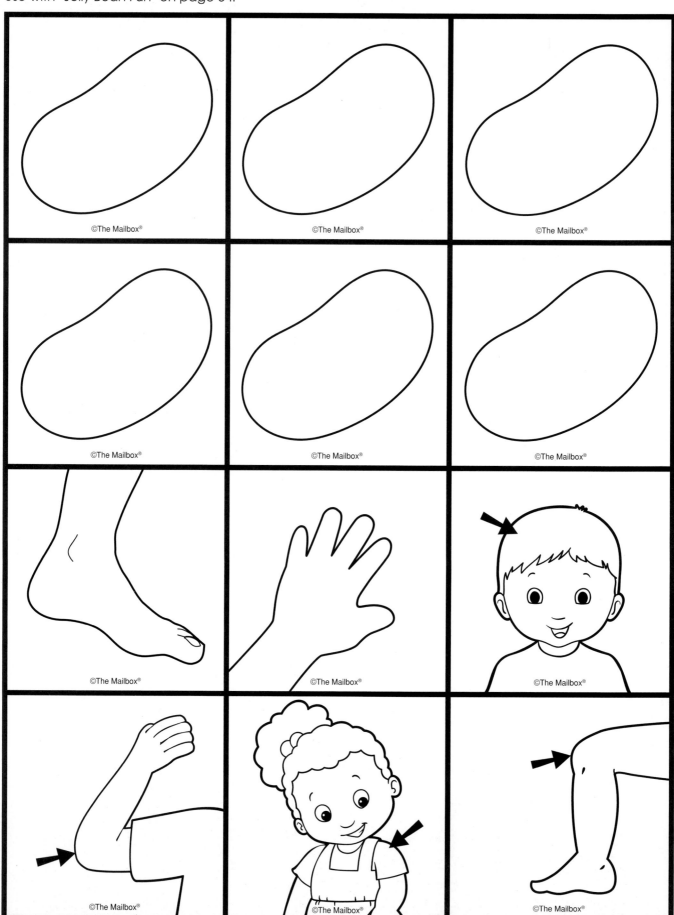

©The Mailbox®
©The Mailbox®
©The Mailbox®
©The Mailbox®
©The Mailbox®
©The Mailbox®
©The Mailbox®
©The Mailbox®
©The Mailbox®
©The Mailbox®
©The Mailbox®
©The Mailbox®

Dear _____,

You are sweet like a strawberry;

Yes, it's true!

Here are some reasons

Why I love you:

_____

_____

_____

Love,

_____

©The Mailbox®

Have a "Berry" Happy Mother's Day!

Glue photo here.

Love,

_____

©The Mailbox®

Snowpal Twins

🖍️ Color the two snowpals in each row that look the same.

Name _____

Wake Up, Groundhog!

Listen for directions.

©The Mailbox® • TEC41077 • Jan./Feb. 2015

Directions 1) Color the pillow blue. 2) Count the hearts on the bedspread. Write the number in the picture frame. 3) Color the hearts red. 4) Color the teddy bear brown. 5) Color the rest of the picture as you like.

Tear.

 Glue.

Note to the teacher: Copy this page on colored paper. Have students tear cotton balls and glue them around the kite so they resemble clouds.

LEARNING CENTERS

Learning Centers

Alphabet Sock
Literacy Center

Tuck several plastic letters (or letter tiles) in the foot of a sock. Place the sock at a center along with a second set of letters that match the ones in the sock. A youngster reaches into the sock and pulls out a letter. Then he finds the matching letter and sets the pair aside. He repeats the process until all the letters are matched. ***Matching letters***

Lozetta Trandem
Trandem Family Day Care/Preschool
Auburn, CA

Tiny Sandboxes
Sensory Center

Fill your sensory table or a large plastic tub with sand. Provide a small plastic scooper and several jewelry box bottoms in assorted sizes. A child uses the scooper to fill a box with sand, counting each scoopful of sand as she works. She repeats the process with a different box to see if it takes more, fewer, or the same number of scoops to fill it. Then she continues in the same way. ***Counting, making comparisons***

Suzanne Moore
Tucson, AZ

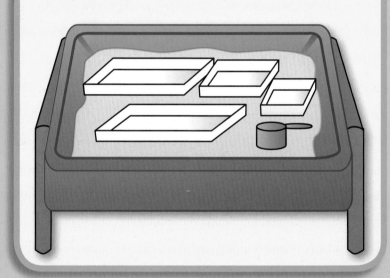

Out to Pasture
Math Center

Cut apart three copies of the farm animal cards on page 107. Divide a green poster board (pasture) into six equal sections; then attach a different animal card to each section. Set out the pasture and place the remaining cards nearby. A student takes a card, locates a matching animal in the pasture, and places the card in that section. He continues with the remaining cards. ***Matching pictures, sorting***

Deborah J. Ryan
Milwaukie, OR

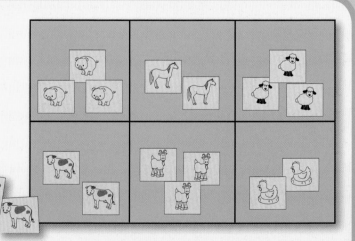

Zigzagging Along
Writing Center

Use masking tape (or craft tape) to make a large zigzag design on a tabletop; then attach a green sticky dot (start) and a red sticky dot (finish) to opposite ends of the zigzag. Provide tools to trace with, such as a large craft feather, a paintbrush, a craft stick, and an unsharpened pencil. A student chooses an item. Starting at the green dot, she uses the item to trace the zigzag from left to right, stopping at the red dot. *Prewriting*

Roxanne LaBell Dearman
NC Intervention for the Deaf and Hard of Hearing
Charlotte, NC

Ten Little Fingerprints
Science Center

Program a class supply of white paper as shown. Place the paper at a table along with a marker, a black ink pad, and a magnifying glass. Help a child trace his hands onto the programmed paper. Then have him press each finger, in turn, on the ink pad and then on the corresponding fingertip of the tracing. When the printmaking is done, encourage him to examine his fingerprints with the magnifying glass. For added fun, teach little ones the song shown. *Observing details*

(sung to the tune of "Ten Little Indians")

One little, two little, three little fingerprints.
Four little, five little, six little fingerprints.
Seven little, eight little, nine little fingerprints.
Ten prints of my own!

Roxanne LaBell Dearman

Cameron's Little Fingerprints

Stamp Bags
Art Center

For this process art, set out construction paper and shallow containers of paint in assorted colors. For each color, provide a bunched-up lunch bag. A youngster dips a bag in paint and then stamps the bag on a sheet of paper. He repeats the process with other bags and colors of paint, overlapping the prints and blending colors. *Expressing oneself through art*

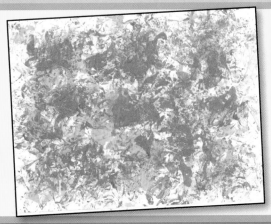

Learning Centers

Name Sanding
Writing Center

This center increases arm strength and name-writing skills! Use a pencil to lightly write each child's name on an inexpensive scrap of plywood. Then give a child his plywood and a sanding sponge. Help him identify the letters in his name. Then encourage him to use the sanding sponge to sand his name off the board! *Forming one's own name, developing fine-motor skills*

Kathy Montilluer
Joli Ann Leichtag Elementary
San Marcos, CA

Excellent for children with motor challenges!

Tracks and Feathers
Art Center

Trim a sponge to resemble a turkey footprint. Then place it at a center along with a shallow pan of paint, craft feathers, and colorful construction paper. A child presses the sponge in the paint and then onto his paper several times, adding more paint when needed. Then he glues feathers around the footprints. *Expressing oneself through art*

Janet Boyce
Hinojosa Early Childhood and Pre-Kindergarten Center
Houston, TX

Counting Cranberries
Math Center

Label foam plates with different numbers and then float them in your water table. Empty a bag of cranberries in the water. (They float as well!) Then post an adult helper at the center. A child points to a plate and identifies the number, with help as needed. Next, he plucks the appropriate number of cranberries from the water and places them on the plate. He continues with each remaining plate. *Be sure to remove the cranberries for safekeeping after center time.* *Counting, making sets*

Janet Boyce

Learning Centers

Matching Plates
Literacy Center

Program pairs of small, seasonal paper plates with matching uppercase letters, lowercase letters, or one uppercase and one lowercase letter. Place the plates facedown. A center visitor turns over two plates. If the plates match, he sets them aside. If the plates do not match, he turns them back over. He continues in this manner until all the letter pairs are matched. **For an extra challenge**, encourage youngsters to identify the letter names. *Matching letters, identifying letters*

Trisha Cooper
Trisha's Preschool
Spanish Fork, UT

Terrific Tree Toppers
Art Center

Set out a class supply of star cutouts (patterns on page 108) and small cardboard tubes along with assorted craft supplies, such as pom-poms, sequins, glitter glue, wrapping paper scraps, and ribbon. A child uses craft materials to decorate a star cutout as desired. Then she glues the star to a cardboard tube. *Expressing oneself with art*

Keely Saunders
Bonney Lake ECEAP
Bonney Lake, WA

Run, Run, Gingerbread Man!
Fine-Motor Area

Cut out a tagboard copy of the gingerbread man patterns on page 109 to make tracers. Set out the tracers, sandpaper pieces, scissors, cinnamon sticks, and black crayons. Assist a child in tracing a gingerbread man shape onto a piece of sandpaper. Then have him cut it out. (For younger preschoolers, have the pieces precut.) Remove the leg holes using scissors or a small circle puncher. Then encourage the child to scrape a cinnamon stick over the gingerbread man to give it a lovely smell. Finally, have him use a crayon to draw a face. During a read-aloud of a favorite version of *The Gingerbread Man*, invite him to place his fingers through the holes on his gingerbread man cutout and make it run at appropriate times. *Developing fine-motor skills*

Natalie Garland
Litchfield Elementary
Litchfield Park, AZ

Snow Writing
Sensory Center

For this sensory-based math activity, place a baking tray containing a thin layer of potato flakes (snow) at a table. Stack a set of number cards face-down near the tray. A child flips the top card and then uses her fingertip to write the number in the snow. Then she uses her hand to smooth out the snow and repeats the activity with a new card. She continues as time allows. *Writing numbers*

Jingle Boxes
Block Center

Add a little holiday jingle to your block area! Gather a number of boxes in various shapes. Put one or more large jingle bells inside each one; then tape the boxes shut and wrap them with holiday gift wrap. A youngster builds various structures with the boxes. What fun to hear the gentle ring-a-ling as the boxes are stacked and the symphony of sound when they topple! *Developing fine-motor skills*

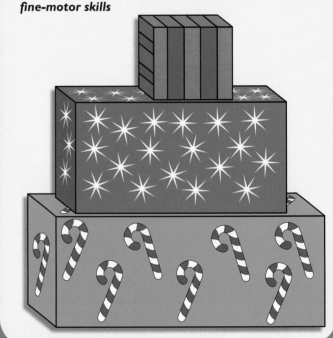

Small Bows, Big Bows!
Math Center

Collect four gift bows in different sizes. Place the bows at a table along with a shallow tray of tempera paint and a class supply of construction paper strips. Invite a youngster to the table and encourage him to choose a paper strip. Then have him press the smallest bow in the pan of paint and use it to make a print on the strip as shown. Have him continue in the same way with each bow from smallest to largest! *Ordering by size*

Learning Centers

So Many Toys!
Literacy Center

Youngsters will be eager to look at environmental print with this catalog-clipping activity. Place several toy catalogs and circulars at a table along with a large stocking cutout and a supply of scissors and glue sticks. Invite students to look through the catalogs, checking out the toy options and familiar name brands. When they see a toy they might particularly enjoy, invite them to cut it out of the catalog and glue it to the stocking. Be sure to comment on letters in the ads that youngsters might find familiar! *Environmental print*

Kwanzaa Feast Mat
Fine-Motor Area

Place masking tape and brown construction paper at a center. A child attaches lengths of masking tape to a sheet of construction paper as shown. (Provide help as needed.) She rubs the side of an unwrapped brown crayon over the surface of the paper. Then she uses scissors to fringe-cut the ends of the paper. *Tearing, rubbing*

Janet Boyce
Hinojosa Early Childhood Pre-Kindergarten Center
Houston, TX

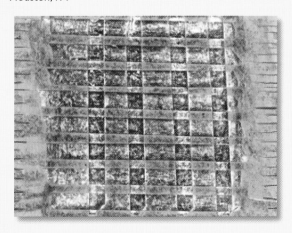

Blue Candle, White Candle
Math Center

Use menorah candles (or colored paper candle cutouts) for practice with simple patterning. Working with a small group, lay several candles on a tabletop to form a pattern. Ask a volunteer to identify the pattern; then help him copy it. After several rounds, pair students and have one child create a pattern for his partner to extend. Then instruct youngsters to switch roles and repeat the activity. *Patterning*

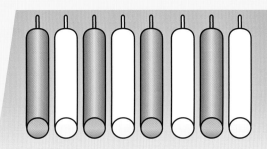

Learning Centers

Winter Wonderland
Discovery Center

Mix salt and silver glitter in a shallow pan so it resembles snow. Set the pan near a collection of items such as feathers, evergreen twigs, pinecones, and a small rag doll. A youngster explores the designs the objects make in the snow. Be sure to encourage the child to use the rag doll to make a snow angel! *Sensory exploration*

Janet Boyce
Hinojosa Early Childhood and Pre-Kindergarten Center
Houston, TX

Sweet Structures
Math Center

Build little ones' spatial skills with this unique center. Use sugar cubes to build several simple structures. Take a photo of each structure before disassembling it. Print the photos and place them near a supply of sugar cubes. A center visitor chooses a photo and then uses it as a reference to build the structure. After a youngster has copied a few structures, invite him to create an original structure. Take a photo of the structure, print it, and then place it at the center for students to copy. *Spatial awareness*

Gail Timpe
St. Mary Cathedral
Cape Girardeau, MO

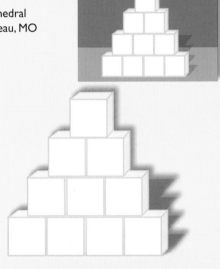

Snowy Scenes
Block Center

Place a length of cotton batting or white felt on the floor of your block center. Set toy vehicles, toy people and animals, small decorative trees, and cotton balls nearby. A child uses the blocks and other materials to create a snowy scene. *Building a seasonal display*

Cindy Hoying
Centerville, OH

H Is for *Heart!*
Literacy Center

Tape several *H* cutouts to a table. Provide large heart cutouts programmed as shown and unwrapped crayons nearby. A child places his heart on top of the *H*s and colors the heart. Then he uses his finger to trace each *H* on his heart as he makes the /h/ sound. *Letter-sound associations*

Hilda Cline
Petal, MS

Box of Chocolates
Math Center

Label several mini cupcake liners with different numbers. Place the liners in a heart-shaped box with a lid and then put a jumbo brown pom-pom (a chocolate) in each liner. A child removes a chocolate from the box, names the number, and then pretends to eat the chocolate. After she has "eaten" all the chocolates, she returns the chocolates to the box to ready the center for the next visitor. *Number identification*

Leanne Swinson
Newport, NC

Eraser Prints
Art Center

Place a rubber eraser in each of several shallow containers of paint. Set the containers near sheets of white construction paper. A child makes colorful prints on his paper until a desired effect is reached. Then he sets his paper aside to dry. *Expressing oneself through art*

adapted from an idea by Cindi Zsittnik
Huntersville, NC

 tip→ Stick a pushpin in each eraser to make it easier for little hands to pick up.

Learning Centers

Making Music
Discovery Center

Place *S*-shaped hooks on the rungs of a ladder ball frame. Then hang a collection of musical instruments and items that can be used to make music on the hooks. Also provide a mallet (or a spoon). A center visitor uses the mallet to tap the instruments and items, exploring the sounds! *Exploring sound*

Jodi Remington, Busy Day Child Care, Okemos, MI

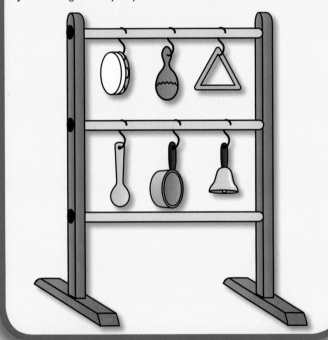

Fluffy Beards
Fine-Motor Area

Take a head shot photo of each child. Then enlarge each photo and print it out. Mix equal parts shaving cream and white glue. Then tint the mixture orange. Invite a child to the center and help her cut out her photo and glue it to a sheet of construction paper. Then have her draw or paint a leprechaun hat above her head on the photo. Next, encourage her to spoon the paint mixture onto her photo and then use the spoon to smooth the mixture so it appears as if she has a leprechaun beard. These projects are so cute! *Fine-motor skills*

Carolyn Jones
St. Athanasius SAFE Program
Louisville, KY

A Golden Path
Math Center

Attach a leprechaun cutout and the pot of gold cutout (patterns on page 110) to a paper strip as shown. Place the strip on a table along with yellow Unifix cubes and a large foam die. A child rolls the die and counts the dots. Then he counts out the appropriate number of cubes, links them together, and places them near the leprechaun. He continues rolling and adding cubes until he reaches the pot of gold! *Counting, exploring length*

Gerri Primak, Holden, MA

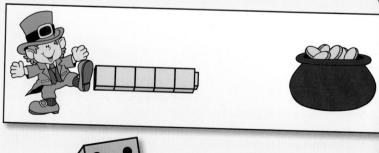

Rainbow Jump
Gross-Motor Area

Cut lengths of streamers in rainbow colors and then place them in parallel rows on your floor, making sure there is space between the streamers. Challenge children to visit the center and jump over each streamer as they name its color!
Jumping

Emily McDowell, LeClaire Christian Daycare
Edwardsville, IL

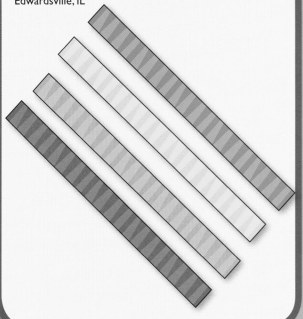

Oval Bunny
Math Center

Cut ovals from tagboard in several different sizes. Then gather two youngsters and show them the tracings. Help them identify the shape. Explain that an oval is similar to the shape of an egg and that it looks like a slightly flattened circle. Then help them trace the ovals and color in the tracings to make a bunny similar to the one shown!
Exploring ovals

Shelley Williams
Children's College
Layton, UT

That's Sweet!
Literacy Center

Gather a bottle of honey, a box of graham crackers, and napkins. Invite students to the center and have each child say the word *honey*. Have children notice the /h/ sound at the beginning of *honey*. Guide them to understand that /h/ is the sound of the letter *H*. Have each child use his finger to make an *H* on the tabletop. Then give each child a napkin and a cracker. Prompt her to squeeze the honey bottle to make an *H* on her graham cracker. As she nibbles on her treat, discuss other words that begin with /h/. *Letter sound /h/*

Tricia Kylene Brown
Bowling Green, KY

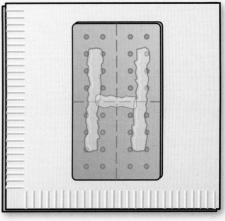

Rain Centers!

Pull a Drop
Math Center

Cover an empty tissue box with cotton balls so it resembles a cloud. Then label raindrop die-cuts with different numbers and place them in the box. A youngster visits the center and removes a drop from the cloud. She identifies the number on the drop and then taps the tabletop that number of times to sound like falling rain. She continues with other numbers. ***Number identification***

Connie Massingill, Dawn Til Dusk Preschool
Zionsville, IN

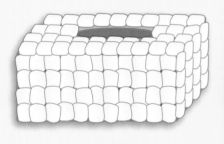

I would like it to rain macaroni and cheese. It would be yummy!

A Unique Downpour
Literacy Center

In advance, mix gray paint with shaving cream to make puff paint. Read aloud *Cloudy With a Chance of Meatballs* to your youngsters. Have each child paint a cloud cutout with the puff paint. Then, when it's dry, ask her, "What would you want it to rain?" Write her idea on a card and hang it from her cloud with fishing line. Display the clouds around the room. ***Responding to literature through art***

Sandy Evans, Hampton First Baptist Academy, Hampton, GA

Rain Sounds
Sensory Table

Place rice and plastic egg halves in your sensory table. Little ones visit the center and investigate the items to make rain sounds. For example, they might pour rice from egg half to egg half or they might seal rice between two halves and shake it. ***Exploring sound***

Janet Boyce
Hinojosa Early Childhood and Pre-Kindergarten Center
Houston, TX

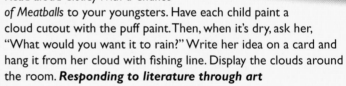

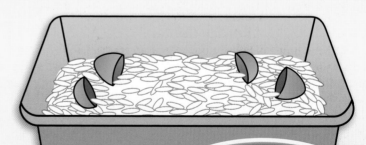

To keep interest high, consider replacing the eggs with other items throughout the week, such as paper plates, metal measuring cups, or mixing spoons. Then challenge youngsters to make rain sounds!

Learning Centers

Counting Petals
Block Center

Youngsters' counting skills are sure to bloom at this center. Label each of several plastic lids with a different number. Place the lids in a tub and set the tub in the block area. A child places a lid on the floor, reads the number, and then arranges a matching number of blocks around the lid so it looks like a flower with petals! *Identifying numbers, counting*

Roxanne LaBell Dearman
NC Intervention for the Deaf and Hard of Hearing
Charlotte, NC

The Cleaning Crew
Dramatic-Play Area

Stock your dramatic-play area with buckets; sponges; dusters; squirt bottles; aprons; gloves; and toy mops, brooms, and dustpans. Post a laminated list of "chores" that youngsters can do around the classroom and set a wipe-off marker nearby. A child chooses a chore and gathers the appropriate items. After she completes the chore, she checks it off the list and chooses another chore. *Participating in pretend play*

Darla Gordon
Orchard Valley Learning Center
Centennial, CO

A Disappearing Treat
Literacy Center

For this center, each child will need a copy of the ice cream bar cards on page 111 and five craft sticks. A child colors his cards and cuts them out. Then he tapes each card to a craft stick. (One craft stick will not have a card.) Next, he arranges the ice cream bars to show the sequence of the bar being eaten. *Sequencing*

Connie Pflaum
Cedar Lake, IN

Learning Centers

Dinosaur Centers

Dino Cafe
Dramatic-Play Area

Serve up some dinosaur fun with this center. Label two bins as shown and place them in your kitchen area. Put play meat foods in the carnivore bin and play fruits and vegetables in the herbivore bin. Set aprons, small notepads, and pencils nearby. Center visitors use the props as they play the roles of cooks, servers, and dinosaur customers. *Participating in pretend play*

Gerri Primak
Holden, MA

Carnivores | Herbivores

Syllable Stomp
Literacy Center

Give each youngster at this supervised center four dinosaur footprint cards (see page 112). Name a word related to dinosaurs. (See the list below for suggestions.) Direct youngsters to repeat the named word as they stomp out the syllables. Then have the group say the word again as each child lays down a footprint card for each syllable. Repeat the activity with other suggested words. *Counting syllables*

Suggested words: *dinosaur, carnivore, herbivore, fossils, gigantic, reptile, spikes, horns, claws, extinct, triceratops, stegosaur, pterodactyl, allosaur, hadrosaur*

Cindy Hoying
Centerville, OH

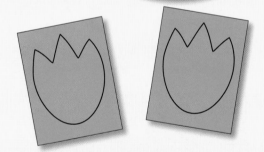

Rep-tile.

Erupting Volcanoes
Snack Center

Set out waffle bowls, cherry pie filling, and plain yogurt along with disposable plates, cups, and spoons. With help, a child pokes a hole in the bottom of a waffle bowl (volcano) to make a crater and then places it upside down on a plate. To make the lava, he places a scoop of pie filling and a scoop of yogurt in a cup and mixes it together. Next, he pours the lava over the volcano. Finally, he enjoys his yummy treat.

Sherry Nakata
Keaau Elementary
Keaau, HI

TEC41074

TEC41074

TEC41074

TEC41074

TEC41074

TEC41074

Star Patterns

Use with "Terrific Tree Toppers" on page 97.

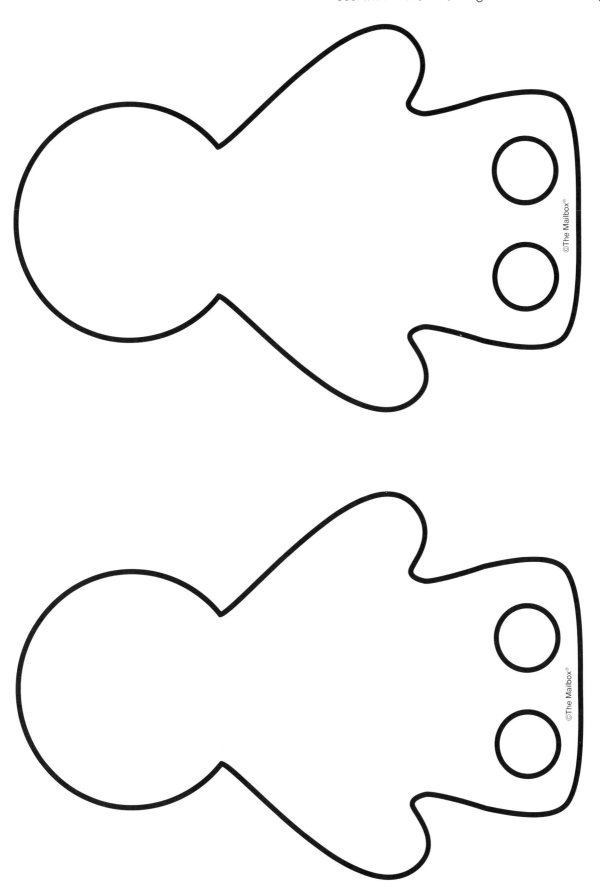

Pot of Gold and Leprechaun Patterns

Use with "A Golden Path" on page 102.

©The Mailbox®

©The Mailbox®

©The Mailbox®

©The Mailbox®

©The Mailbox®

©The Mailbox®

Footprint Cards

Use with "Syllable Stomp" on page 106.

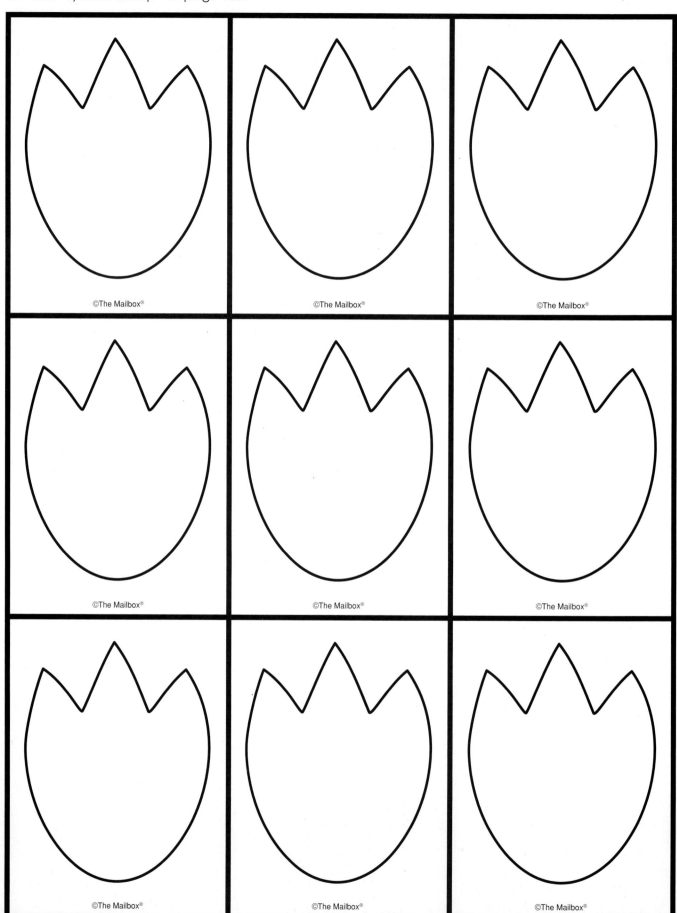

©The Mailbox®

©The Mailbox®

©The Mailbox®

©The Mailbox®

©The Mailbox®

©The Mailbox®

©The Mailbox®

©The Mailbox®

©The Mailbox®

OUR READERS SHARE

Our Readers Share

Birthday Numbers

To celebrate a child's birthday, I cut a large poster board number to represent his age. On the day of his birthday, I set out the number along with crayons, markers, stickers, stampers, and ink pads. Then I invite the birthday child and his classmates to decorate the number. After they finish decorating the number, I display it. At the end of the day, I send the number home with the child.

Suzanne Foote, East Ithaca Preschool, Ithaca, NY

A Successful Display

At the beginning of the year, I ask each child to bring one yard of ribbon. I attach a nametag to one end of the ribbon and then display the ribbons in a child-accessible location. When a child masters a skill, I give her a cutout related to that skill to attach to her ribbon. Students are proud of their ribbons, plus you can see at a glance who has mastered a certain skill. *Brenda Taylor, Clements/ Parsons Elementary, Copperas Cove, TX*

See page 122 for skill patterns to use with this idea!

Learning About Letters

Here's a simple way for a youngster to learn the first letter of his name. For each child, I die-cut the first letter of his name in a few colors. I send one of the letters home with the child along with a note to his family. I ask the family to decorate the letter, display it, and review it often. I use the remaining letters for review activities at school.

Susan Jacobs, Vernon E. Whightman Primary, Bath, NY

"Heart-y" Hugs

To ease little ones' worries at school, I have each family create a hug from home. The family decorates a large heart cutout with pictures and reassuring messages. They return the heart to school, and we place them in a special box that my students have decorated. Whenever a child is feeling a little sad, she can take her hug from the box and keep it with her as long as she needs it.

Sheryl Keseian, Avon Nursery School, Avon, MA

Our Readers Share

What Do You See?

My little ones wear Halloween costumes to school for our fall celebration. I take a photo of each child. Then I put the photos in an inexpensive photo album and caption them in the style of *Brown Bear, Brown Bear, What Do You See?* by Bill Martin Jr. and Eric Carle. After reading the book to my youngsters, I place it in the reading center. **Kathy Henson, First United Methodist Church Preschool, Warrensburg, MO**

Kitty cat, kitty cat, what do you see?

I see a princess looking at me.

I saw a little turkey
Standing by the tree.
It gobbled, and it wobbled.
Then it ran away from me!
Oh, turkey, turkey, turkey,
Please come out and play!
I promise not to eat you
On Thanksgiving Day!

Turkey Treats

Before Thanksgiving Day, I have each child make Gobbler Goodie Bags for the wild turkeys in our area. A child puts one scoop each of millet, cracked corn, and soybeans in a resealable plastic bag. After sealing the bag, he attaches a copy of the poem shown to it. Then I send home the child's bag and a note encouraging his family to help him spread the contents of the Gobbler Goodie Bag in a wooded or open field so the wild turkeys can enjoy a tasty treat. **Carrie Newell, Palco Enhancement Preschool, Palco, KS**

Shape Trains

I use these trains for fine-motor practice and a shape review! I give each child a long tagboard strip, several address labels, and colorful sticky dots. I help a child cut one of the address labels to make a rectangle and a square. Then I encourage him to attach the labels and dots to make a train as shown. When he's finished, I prompt him to identify the shapes. **Cindy Hoying, Centerville, OH**

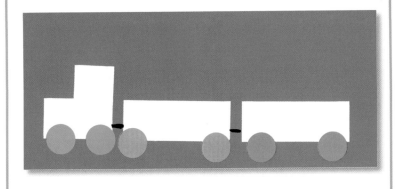

Cornmeal Play Dough

During the fall, my youngsters enjoy using this unique textured dough. I mix together 1½ cups of flour, 1½ cups of cornmeal, 1 cup of salt, and 1 cup of water. Add more water and flour, if desired, to reach an appealing consistency. Store the dough in an airtight container in the refrigerator when you're not using it. **Tina Rabas, St. Mary's Day Care, Green Bay, WI**

Wheat Flour

Corn Meal

SALT

Our Readers Share

Ornaments That Sparkle

For each child, I run a length of ribbon through the center of a discarded CD and tie the ends together. Then I have him glue a felt circle to the back of the CD and a circle-shaped photo of himself to the front. Next, I direct him to glue a piece of tinsel garland around the photo. To complete the ornament, I invite him to glue holiday-themed confetti to the garland. **Sheryl Gulan, DUMC Preschool, Davidson, NC**

Snow Painting

Youngsters practice writing their names with this fun outdoor activity for a snowy day. I put diluted paint in several clean spray bottles. Then I take my youngsters outside. I have each child spray paint on the snow to make the letters in her name. After she spells her name, I invite her to use the paint to make pictures in the snow. **Shaindy Spitzer, Lakewood, NJ**

Ice Fishing

During my winter unit, I use my sensory table to give my youngsters a cool fishing experience. I put a couple inches of water into the sensory table and set it outside. To create ice fishing holes, I place a few small weighted-down buckets in the water. The next day, I bring the sensory table inside and remove the buckets. Then I pour some more water in the table. This causes the ice to lift from the bottom and float. Finally, I put plastic fish in the table and set play fishing poles nearby. **Heidi Braun, Redeemer Lutheran Preschool, Winona, MN**

tip If the temperatures in your area aren't cold enough for this idea, put water and weighted-down cans in a dish pan and then put it in the freezer.

Recipe Re-creations

Each week, my youngsters work together to follow a recipe to make a snack. After the snack is finished, I put the empty food packages from the snack ingredients in our play kitchen area. When a child visits the kitchen area, he uses the food packages and other items in the area to recreate the recipe. **Christine Cavin, YMCA of Frederick, Frederick, MD**

Our Readers Share

Boo-Boo Butter

I keep raw, organic shea butter (boo-boo butter) in my classroom. When a child gets a small scratch or an itchy patch, I rub a little boo-boo butter on it. The boo-boo butter is soothing, plus the extra attention helps the boo-boo too! *Shawn F. Blunt, Westview Primary School, Goose Creek, SC*

Birthday Buddies

Staff birthdays are a big deal at our school. Each staff member is assigned a surprise birthday buddy! The birthday buddy plans a special birthday treat, such as a cake and a crown to wear or yummy snacks and a little gift! It's always fun to see what surprises are in store for your birthday. *Karen Gerton, B'nai Israel Schilit Nursery School, Rockville, MD*

Xs and Os

I have found the perfect manipulatives for Valentine's Day! At the hardware store, I purchase a supply of plastic tile spacers and large metal washers. They look like *Xs* and *Os*! My youngsters use them for patterning and sorting as well as playing the classic game tic-tac-toe. *Karen Smith, Little Tid-Bits, Fresno, CA*

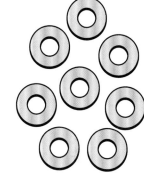

Stop!

I attach several stop sign cutouts to separate spring-type clothespins. Then I put the stop signs in a student-accessible location. At cleanup time, if a child is not finished building or creating something, he places a stop sign nearby. This lets his classmates know not to clean it up because he is still working on it. *Cynthia Zimmerman, Beth Israel Preschool and Kindergarten, Eagle, PA*

Our Readers Share

Lamination Elimination

Instead of laminating activity cards and picture cards to make them sturdy, I save time and money by printing them on photo paper. Photo paper is strong and holds up well. Plus it makes the cards look glossy and lovely! *Fran Ludy, Franny's Home Daycare, Jonesburg, MO*

Fluffy Tails

For a fun springtime treat, I make a batch of bunny-shaped sugar cookies. I give each child a cookie and have her spread white or pink icing on her cookie. Then I invite her to add a cotton candy tail to her cookie. My kids love making these cute cookies as much as eating them. *Rachel Garman, Tri-County Co-Op Preschool, Wooster, OH*

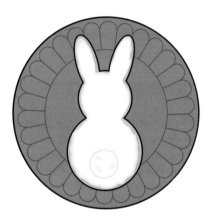

I See It!

I attach large wiggly eyes to craft sticks. Then I give one to a child when we are looking at a book or a letter chart together. I tell the child, "Put your eye on the letter [letter name]," and the child can touch the stick to the letter. I've also adapted this practice for work with our iPads! I simply attach a pom-pom on the opposite side of the eye, and then the child can gently touch the pom-pom to the screen without making the iPad flip to the next page! *Laura Johnson, South Decatur Elementary, Greensburg, IN*

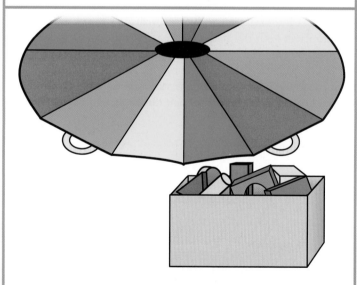

Parachute Sort

To reinforce sorting by color, I bring out my parachute! I provide a box full of colorful manipulatives, such as pom-poms, play food, toy vehicles, magnetic letters, and building blocks. Then I have my students sort the items onto the colorful sections of the parachute. For added fun, set a timer and have students correctly place all the items on the parachute within the designated time frame! *Nancy Jandreau, Kids Cottage Day Care, Ballston Lake, NY*

"Ribbit-ing" Rewards

Count on students to go buggy over this approach to recognizing their hard work! For each child, cut a lily pad from a folded piece of construction paper as shown. Label it with the child's name and decorate the front of it with a frog sticker. Attach each youngster's folded lily pad to his desk or work area. When a child completes a certain task, open his lily pad and place an insect sticker inside. After he has a predetermined number of stickers, reward him with a small prize or special privilege.

Ready to Take Home

Students have trouble taking large projects home without damaging them. Solve this problem with cardboard tubes. Cut paper towel tubes in half to make a supply. When a child has a large poster or paper project to take home, roll it up, slide it into a tube, and then label the tube with the child's name. Students are always pleased to know that their special projects will arrive home safely!

Perfect for Pencils

This idea for making pencil cups is so easy that you'll want to make cups for several different classroom areas. Simply decorate clean, empty frosting containers with stickers. Then stand several sharpened pencils in each container. The resulting pencil cups are durable, convenient, and free from sharp edges.

Growing Appreciation

Looking for a creative way to thank a classroom volunteer or school staff member? Try this! To make one thank-you note, glue a small, circular photo of each student on a large circle. (The photos may overlap slightly.) Glue student-made petals to the circle and add a stem and two leaves. Write a message on the leaves, and this classy blossom is ready to be delivered!

Our Readers Share

My masterpiece for Mom

MOM

Mail for Mom

This idea is perfect for Mother's Day and for reinforcing the letter *M*! I give each child a sheet of paper labeled as shown and invite him to draw a picture for his mom. I help him put the picture in an envelope and address it to his mom. Then I mail the letters. My youngsters can hardly contain their excitement when they share about their moms receiving this special mail! *Kara Dozier, The Bowman Academy, Tampa, FL*

Perfect Pickles!

For my garden unit, I have little ones make these quick pickles! I cut small cucumbers so they won't roll around. Then I have each youngster use a plastic knife to cut a cucumber into chunks. I have her place the chunks in a quart-size resealable bag. Then we add a few green pepper and onion chunks, 2 tablespoons of sugar, ½ teaspoon of salt, ½ teaspoon of celery seed, and ¼ cup of cider vinegar. I help the child close the bag securely and shake it gently. Then I send the pickles home to be refrigerated. They're ready to eat by suppertime! *Karen Canfield, Family of Christ Preschool, Chanhassen, MN*

VINEGAR

Gross-Motor Game

When you need an easy-to-prepare gross-motor center, try this! Simply set a classroom chair in an open space in your room. Then place several balls in a basket and set it a few feet away from the chair. Youngsters visit the center and attempt to roll the balls between the legs of the chair.

Warm Fuzzies

Encourage students to remember manners and be kind to others with a warm fuzzy jar! Simply place a cotton ball in a plastic jar each time you witness positive behavior. A full jar of warm fuzzies will earn little ones a special snack or movie.

Please Feed the Dog

To encourage little ones to throw away paper scraps, attach a picture of a dog to each of the trash cans. When there are paper scraps on or under tables, simply say, "Please feed the dog." Little ones will love "feeding" the dog all the scraps.

Dad's Bank

To make this Father's Day gift, I first gather a class supply of plastic containers with lids. (Frosting containers work well!) I cut a slit in each container's lid. Then I help a child cover the can with a piece of solid-color Con-Tact covering cut to fit. On each bank, I write "When Daddy spends time with me, I'm the richest kid in the world." Then the child decorates the bank with money-themed stickers.
Lainey Bradley, Alpharetta First United Methodist Preschool, Alpharetta, GA

When Daddy spends time with me, I'm the richest kid in the world.

Water Table Fun

For some unique outside water table exploration, I gather a short length of clear plastic tubing, a funnel, and an empty one-liter soda bottle. I attach the tubing to the side of the water table. Then I arrange the funnel and bottle as shown. Little ones use containers to pour water into the funnel and fill up the soda bottle. Then they can dump the water back in the table. This always encourages a lot of prediction and observation during outdoor play!
Evelyn Casil, Meo Lahaina Head Start, Lahaina, HI

An Attendance Twist

At the end of the school year, add a fun twist to taking attendance. Give students a question, such as "What is your favorite breakfast food?" or "What is your middle name?" Then, when you call each child's name for attendance, have her answer the question using a complete sentence.

My favorite breakfast is pancakes.

Skill Patterns

Use with "A Successful Display" on page 114.

I know my colors!

TEC41074

I know my address!

TEC41074

I know my telephone number!

TEC41074

I know my shapes!

TEC41074

PROBLEM SOLVED!

Problem Solved!

Your Solutions to Classroom Challenges

If my little ones are having a difficult time remembering to raise their hands, we **sing this little song**. It's a great reminder!

Melody Kugel, Lincoln Christian Preschool, Lincoln, NE

("sung to the tune of "Hickory, Dickory, Dock")

If you have something to say,
Just raise your hand right away.
Then wait for your turn
To share what you've learned
If you have something to say.

I make a **reminder puppet**! I attach a tagboard hand cutout to a jumbo craft stick. If a youngster is interrupting, I simply continue with the class conversation and hand the puppet to the child. It's a great reminder that doesn't stop the flow of instruction!

Rosemary Blessman, Manning School, Westmont, IL

I have each child practice raising her hand and using **her other hand to cover her mouth**. After using this method for a while, my students don't need their helper hands at all!

Kelly Tincher, Saint Edmond, Fort Dodge, IA

To help little ones remember to raise their hands, simply **sing this song** as a reminder before circle time!

adapted from an idea by Robin Wilhelm, Douglas Child Care, Box Elder, SD

(sung to the tune of "Row, Row, Row Your Boat")

Raise, raise, raise your hand
Way up high with me!
Raise it quickly; raise it slowly.
Raise it thoughtfully.

Raise your hand.

Raise it quickly and then slowly.
Tap head with finger.

It's your turn!
TheMailbox.com/submitideas

How do you manage *student bathroom breaks?*

Your Solutions to Classroom Challenges

 To make bathroom transition times go more smoothly, I attach a **plastic sleeve** to the wall next to our bathrooms. I stock it with songs, fingerplays, and simple movement activities to do with youngsters while they wait their turns. I make sure to change out the activities each month to keep interest high!

Angela Lenker, Montgomery Early Learning Centers, Pottstown, PA

 I have a laminated **two-sided sign** on the single bathroom in my classroom. One side is a red "stop" sign and the other side is a green "go" sign. Before a child goes into the bathroom, she knows to flip the sign to show "Stop." Then, when she leaves, she flips the sign back to "Go." My kids always know when the bathroom is available!

Darlene Taig, Willow Creek Cooperative Preschool, Westland, MI

 While youngsters are waiting to use the restroom, I teach my students **Bible verses**. (Other options could include learning a favorite **poem** or an unfamiliar **nursery rhyme**.) We begin slowly and add more words each day. Youngsters' parents are always impressed with their memorization!

Mary Ann Craven, Fallbrook United Methodist Christian School, Fallbrook, CA

 I always let my little ones go to the restroom when they ask, but I found that I had a tough time telling when they had their hands up for a question and when they needed to use the restroom. So I taught my youngsters how to make the American Sign Language **sign for the letter *R***. Now, if a child needs to use the restroom, he holds up his hand forming an *R*. I can just nod my head without interrupting the activity.

Elizabeth Egesdahl, Frangus Elementary, Orlando, FL

It's your turn!
TheMailbox.com/submitideas

Problem Solved!

Your Solutions to Classroom Challenges

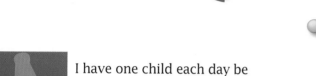 **How do you add zip *to your calendar time?***

On the final school day of a month, I lead little ones in singing the first verse of the **song** below. Then, on the first school day of the next month, we sing the second verse!

Shelley Hoster, Jack & Jill Early Learning Center, Norcross, GA

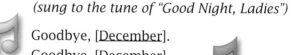

(sung to the tune of "Good Night, Ladies")

Goodbye, [December].
Goodbye, [December].
Goodbye, [December].
We will see you next year!

Hello, [January].
Hello, [January].
Hello, [January].
We're happy that you're here!

I have one child each day be in charge of the **daily news**. During calendar time, the chosen youngster tells me some news she would like to share with the class. I write her words on chart paper. Then I have students search the message for our letter of the week. A volunteer circles the letter each time it is found.

Ruth Zabelin, Riviera, TX

To add excitement to our calendar time, I have little ones climb aboard a **pretend airplane**. (I even have a cardboard control panel I made to add extra fun to this activity.) While we are "flying" in our airplane, we look out the windows and check out the weather so we can note it in our calendar area. We also share any other interesting things we "see" out the window before landing and finishing calendar time.

Michelle Jeanveau, Lethbridge, Alberta, Canada

I picked up a few **props** in the after-Halloween sales one year, including a pink wig, huge silver sunglasses, and a wand. To add zip to calendar time, I don some of these props and do calendar time as a different character. My little ones love to teach this new character all about the procedures we follow for calendar time!

Carrie Sturges, Castleton United Methodist Church Nursery School, Indianapolis, IN

It's your turn!
TheMailbox.com/submitideas

Problem Solved!

Your Solutions to Classroom Challenges

How do you teach youngsters to *control their anger*?

When a youngster is angry, I encourage her to hug herself. Wrapping your arms around yourself and giving a good squeeze releases tension!

Sandy Rothstein, Long Beach, NY

I teach little ones this song to give them an outlet for their anger!

Betty Silkunas, Fernandina Beach, FL
Sandy Rothstein, Long Beach, NY

(sung to the tune of "If You're Happy and You Know It")

If you're angry and you know it, [use your words—I'm angry]!
If you're angry and you know it, [use your words—I'm angry]!
If you're angry and you know it
And you really want to show it,
If you're angry and you know it, [use your words—I'm angry]!

Continue with the following: *walk away, stomp your feet, get a drink*

I take the child's hands in mine and encourage him to take deep, calming breaths with me. The child calms himself, and then the problem can be addressed.

Ann Morris Bruehler, Mattoon, IL

If a little one needs an outlet for his aggression, I provide a square of Bubble Wrap cushioning material! After he stomps on the Bubble Wrap, he usually feels much calmer.

Ann Morris Bruehler

It's your turn!
TheMailbox.com/submitideas

Problem Solved!

Your Solutions to Classroom Challenges

Sharing squabbles? How do you *teach youngsters to share?*

 I make sure I model good sharing behavior! I frequently sit down with three children at a time, and we color together with only one box of markers. I ask youngsters to share various markers with me and model using the words *please* and *thank you*. Modeling a desired behavior works wonders!

Darlene Butler Taig, Willow Creek Co-op Preschool, Westland, MI

 To encourage sharing, I jot down ways to share on separate cards and keep them in a basket on my desk. At the beginning of the week, I have a child pull a card. I read the card aloud. Then we do our best throughout the week to follow the sharing suggestion on the card.

Marianne Cerra, St. Ignatius R. C. School, Sinking Spring, PA

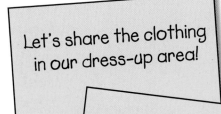

Let's share the clothing in our dress-up area!

Let's share cleaning up our classroom after centers!

 I teach my little ones to ask, "May I have a turn when you're done?" Then we flip a three-minute or five-minute sand timer. My little ones know that when the timer is done, it's their friend's turn to play with the toy. This method works really well in my classroom!

Kim Angel, Columbia College Child Development Center, Sonora, CA

See pages 129 and 130 for **sharing awards** and a **coloring page** that reinforce sharing!

 My students know to sing this little song while they're waiting their turn. It gives them something to do and reminds them to be patient.

(sung to the tune of "The Farmer in the Dell")

I'm waiting for my turn.
I'm waiting for my turn.
I am so patient.
I'm waiting for my turn.

Jeanne-Marie Peterson, Charlottesville, VA

It's your turn!
TheMailbox.com/submitideas

_____
name

was spotted sharing.
Way to go!

_____   _____
teacher   date

©The Mailbox®

_____
name

was spotted sharing.
Way to go!

_____   _____
teacher   date

©The Mailbox®

I can share.

Note to the teacher: To reinforce sharing behaviors, have little ones color a copy of this page and discuss what is happening in the picture.

Songs & Such

Songs & Such

Clean Hands!

Youngsters get a hand-washing lesson with this fun action chant!

Put your right hand in.
Put your left hand in.
Put the soap in the middle
And squish it all around.
Wash the tops and bottoms
And your fingers in between.
And now your hands are clean!

Hold out your right hand.
Hold out your left hand.
Clap hands on soap; then rub hands.

Pretend to wash tops, bottoms, and fingers.

Clap to the beat.

Audrey Grizanti
First Baptist Church Preschool
Vero Beach, FL

Color Names

Here's a song that spotlights beginning sounds and colors.

(sung to the tune of "Bingo")

What is the color of a [plum]?
Why, [purple] is its name-o!
[/p/, /p/, purple, purple],
[/p/, /p/, purple, purple],
[/p/, /p/, purple, purple],
[Purple] is its name-o.

Continue with the following: *sun, yellow, /y/;*
yam, orange, /ŏ/; leaf, green, /g/; rose, red, /r/; sky,
blue, /b/; snow, white, /w/; bat, black, /b/

Jacqueline Schiff
Moline, IL

Something Good!

This uplifting little action poem emphasizes patience!

Something good will happen;   *Hug self.*
Wait and see.   *Shake finger.*
The seed under the ground   *Touch floor.*
Will become a tree.   *Stand tall like a tree.*

Something good will happen,   *Hug self.*
Though it's seldom quick.   *Shake finger.*
Out from the egg   *Cup hands.*
Will pop a baby chick.   *Flap elbows.*

Something good will happen,   *Hug self.*
But not too soon!   *Shake finger.*
The butterfly will leave   *Flap arms*
Its cozy cocoon.   *Roll arms.*

Arlene Clare Muller
Glendale, NY

The Only Me

Promote self-esteem with this catchy song! If desired, give youngsters crepe paper streamers (or gauzy scarves) and have them sway as they sing, moving the streamers through the air.

(sung to the tune of "O Christmas Tree")

There's just one me.
There's just one me.
That's all you'll see!
There's just one me.
I'm glad to be
The only me!
The only one
That's made like me!

Cindy Hoying
Centerville, OH

Songs & Such

One Hungry Worm

This action rhyme is perfect for the beginning of the school year!

One hungry worm | Show pointer finger.
In an apple so red, | Close other hand around finger.
Stuck his head out | Poke finger through fist.
And then he said,
"Come on in! | Wiggle finger.
This apple's really yummy."
Then he popped back in | Pull finger back into fist.
To fill his tummy.

LeeAnn Collins
Sunshine House Preschool
Lansing, MI

Teeth Are Not for Biting!

What are teeth for? Youngsters discuss the uses of teeth with this antibiting rhyme!

These teeth are not for biting. | Move hand like a biting mouth.
Yes, what we say is true.
These teeth are not for biting.
That's bad for me and you.

These teeth are made for brushing, | Pretend to brush with finger.
And that's just what we do.
These teeth are made for brushing.
That's nice for me and you!

These teeth are made for chewing, | Make a chewing motion with hand.
And that's just what we do.
These teeth are made for chewing.
That's nice for me and you!

These teeth are made for cheesing, | Make a big cheesy smile!
And that's just we do.
These teeth are made for cheesing.
That's nice for me and you!

Kelly Williams
Detroit Diesel Child Development Center
Detroit, MI

Songs & Such

The Little Leaf

This little fall leaf goes from the tree to the ground! Have a child color and cut out a copy of a leaf pattern on page 149. Then have her use it as a prop during a performance of this chant!

The little fall leaf stays on the tree	*Hold the leaf in the air.*
Until the wind comes round.	*Flutter the leaf.*
The leaf sails right.	*Flutter the leaf right.*
The leaf sails left.	*Flutter the leaf left.*
Then it tumbles to the ground!	*Release the leaf.*

Suzanne Moore
Tucson, AZ

Fall Sounds!

What might your youngsters hear in the fall? Have them sing this little song to find out!

(sung to the tune of "If You're Happy and You Know It")

Can you [hoot like the owls] just like me? [Hoot, hoot]!
Can you [hoot like the owls] just like me? [Hoot, hoot]!
Let's make sounds, one and all,
That we might hear in the fall!
Can you [hoot like the owls] just like me? [Hoot, hoot]!

Continue with the following:
whoosh like the wind; Whoosh, whoosh
crunch like the leaves; Crunch, crunch
flap like the bats; Flap, flap
boo like the monsters; Boo, boo
gobble like the turkeys; Gobble, gobble

Bonnie C. Krum
St. Matthew's Early Education Center
Bowie, MD

Songs & Such

Halloween Is in the Fall

Sing this song to help little ones remember the season in which Halloween falls!

(sung to the tune of "Twinkle, Twinkle, Little Star")

Halloween is in the fall.
Cool winds blow, and corn is tall.
Pumpkins grin and shine so bright,
Trick-or-treaters out at night,
Caramel apples, fun for all!
Halloween is in the fall.

Jacqueline Schiff
Moline, IL

The Pumpkin Chant

Get the wiggles out with this fun action chant!

Pumpkin, pumpkin, seed in the ground.   *Touch the floor.*
Pumpkin, pumpkin, big and round.   *Hold arms in a big circle.*
Pumpkin, pumpkin, stretch your vine.   *Stretch arms outward.*
Pumpkin, pumpkin, you look fine!   *Pose with one hand on hip, other*
                                                *   hand on side of head.*
Pumpkin, pumpkin, I can't lie—   *Shake head.*
Pumpkin, pumpkin, you'll make a great pie!   *Rub tummy.*

Lola Anderson
Canby Head Start
Canby, MN

Laughter guaranteed!

Thanksgiving Action!

You'll hear plenty of giggles when little ones perform this action rhyme!

Do the strut—do the turkey strut! *Strut like a turkey.*
Do the mash—do the potato mash! *Clap hands with palms facing up and down.*
Do the slide—do the corncob slide! *Pretend to eat corn on the cob.*
Do the wavy—do the wavy gravy! *Move like a wave with arms overhead.*
Do the roll—do the dinner roll! *Roll arms.*
Do the jiggle—do the gelatin jiggle! *Jiggle your whole body.*
Put them all together, and what do you get? *Throw arms out to sides.*
Thanksgiving dinner! *Jump up and down.*

Pat Karpinski
Ebenezer Preschool
Newark, DE

I Am Thankful

Remind youngsters of the many things to be thankful for with this poem.

I am so thankful for all that I see: *Point to self and then to eye.*
The birds in the sky, *Flap arms.*
The leaves on the tree, *Arms up; wiggle fingers.*
The flowers to smell, *Cup hands like a tulip and sniff.*
And food that I eat, *Rub tummy.*
The home that I have, *Form arms like a roof.*
The sun and its heat. *Round arms.*
I'm thankful for lots— *Hold out arms.*
These are just a few— *Hold finger and thumb close together.*
But mostly, I'm thankful for friends like you! *Shake finger; then point at a classmate.*

Barb Stefaniuk
Kerrobert Tiny Tots Playschool
Kerrobert, Saskatchewan, Canada

Songs & Such

Hanukkah Is Here!

(sung to the tune of "Twinkle, Twinkle, Little Star")

Hanukkah is finally here.	*Nod.*
Time for laughter, time for cheer.	*Put hands in air and sway.*
Time for candles every night—	*Touch fingers.*
One by one, they burn so bright.	*Continue touching fingers.*
Hanukkah is finally here.	*Nod.*
Time for laughter, time for cheer.	*Smile and sway arms side to side.*
Hanukkah is finally here.	*Nod.*
Time for laughter, time for cheer.	*Put hands in air and sway.*
Make the latkes nice and round—	*Pretend to form latkes.*
Cook them till they start to brown.	*Wiggle fingers.*
Hanukkah is finally here.	*Nod.*
Time for laughter, time for cheer.	*Smile and sway arms side to side.*

Christmastime Is Here!

If desired, have little ones play jingle bell bracelets as they sing this song!

(sung to the tune of "Mary Had a Little Lamb")

Decorate the Christmas tree,
Christmas tree, Christmas tree!
Twinkly lights for you and me!
Christmastime is here.

Put the tinsel here and there,
Ornaments everywhere!
Put the topper on the tree.
Christmastime is here.

Suzanne Moore, Tucson, AZ

Songs &Such

Five Little Elves

Here's an adorable counting rhyme that's sure to be popular with your little ones! Lead students in performing the rhyme five times, subtracting one from the number each time.

[Five] little elves filled with joy— | Hold up five fingers.
One hit his thumb when he hammered a toy! | Hold up thumb; then pretend to hammer.
Santa put a bandage on that little boo-boo, | Wrap hand around thumb on opposite hand.
And the elf said, "That's much better. | Say with a squeaky voice.
   Thank you!"

Christine Wagner, Tender Care Learning Center—Jefferson
Clairton, PA

Do you want to use **elf patterns** with this chant? Check out page 150!

Oh, Santa Claus!

(sung to the tune of the chorus of "Jingle Bells")

Oh, Santa Claus, Santa Claus,
Bringing Christmas cheer;
Bringing toys to girls and boys,
'Cause it's that time of year!
Santa Claus, Santa Claus,
Bringing lots of joy;
Leaving lots of Christmas gifts
For good girls and good boys.

Songs & Such

Kwanzaa Days

After a discussion of Kwanzaa, lead students in singing this engaging song!

(sung to the tune of "Twinkle, Twinkle, Little Star")

Kwanzaa colors that I see,
Black, red, green—they shine for me.
Candles gleam for seven days.
Families gather to give praise.
Handmade presents, poems, and plays,
Dance to drums on Kwanzaa days.

Jacqueline Schiff
Moline, IL

Winter Gear

It's tough for little ones to put on their winter clothing in the correct order! So here's a fun little ditty to help streamline this process. To add actions to this song, see the "accompanying actions" given below.

(sung to the tune of "Head and Shoulders")

Snow pants, boots, coat, and hat—gloves are last.
Snow pants, boots, coat, and hat—gloves are last.
Please remember to get ready fast.
Snow pants, boots, coat, and hat—gloves are last!

Accompanying actions:
snow pants—pat legs
boots—touch feet
coat—pat chest
hat—pat head
gloves—clap hands

Kelly Schroeder, Moppet Play House, Waunakee, WI

Songs & Such

Where's the Snow?

Perhaps you live in a location that doesn't get snow, or your little ones are antsy for that first snowfall. If so, this song is for you and your youngsters!

(sung to the tune of "The Farmer in the Dell")

My snowman needs a hat,
A mouth, two eyes, a nose.
But I can't build a snowman yet.
I really hope it snows.

My snowman needs a scarf
And arms and buttons too.
It's wintertime, but there's no snow!
It makes me feel so blue.

Suzanne Moore
Tucson, AZ

A Macaroni Penguin

Show youngsters a photo of a macaroni penguin. (An Internet image search will turn up plenty of options.) Prompt students to notice the distinctive yellow feathers, or crest, on its head. Next, give each child a yellow craft feather. Lead them in singing the song as they hold the feather on their heads and lean from side to side as if waddling.

(sung to the tune of "If You're Happy and You Know It")

I'm a macaroni penguin; yes, I am!
I'm a macaroni penguin; yes, I am!
See my feathers, golden yellow.
I'm a funny-looking fellow!
I'm a macaroni penguin; yes, I am!

Cindy Hoying, Centerville, OH

A Little Groundhog

Explain Groundhog Day to your little ones. Then lead them in performing this adorable action rhyme.

I'm a little groundhog furry and round.
I live in a burrow underground.
On February 2, I'll let you know
Whether you will see spring rain or snow!

Wiggle in an adorable manner!
Pat the floor.
Hold up two fingers.
Wiggle fingers downward.

Samantha Kyzer
PG's Kiddie College
Rockaway, NJ

Two Little Friends

This sweet little fingerplay is sure to get lots of requests!

One little friend came to school one day.
He went to the blocks and began to play.
A second little friend said, "Can I play too?"
The first little friend said, "I'll share with you!"
So they worked together and built a big town.
Then when they were finished, they knocked it all down!

Hold up index finger.
Bob hand to indicate movement.
Hold up remaining index finger and wiggle it.
Wiggle the first index finger.
Wiggle both fingers.
Clap hands together.

Suzanne Moore
Tucson, AZ

I Love You!

What are some ways to say "I love you!"? Little ones demonstrate with this chant that features American Sign Language!

Give a heart.

heart

Give a flower.

flower

Give some candy too!

candy

These are some ways to say,

"I love you!"

I love you

Tricia Kylene Brown
Bowling Green, KY

Songs & Such

Be the Dinosaur

Your little ones won't be able to resist a dinosaur song that incorporates roaring! Cut out a copy of the dinosaur patterns on page 151 and transform them into stick puppets. Explain to little ones the difference between a carnivore and an herbivore, using the puppets as props. Then give each prop to a different child. Lead youngsters in singing the song, prompting each child to hold up his prop when appropriate. After the sing-along, ask each child which type of dinosaur he would prefer to be.

(sung to the tune of "The Muffin Man")

If you could be a dinosaur, a dinosaur, a dinosaur,
Oh, would you be a carnivore?
Let's give a dino roar!
(Spoken) Roar!

If you could be a dinosaur, a dinosaur, a dinosaur,
Oh, would you be an herbivore?
Let's give a dino roar!
(Spoken) Roar!

adapted from a song by Jennifer Rauber
St. Angela's Children's Center
Pacific Grove, CA

It's a Leprechaun!

Here's a festive St. Patrick's Day action song!

(sung to the tune of "If You're Happy and You Know It")

If you see a little rainbow in the sky,   *Move finger in an arc.*
Then there just might be a leprechaun nearby!   *Place finger against lips.*
He'll be small and very old,   *Show thumb and finger inches apart.*
Sitting on his pot of gold,   *Cross arms.*
If you see a little rainbow in the sky!   *Move finger in an arc.*

Puddle Jumping!

Spotlight spring rain with this active rhyme!

Hopping, skipping
In the sun—
Along comes rain.
Inside we run!
On go the boots.
Outside we dash,
Straight for the puddles—
Splish and splash!

Hop twice on each leg.
Hold arms in a circle over head.
Wiggle fingers downward.
Run in place.
Pat each foot.
Run in place.
Run in place.
Jump up and down.

Donna Cangelosi
Wayne, NJ

The Rainbow Song

Help little ones learn the conditions necessary for a rainbow—and the colors in a rainbow—with a quick and cute song!

(sung to the tune of "Row, Row, Row Your Boat")

Red, orange, yellow, green,
Blue, and violet.
First the sun
And then the rain—
A rainbow's what you get!

Jennifer Schear
Clover Patch Preschool

Songs & Such

All About Insects!

Here's a simple song that teaches little ones about the parts of an insect!

(sung to the tune of "The Farmer in the Dell")

An insect has three parts.
An insect has three parts.
Head, thorax, abdomen,
An insect has three parts.

An insect has six legs.
An insect has six legs.
One, two, three, four, five, six!
An insect has six legs.

Cindy Hoying
Centerville, OH

Hooray for Mom!

Have your little ones sing this song for a Mother's Day celebration!

(sung to the tune of "If You're Happy and You Know It")

[If you love your mom so grand, clap your hands]!
[If you love your mom so grand, clap your hands]!
For the love she always gives
And the caring way she lives,
[If your love your mom so grand, clap your hands]!

Continue with the following:
If you love your mom so sweet, stomp your feet.
If you love your mom today, shout hooray!

Cindy Hoying

Playful Pets!

Have each child cut out and color copies of the pet patterns on page 152. Then help her transform them into stick puppets. Lead little ones in singing the song, holding up and moving each puppet when appropriate! Follow up a performance of this song with a discussion about pets and their antics!

(sung to the tune of "I Have a Little Dreidel")

I have a little puppy.
She is so very small.
She likes to chew my shoestrings and chase a little ball.
My puppy, puppy, puppy, she is so very small.
My puppy, puppy, puppy, she is the best of all.

I have a little kitty.
He is so very small.
He likes to chew my shoestrings and chase a little ball.
My kitty, kitty, kitty, he is so very small.
My kitty, kitty, kitty, he is the best of all!

Sara Andrew
Jefferson Preschool Center
Charlottesville, VA

Showing Respect

Explain to youngsters what it means to respect people and property. Then lead them in singing this catchy little song with a fabulous message!

(sung to the tune of "This Old Man")

Keep your hands to yourself.
Put all toys back on the shelf.
Please respect all people
And their property!
R-E-S-P-E-C-T!

Cindy Hoying
Centerville, OH

Songs & Such

Critters in the Garden!

Lead little ones in performing this fun song about garden critters! During the final verse, replace "day" with "night" to reflect when crickets come out and chirp!

(sung to the tune of "The Wheels on the Bus")

The [bees] in the garden go [buzz, buzz, buzz],
[Buzz, buzz, buzz, buzz, buzz, buzz].
The [bees] in the garden go [buzz, buzz, buzz]
All [day] long.

Continue with the following:
ants; march, march, march
flies; zip, zip, zip
moths; flutter, flutter, flutter
worms; wiggle, wiggle, wiggle
crickets; chirp, chirp, chirp

Jenna Dunlop
Mason, OH

Splash!

Spotlight vacation season with this happy little song about preparing for the beach!

(sung to the tune of "There's a Hole in the Bucket")

Got my [sunglasses] on—   *Make circles with fingers and put against eyes.*
Let's go to the beach!
Got my [sunglasses] on—
Let's go to the beach!

Continue with the following:

swimming suit	*Wiggle hips.*
sunscreen	*Rub arms.*
floppy hat	*Wave hands next to head.*
flip-flops	*Alternate lifting flattened hands.*

Cindy Hoying
Centerville, OH

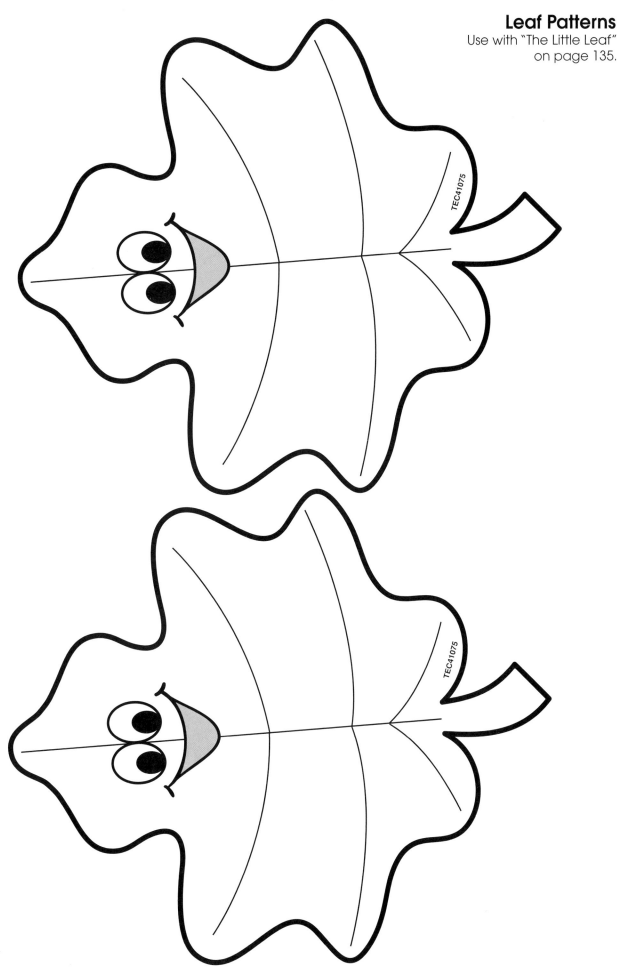

Elf Patterns

Use with "Five Little Elves" on page 139.

TEC41076

TEC41076

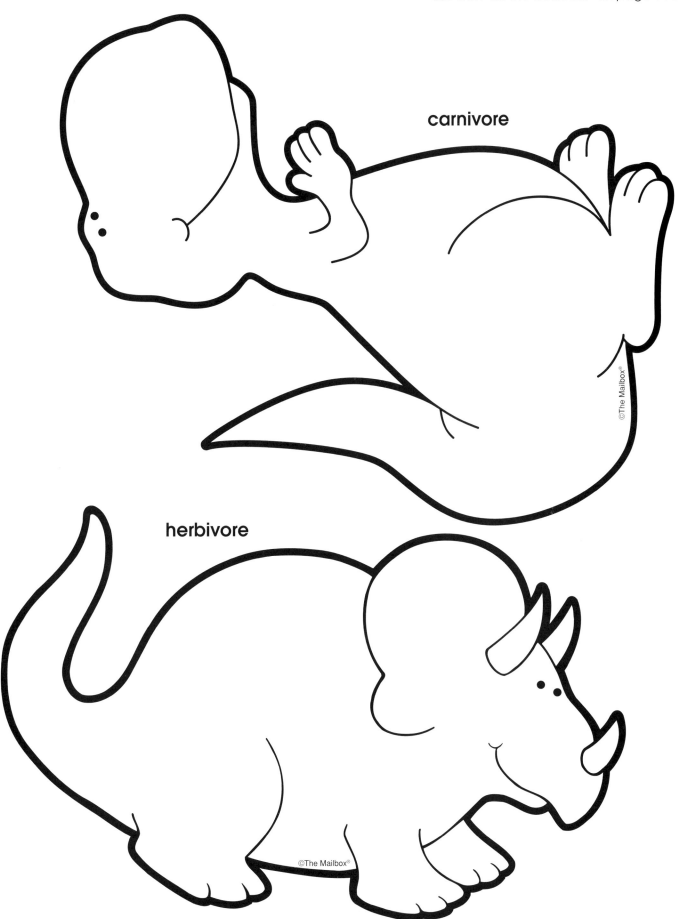

carnivore

herbivore

©The Mailbox®

©The Mailbox®

Pet Patterns

Use with "Playful Pets!" on page 147.

©The Mailbox®

©The Mailbox®

STORYTIME

Brown Bear, Brown Bear, What Do You See?
Written by Bill Martin Jr.
Illustrated by Eric Carle

What does Brown Bear see? He sees a red bird! This beloved book continues with Yellow Duck, Blue Horse, and other colorful critters until a group of children get the last look!

ideas contributed by Cindy Hoying
Centerville, OH

Bill Martin Jr / Eric Carle

Brown Bear, Brown Bear, What Do You See?

● ● ● Before You Read ● ● ●

Show students the book cover and read the title aloud. Pose the question "What do you think Brown Bear will see?" Pass a stuffed toy bear or bear cutout to a child and invite him to share what he thinks Brown Bear will see. Continue in this manner until each child has made a prediction. Then read the story aloud to find out if any of the predictions are correct. **Predicting**

I see a yellow duck looking at me.

● ● ● After You Read ● ● ●

In advance, prepare a simple spinner that features the colors of the animals in the story. Pass the spinner to a child and then lead the other students in saying the first two lines of the chant shown. The child spins the spinner and says the last two lines of the chant, inserting the color and animal from the story with prompting as needed. Continue until each child has had a turn. **Recalling story details**

[Child's name], [child's name],
What do you see?

I see a [color] [animal]
Looking at me.

Ladybug Girl and Bumblebee Boy

Written by Jacky Davis
Illustrated by David Soman

Lulu and Sam just can't seem to agree on what to play. Then Lulu becomes Ladybug Girl and shows off her superpowers. Sam is interested and quickly joins her as Bumblebee Boy. As Ladybug Girl and Bumblebee Boy, Lulu and Sam figure out that when they work together, they can create fun games that they both like to play.

I think Ladybug Girl will have spots!

● ● ● Before You Read ● ● ●

Post a picture of a ladybug and a picture of a bumblebee. Gather youngsters near the pictures and tell them that the main characters in the book are Ladybug Girl and Bumblebee Boy. Invite students to share their thoughts about how the main characters of the story might look. Then have them settle in for this fun read-aloud! *Speaking*

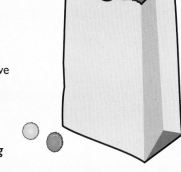

● ● ● After You Read ● ● ●

Place red and yellow pom-poms (mostly red) in a paper lunch bag. Have youngsters sit in a circle and pass the bag to a child. Invite her to take a pom-pom from the bag. If the pom-pom is red, have her tell something about Ladybug Girl. If the pom-pom is yellow, have her tell a story detail about Bumblebee Boy. After sharing, direct her to pass the bag to a child beside her. Continue in this manner until each child has shared. *Recalling story details*

 tip → For extra fun, have students make a pattern with the pom-poms and then read the pattern! Ladybug Girl, Bumblebee Boy, Ladybug Girl, Bumblebee Boy,…

Storytime

Literacy Ideas for Teachers®

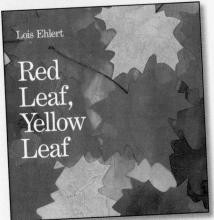

Red Leaf, Yellow Leaf
by Lois Ehlert

A child tells the story of her sugar maple tree, from its beginning as a whirling seed to its transition to a tree by her home.

ideas contributed by Tricia Kylene Brown
Bowling Green, KY

● ● ● **Before You Read** ● ● ●

Tell students you are going to read a story about a maple seed that grows into a tree. Explain that many seeds are small and round. Prompt each student to curl up into a ball just like a little seed. But maple seeds are very long and, when they fall from a tree, they whirl and twirl through the air. Have students whirl and twirl as if they were maple seeds. Then have them sit down and listen to the story.

● ● ● **After You Read** ● ● ●

Draw a simple tree, minus foliage, on a length of bulletin board paper. Then attach the paper to a wall. Place red and yellow construction paper scraps and glue nearby. A child tears a piece of paper and then glues it to the tree. Youngsters continue until this sugar maple is covered with red and yellow foliage!

Pumpkin Pumpkin

by Jeanne Titherington

Jamie plants a pumpkin seed. He watches his seed grow all summer long until he finally has a huge pumpkin. Then he turns it into a jack-o'-lantern and saves seeds for the next season.

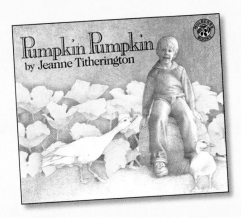

I think it might be a tree!

● ● ● **Before You Read** ● ● ●

Show students a pumpkin seed and ask them what they think the seed grows into. After several guesses, reveal that the seed grows into a pumpkin! Then explain that the book you're about to read is about a little boy who plants a pumpkin seed.

● ● ● **After You Read** ● ● ●

Give each child a 6" x 18" strip of construction paper folded into fourths and a copy of the sequencing cards on page 169. Have each child color and cut out the cards. Then have her put them in order on the strip to tell the story of Jamie's pumpkin. After approving the order, have the child glue the cards in place.

Try this data collection activity after reading *Red Leaf, Yellow Leaf* and *Pumpkin Pumpkin*! Have little ones draw either a red (or yellow) leaf or a pumpkin on a paper square to show which book out of the two was their favorite. Place the books on the floor. Then have each student place her square on the appropriate book. Help students count and compare the results.

Literacy Ideas for Teachers®

Gingerbread Baby

Written and Illustrated by Jan Brett

When the Gingerbread Baby escapes from Matti's oven, he is chased around the countryside by a variety of people and animals. Meanwhile, Matti remains at home cooking up a way to catch this mischievous cookie!

ideas contributed by Suzanne Moore, Tucson, AZ

What's in the bag? Let's take a look.

A [spoon] is a clue about our book!

Gingerbread Mix

Before You Read

Serve up clues about the story with a sack full of mystery items! Place in a paper sack the following clues about the story: a mixing spoon and bowl, a box of gingerbread mix (or a sack of sugar), and a gingerbread man cookie cutter. Recite the rhyme shown, removing the spoon from the sack after the second line. Then invite youngsters to guess what the story might be about based on this clue. Continue in the same way for each remaining clue. Once all the items have been revealed, present the book with great fanfare. Then invite youngsters to settle in for a tale about a gingerbread cookie on the run!

After You Read

With this sweet activity, little ones create a house for the Gingerbread Baby just like Matti does! Help each youngster cut out a construction paper copy of the house pattern on page 170; then have her decorate it with craft supplies to resemble a gingerbread house. Staple the house atop a sheet of construction paper, as shown, to make a flap. Next, instruct her to draw a picture of the Gingerbread Baby under the flap. Invite little ones to retell the story and flip open their houses to reveal the conclusion!

The Polar Express
by Chris Van Allsburg

On Christmas Eve, a boy boards the Polar Express train and is taken to the North Pole with other boys and girls. While there, Santa grants him the first gift of Christmas and the boy asks for one of his sleigh bells. The bell is lost on the journey home but shows up beneath the Christmas tree the next morning.

ideas contributed by Janet Boyce, Tomball, TX

Choo, choo, choo, choo...!

● ● ● Before You Read ● ● ●

Give each child a pair of large craft sticks. Then have children tap their sticks together so the sound resembles the clackety-clack of a train on the tracks. While youngsters continue tapping, have them say, "Choo-choo, choo-choo" and make sounds similar to a train whistle. Ask them what sound they are imitating, encouraging them to notice that they sound like a train. Next, show youngsters the book and have them settle in for this classic holiday story.

● ● ● After You Read ● ● ●

For each child, thread a jingle bell onto a pipe cleaner. Then twist the ends of the pipe cleaner together. Give each youngster a bell and prompt youngsters to ring it. Ask little ones if they can hear the bells and pronounce that they have excellent holiday spirit! Then use the bells to play a game of "Santa Says" similar to "Simon Says." For example, say, "Santa says ring your bell above your head," "Santa says ring the bell behind your back," or "Santa says ring the bell between your feet." Collect the bells after the game for safekeeping.

Storytime

Literacy Ideas for Teachers®

A Penguin Story

by Antoinette Portis

Edna the penguin sees the white ice, the black night sky, and the blue water. Everything is white, black, and blue. There must be something else out there! Edna goes on a search and finds scientists wearing orange. How exciting!

ideas contributed by Janet Boyce, Tomball, TX

A Penguin Story

Antoinette Portis
Creator of the bestselling NOT A BOX

● ● ● Before You Read ● ● ●

Ask your little ones, "Where do you think penguins live?" After a brief discussion, explain that penguins live in the southern part of the world, including Antarctica. Point out Antarctica on a globe. Next, ask students what they think penguins would see there, guiding them to understand that penguins might see white snow. Next, show the cover of the book and explain that today's story is about a penguin named Edna who goes on an adventure to see "something else."

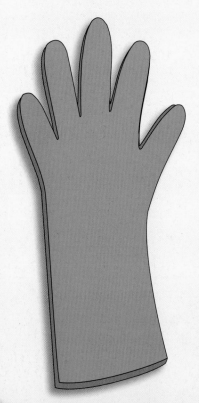

● ● ● After You Read ● ● ●

Cut a glove shape from orange craft foam. First, lead students in singing the song shown. Then hold the glove in the air as you waddle about the room, prompting youngsters to follow you just as the penguins did with Edna in the story. Take a few laps about the room, having youngsters take turns being the leader.

(sung to the tune of "The Bear Went Over the Mountain")

Edna went over the snow.
Edna went over the snow.
Edna went over the snow
To look for something else.
And what did Edna find?
And what did Edna find?
Edna found something else.
Edna found something else.
Edna found something else,
And it was something orange!

 See page 171 for a reproducible to go with this story!

The Quiet Book
Written by Deborah Underwood
Illustrated by Renata Liwska

There are many different kinds of quiet: first one awake quiet, jelly side down quiet, don't scare the robin quiet, and many others!

Fish are quiet.

● ● ● Before You Read ● ● ●

Dim the lights in the classroom and then whisper the chant shown. Prompt students to whisper as they name situations, critters, or items that are very quiet. Then explain that the book you're about to read is called *The Quiet Book* and it talks about different kinds of quiet times. **Speaking**

Whisper, whisper quietly.
Name some quiet things for me!

● ● ● After You Read ● ● ●

Little ones contribute to this class book! Take a head-shot photo of each child with her finger to her lips, saying, "Shhhh!" Print out the photos. Then help each child cut out her photo and glue it to the bottom of a sheet of construction paper. Draw a thought bubble above the child's head and have her describe a time when she was very quiet. Write her words in the thought bubble. Then bind the pages together with a cover titled "Our Class Quiet Book." **Dictating information to be written down, contributing to a class book**

Don't want to make a class book? These projects look adorable displayed on a wall!

I was quiet when I went to a wedding.

Storytime

The Lion & the Mouse

by Jerry Pinkney

This nearly wordless picture book is a retelling of the classic Aesop's fable. A lion goes against its instinct and lets a mouse run free. The mouse returns the favor by saving the lion when it is trapped by poachers.

ideas contributed by Cindy Hoying, Centerville, OH

The Big Lion Ate a Mouse!

● ● ● Before You Read ● ● ●

Show youngsters the cover of the book and have them notice what is missing (the title). Then show youngsters the back cover as well. Ask little ones to guess what the title of the story might be and what it will be about. Then ask youngsters why they think the title was left off the book. After students share their thoughts, have them settle in to explore the book. *Predicting*

● ● ● After You Read ● ● ●

Give each child a copy of page 172 and help her transform the patterns into stick puppets. Encourage her to use the stick puppets to retell the story by wrapping the lion puppet with yarn (the net) and using scissors (the mouse's teeth) to cut through the net. Prompt her to take her puppets home to share the story with her family. *Retelling a story*

What else can you do with the puppets? Say a word that begins with /l/ or /m/. If it begins with /l/, the child raises the lion puppet. If it begins with /m/, she raises the mouse puppet. Continue with other words.

Olivia

by Ian Falconer

Olivia is a precocious little pig. She loves to dance, try on clothing, build sand castles, and visit the art museum. Olivia is quite a handful!

I'm good at running fast!

● ● ● Before You Read ● ● ●

Explain that you are going to read a book about a little pig named Olivia. Olivia is good at many things. Ask, "What are you good at?" After youngsters discuss things they're good at, have them settle in for a read-aloud of this adorable story! **Speaking**

● ● ● After You Read ● ● ●

Do your little ones like to do the same things Olivia likes to do? They'll find out with a little bit of data collection! Place a plastic hoop or a circle of yarn on the floor. Then give each child a small manipulative, such as a linking cube. Say, "Olivia likes to try on clothes. Do you like to try on clothes?" If youngsters like to do this, have them place their manipulatives in the circle. If they don't, have them place the manipulatives outside the circle. Lead youngsters in counting and comparing the two sets. Then repeat the activity with other Olivia favorites, such as building sand castles, dancing, basking in the sun, and looking at artwork. ***Organizing data, counting sets, comparing sets***

Storytime

Down by the Cool of the Pool

Written by Tony Mitton
Illustrated by Guy Parker-Rees

Frog, Duck, Pig, and a variety of other critters flap, wiggle, and dance their way around a pond.

ideas contributed by Ada Goren, Winston-Salem, NC

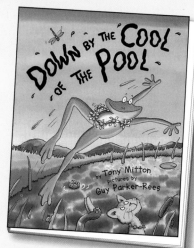

● ● ● Let's Dance! ● ● ●

Before reading this story, show youngsters the cover of the book and explain that the characters in the story just love to dance. Next, play one of your class's favorite music selections and encourage youngsters to freestyle dance about the room. Then have them settle in to see how the animals in the story dance. ***Gross-motor skills***

● ● ● Act It Out ● ● ●

All you need to act out this story is a blue blanket or sheet! Place it on the floor so it resembles a pond. Then assign each child a character from the story. Reread the story, prompting students to dance their character's signature moves. When you reach the part of the story where all the characters splash into the pool, have the students fall carefully onto the blue blanket. Continue reading, having little ones continue their moves and eventually exit the pool when indicated. Youngsters will love this dramatic reading! ***Dramatizing a story***

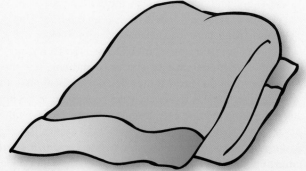

Don't Let the Pigeon Stay Up Late!
by Mo Willems

The pigeon really wants to stay up late! He tries pleading, bargaining, and begging but ends up falling asleep anyway.

ideas contributed by Cindy Hoying
Centerville, OH

● ● ● What Would You Do? ● ● ●

For this prereading activity, get a moon or star cutout. Then tell your little ones about something you would do if you decided to stay up late. Give the cutout to a child and say, "[Child's name, child's name], how about you? Tell me something you would do." After the child shares, have him pass the cutout to a classmate. Continue until each child has an opportunity to respond. Then have little ones settle in for a book about a pigeon that really wants to stay up late! **Speaking to share an opinion**

● ● ● A Very Excited Pigeon! ● ● ●

Draw an exclamation point on the board and introduce it to youngsters. Explain that the mark means that something is said with very strong feelings or shouted. The pigeon in the story definitely has strong feelings, so there are plenty of exclamation points! Reread the story and have little ones help you draw a tally mark on the board for every exclamation point. Then guide them in counting the tallies. That little bird definitely does not want to go to bed! **Introducing punctuation, making tally marks, counting**

"Yertle the Turtle"
by Dr. Seuss

Yertle, the turtle king, wants his throne to be higher. So he orders the turtles in the pond to pile up and sits atop them. But when the one little turtle at the very bottom of the stack gets a little bit mad, Yertle's throne falls apart!

ideas contributed by Roxanne LaBell Dearman
NC Intervention for the Deaf and Hard of Hearing
Charlotte, NC

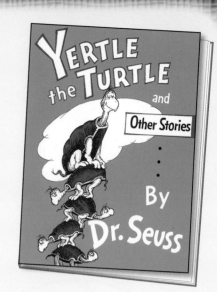

● ● ● Make a Turtle Stack! ● ● ●

Transform your block center into a storytelling area for "Yertle the Turtle"! To represent the turtles in the story, attach turtle cards to separate blocks in your block center. (See page 173 for turtle cards.) Place the book at the center. Then encourage little ones to visit and stack the turtles to retell the story! ***Retelling a story***

● ● ● The King of Rhyming ● ● ●

In advance, cut out a copy of the animal cards on page 174 and place them in a bag. Explain to little ones that the name *Yertle* rhymes with *turtle.* Then say, "Let's pretend that different animal kings need to have rhyming names as well!" Have a child pull a card from the bag and identify the animal. Help students come up with a silly royal rhyming name for the animal king, such as Foose the Moose or Bippo the Hippo. You're sure to hear lots of giggles with this rhyming practice! ***Rhyming***

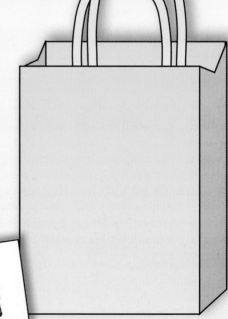

I Fall Down
Written by Vicki Cobb
Illustrated by Julia Gorton

A boy notices that objects fall down—and they fall down at the same rate. This introduction to gravity is perfect for preschoolers!

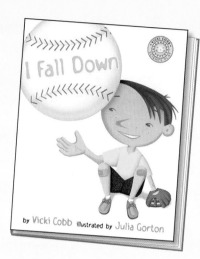
by Vicki Cobb illustrated by Julia Gorton

● ● ● Can I Fall Up? ● ● ●

Get ready for laughter with this prereading activity! Ask youngsters to recall a time when they've fallen. Then ask, "When you fell, did you fall down or up?" Of course, youngsters will reply that they fell down. Ask, "Do you think we could fall up if we tried?" Then prompt students to try their best to fall up. They will surely notice that they can jump up but will inevitably fall back down. After lots of jumping and pretend falling, bring out the book and have students settle in for storytime. *Gross-motor skills*

> **Have little ones try the simple gravity experiments mentioned throughout the book!**

● ● ● Gooey Stuff! ● ● ●

I Fall Down emphasizes that gravity pulls down a sticky strand of honey as it oozes back into the jar. Have little ones explore how gravity affects a variety of gooey substances! Pour several gooey substances in separate bowls. You might want to consider using honey, maple syrup, corn syrup, and molasses. Place a spoon in each bowl and then put the bowls at a center. Encourage youngsters to scoop up a spoonful of each substance, tilt the spoon, and then watch as gravity pulls the item back into the bowl. *Exploring textures*

Ladybug Girl and Bumblebee Boy
Written by Jacky Davis
Illustrated by David Soman

Ladybug Girl and Bumblebee Boy are friends.

Color to show what they play on together.

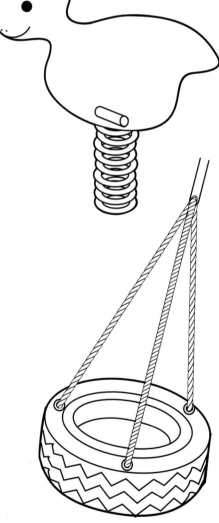

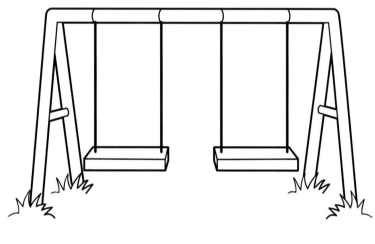

Note to the teacher: Have each child complete a copy of this page after the read-aloud of *Ladybug Girl and Bumblebee Boy* featured on page 155. Help her recall that the two friends do not both play on the seesaw together.

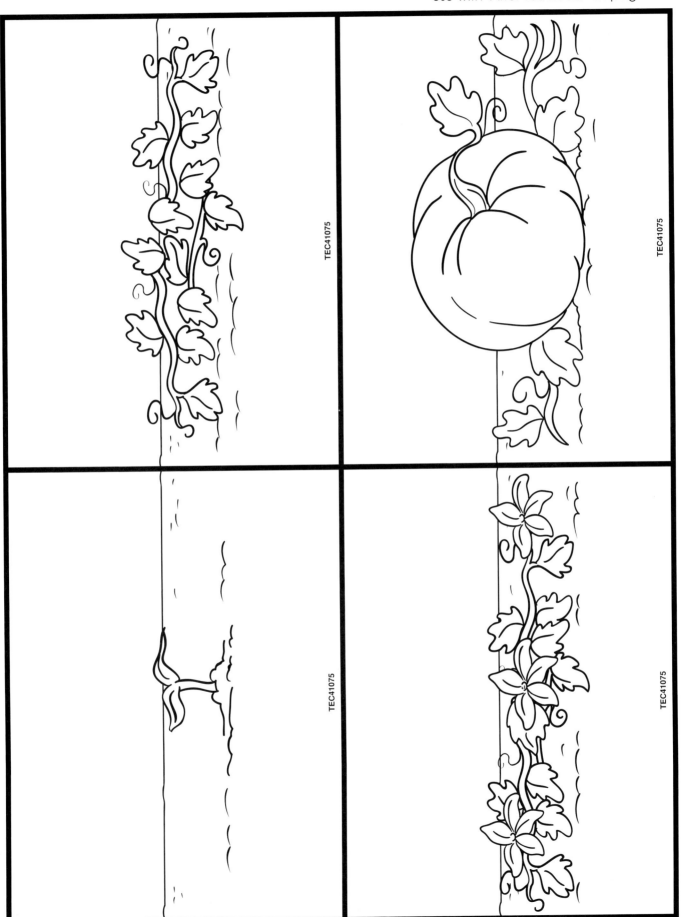

House Pattern

Use with "*Gingerbread Baby*"
on page 158.

TEC41076

A Penguin Story
by Antoinette Portis

Edna finds something orange.

Other things can be orange too.

Name the items. Color them orange.

Note to the teacher: Use with "*A Penguin Story*" on page 160.

Lion and Mouse Patterns
Use with "After You Read" on page 162.

©The Mailbox®

©The Mailbox®

©The Mailbox®

©The Mailbox®

©The Mailbox®

©The Mailbox®

©The Mailbox®

©The Mailbox®

©The Mailbox®

©The Mailbox®

Animal Cards

Use with "The King of Rhyming" on page 166.

©The Mailbox®

©The Mailbox®

©The Mailbox®

©The Mailbox®

©The Mailbox®

©The Mailbox®

©The Mailbox®

©The Mailbox®

BOOK UNITS

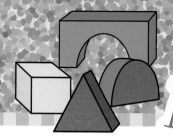

Llama Llama Misses Mama

by Anna Dewdney

Llama Llama gets up, gets ready, and goes to his first day of school. But school is full of new faces and new toys, and Llama Llama misses his mama! After being reassured by his teacher that Mama Llama will be back for him, Llama Llama ends up having a good day with new friends!

ideas contributed by Roxanne LaBell Dearman
NC Intervention for the Deaf and Hard of Hearing
Charlotte, NC

Llama Happy, Llama Sad
Identifying emotions
Llama Llama feels happy and sad at various times during the story. Help students identify his emotions with the help of these cute stick puppets! Make two simple Llama stick puppets, similar to the ones shown, and place them nearby. Next, show a page in the book and ask, "How does Llama Llama feel?" Prompt a child to choose a puppet that matches the emotion and hold it up. Encourage students to say, "Llama Llama feels [emotion]." Then have the child replace the puppet. Continue with different pages and youngsters.

L or M?
Beginning sounds
Cut out a copy of the cards on page 177 and place them in a bag. Open the book to the page that shows Llama Llama in bed and Mama nearby. Then have students say the words *Llama* and *Mama*, noticing that *Llama* begins with /l/ and *Mama* begins with /m/. Have a child choose a card and name the picture. Help students decide whether it begins with /l/ or /m/ and then lightly tape the picture appropriately to either the page with Llama Llama or Mama.

That Sounds Different!
Manipulating phonemes, rhyming, understanding that print has meaning
Write the name of the book on sentence strips and place it in your pocket chart. Gather several consonant cards. Read the title aloud as you follow the words with your finger. Then say, "I wonder what would happen if I put a different letter in the title?" Take a card and place it over the *M* in *Mama*. Then reread the title. You're sure to hear lots of giggles! Remove the card and repeat the process, encouraging youngsters to help you place the cards.

TEC41074

TEC41074

TEC41074

TEC41074

TEC41074

TEC41074

There Was an Old Lady Who Swallowed a Fly

Little ones will eat up these activities that go with any version of the classic story!

What Did She Eat?

Letter-sound association

After a read-aloud of the story, cut out two copies of the old lady pattern on page 180 and attach a resealable plastic bag to each lady's belly. Write a different letter on each bag. Then display the ladies in your room. Send letters home to youngsters' families requesting that they send in pictures from magazines or the Internet with names that begin with the letters. Help youngsters place the pictures in the appropriate bags. After a few days, gather youngsters around and say, "Let's see what the [letter name] lady has eaten." Remove each picture; then have students name it and determine if it begins with the correct sound.

Marcell Gibison
Ephrata Church of the Brethren Children's Center
Ephrata, PA

Rhyme Time

Rhyming

Get a plastic fly (or a black pom-pom). Have students sit in a circle and give one child the fly. Have youngsters pass the fly around the circle as you say the couplet shown. When the couplet is finished, help the child with the fly name a word that rhymes with *fly* (accept nonsense words). Then repeat the game, reciting the couplet again but replacing the word *fly* with the word suggested by the child.

There was an old lady who swallowed a [fly].
I don't know why. Perhaps she'll die.

Old Lady Art

Recalling story details, expressing oneself through art

Before You Read: Fold a sheet of skin-tone paper in half for each child. Then cut a shape from the paper similar to the one shown. To begin, show her the book cover and read the title. Then ask, "What else do you think the old lady ate?" After a brief discussion, have her unfold the cutout and glue it to a sheet of paper. (If desired, add a nose and glasses.) Then have her glue eye cutouts or jumbo wiggle eyes to the project. Have her pull cotton balls and glue them, as shown, so they resemble hair.

After You Read: Have little ones recall what the little old lady ate in the story and have each child draw corresponding pictures in the old lady's mouth.

Colleen Dabney
Williamsburg, VA

Marvelous Motions

Participating in an interactive read-aloud

Now that youngsters are comfortable with the book text, have them help you come up with a motion for each critter mentioned. For example, for the fly, students could clap their hands together as if trying to slap a fly; for the spider, youngsters could wiggle their fingers; and for the bird, students could flap their arms. Then reread the story or sing the traditional song, prompting little ones to add in the motion for each critter!

Time for Questions!

What questions could you ask your students after a read-aloud of this classic? Here are some ideas!
- What was the smallest thing the old lady swallowed?
- What was the biggest thing the old lady swallowed?
- Is this story make-believe or real? Why do you think so?
- Why do you think the woman swallowed all those critters?
- Do you like this story? Why or why not?

Rebecca Tuggle Landreth
Erdenheim Elementary
Flourtown, PA

Old Lady Pattern

Use with "What Did She Eat?" on page 178.

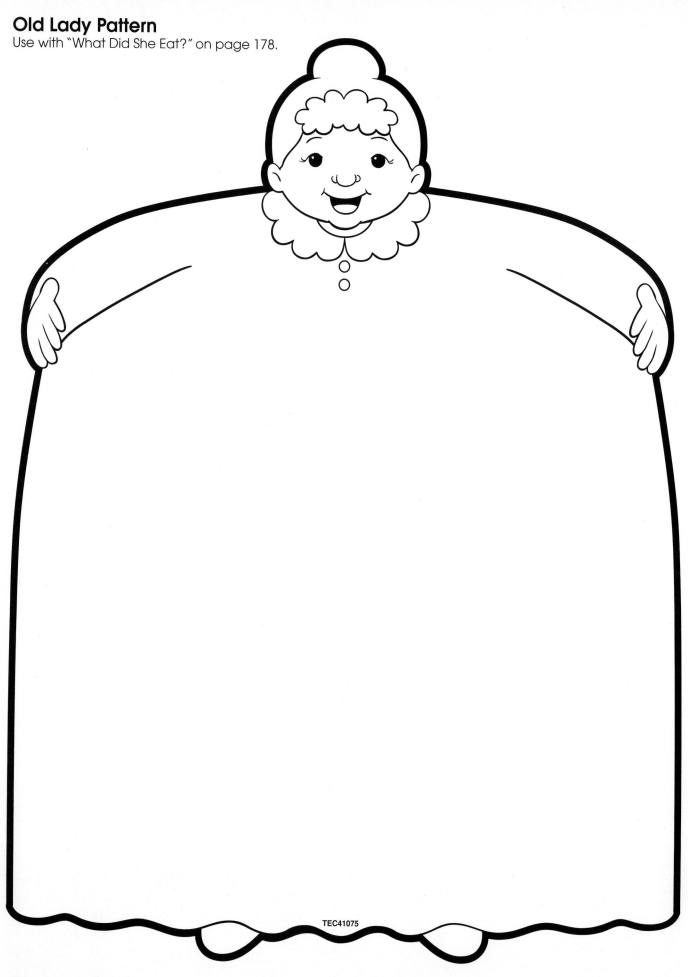

TEC41075

How Do Dinosaurs Say Good Night?

Written by Jane Yolen
Illustrated by Mark Teague

How do dinosaurs say good night? Do they whine and cry and make a fuss? Of course not! They go to bed like big dinosaurs should.

ideas contributed by Tricia Kylene Brown
Bowling Green, KY

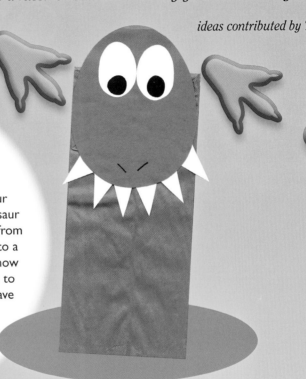

Bedtime Attitudes
Speaking to share an opinion

Find out youngsters' opinions on dinosaur bedtime habits with this activity. Get a dinosaur puppet (or make a simple dinosaur puppet from a paper bag as shown) and give the puppet to a child. Then have her use it to demonstrate how the dinosaur would act when it's time to go to bed. Repeat the activity a few times. Then have little ones settle in for this fun story!

More, roar, for!

Dinosaur Roar!
Rhyming

Turn to the spread in the book that has the text, "Does a dinosaur stomp his feet on the floor and shout: 'I want to hear one book more!'?" Read this page and the next page to youngsters. Then have little ones say the words *more* and *roar* and encourage them to notice that the words rhyme. Hand a toy dinosaur to a youngster and prompt him to say, "More, roar, [additional rhyming word]." Accept nonsense words. Then direct him to hand the dinosaur to another child. Continue for several rounds.

Good Night!

Participating in an action rhyme

Little ones will love this action rhyme based on the events in the story!

One little dinosaur — *Hold up one finger.*
Was sent to bed. — *Place hands beneath cheek as if asleep.*
He stomped his feet, — *Stomp feet.*
And he shook his head! — *Shake head.*

Two big dinosaurs — *Hold up two fingers.*
Said, "No, no, no! — *Shake finger.*
I want to stay up. — *Cross arms.*
I will not go!" — *Shake head.*

Three loving dinosaurs — *Hold up three fingers.*
Hugged each other tight. — *Hug self.*
They gave a big kiss — *Substitute "kiss" with a kissing noise.*
And said, "Good night!" — *Place hands beneath cheek as if asleep.*

How does _a tiger_ say good night?
He growls and chews on the pillow!

Bedtime Antics

Creating a story innovation, adding to a class book

Have each child color and cut out a copy of the bed pattern on page 183. Then have him attach it to a sheet of construction paper labeled with the heading shown. Next, prompt him to draw a desired animal in the bed. Then ask him how this animal might say good night, prompting him to craft a response that is individual to that animal. Write the name of the animal on his paper and add his description. Then bind the completed pages together. Read the resulting class book to your little ones.

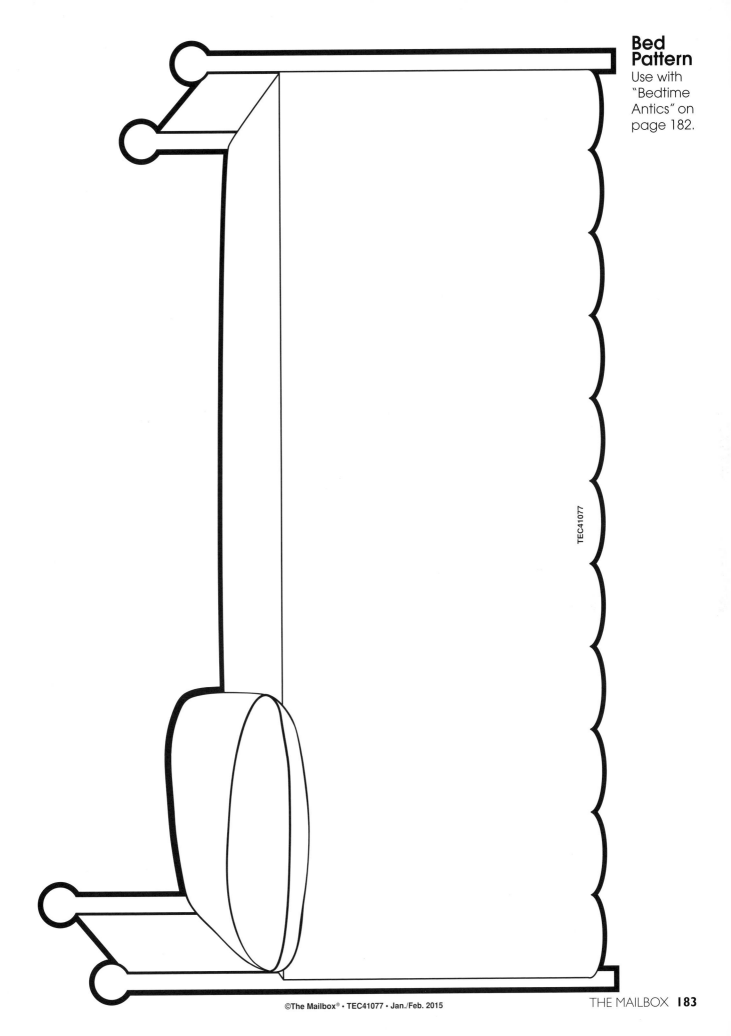

TEC41077

Books With BIG MACHINES

Rumble, crunch, vroom! Build enthusiasm for big machines with this incredibly fun book selection.

Demolition

Written by Sally Sutton
Illustrated by Brian Lovelock

In this rhyming book, workers demolish a building and construct a park and playground in its place!

ideas contributed by Tricia Kylene Brown
Bowling Green, KY

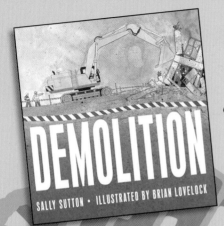

BUILD IT UP!

Rhyming

Little ones will love to play demolition! Program a set of index cards with words, making sure that many of the words rhyme but others do not. Attach the cards to separate boxes (or blocks). Help youngsters notice some of the rhyming words in the story. Then have them play this rhyming game that allows them to "demolish" a building! Have a child say the words on two rhyming boxes and then stack them. Next, have her place a third box on the stack. If the word on the box rhymes with the first two, have her add another block. If it doesn't rhyme, have her demolish the stack! Continue playing until a nonrhyming word is introduced and the stack is demolished.

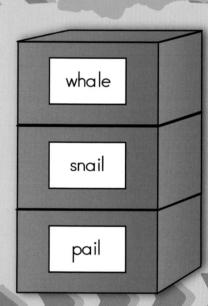

ADD SOME ACCOMPANIMENT

Taking part in an interactive read-aloud, exploring musical instruments

Bang! Clang! Crack! Add extra zip and encourage little ones' listening skills by adding musical instruments to the onomatopoeia in the story. Give youngsters rhythm instruments, such as tambourines, hand drums, maracas, and rhythm sticks. Then reread the story, prompting little ones to play their instruments during each trio of sound words. Thud! Creak! Wham!

tip ⟶ No traditional instruments? No problem! Have little ones tap cardboard tubes or dowel rod pieces, bang on pots and pans with wooden spoons, and shake empty water bottles containing beans or rice. There's more than one way to make a band!

Mike Mulligan and His Steam Shovel

by Virginia Lee Burton

Mike Mulligan and his steam shovel, Mary Anne, dig holes for canals and cellars and roads. Then one day, steam shovels aren't wanted anymore in the big city. Mike and Mary Anne go to a small town in the country and try to dig a town hall cellar in one day. They succeed but forget to leave a way out of the hole!

Scoop It Up!

Developing spatial skills, comparing volume

Encourage little ones to pretend to be Mary Anne at this center! Moisten the sand in your sand table. Then provide scoops, measuring cups, and small containers. Prompt little ones to visit the center and use the props to dig a cellar just like Mary Anne did in the story! As they work, encourage youngsters to compare the containers they use for scooping.

Name Change

Writing letters, manipulating phonemes

In advance, write "Mike Mulligan" on a sentence strip and place it in your pocket chart. Make pairs of consonant cards and place them nearby. Have little ones identify the main character in the story, Mike Mulligan. Then direct their attention to his name, prompting little ones to notice that both *Mike* and *Mulligan* begin with *M*. Next, show a pair of cards and have students identify the letter and its sound. Then have a child place a card over each *M*. Read aloud the new name and prepare to hear giggles! Continue with each card pair.

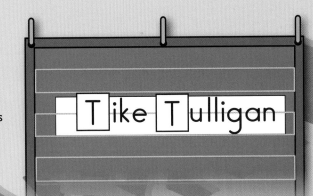

When?

Distinguishing between the past and the present

Ask little ones to notice the clothing people are wearing and cars they are driving in the illustrations. Ask, "Do these clothes and cars look the same as the clothing and cars you see when you're out with your family?" Prompt students to conclude that the events of this book take place a long time ago. Ask, "What else do you think was different a long time ago?" Discuss little ones' thoughts. Then explain that this book was written 76 years ago. Now that's a classic!

My Truck Is Stuck!

Written by Kevin Lewis
Illustrated by Daniel Kirk

Two dogs are taking a load of bones for a delivery when their truck gets stuck. Multiple vehicles try to pull them out, but in the end, only a tow truck will do! Unfortunately, a bunch of mischievous prairie dogs have stolen their load of bones.

Sandy Illustrations

Describing the job of an illustrator, extending a story through art

In advance, mix sand with several colors of tempera paint. Tell little ones that the illustrator of the book is Daniel Kirk. Help students describe what an illustrator does, with help as needed. Point out the clouds on the pages and have students notice that they are bumpy and gritty in appearance. Explain to little ones that the artist used sand with his paint to make that texture. Then explain that they can do this too! Allow little ones to paint a masterpiece with the sand and paint mixture.

What Would You Do?

Dictating information, speaking to discuss an opinion

Have a child color and cut out a copy of the truck on page 187. Cut a slit in a sheet of construction paper programmed as shown and help the child slide the front wheel of the truck cutout into the slit, as if the truck has fallen into a hole. Glue the truck in place. Have the youngster complete the prompt. Then write his words in the space provided. If desired, bind the finished projects with the title "One Stuck Truck."

Stealing Bones

Representing subtraction with images, dramatizing a story

Cut out two copies of the bone cards (see page 188). Have two youngsters sit on the floor and pretend to be the drivers of the stuck truck. Then scatter the bone cards behind the youngsters. Help students count the bones aloud. Then gently tap two youngsters on the shoulder. Have each child pretend to be a prairie dog, sneak up to the bones, take one, and then sit back down. Help little ones count the bones again. Continue in the same way until all the bones have disappeared!

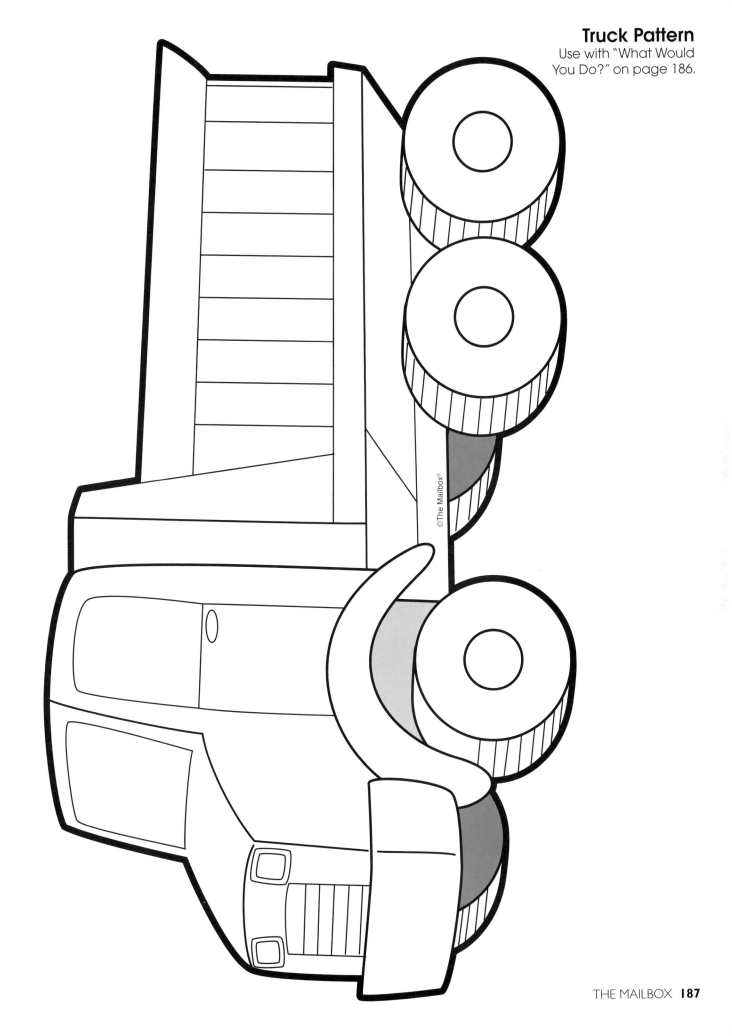

Truck Pattern
Use with "What Would You Do?" on page 186.

©The Mailbox®

Bone Cards
Use with "Stealing Bones" on page 186.

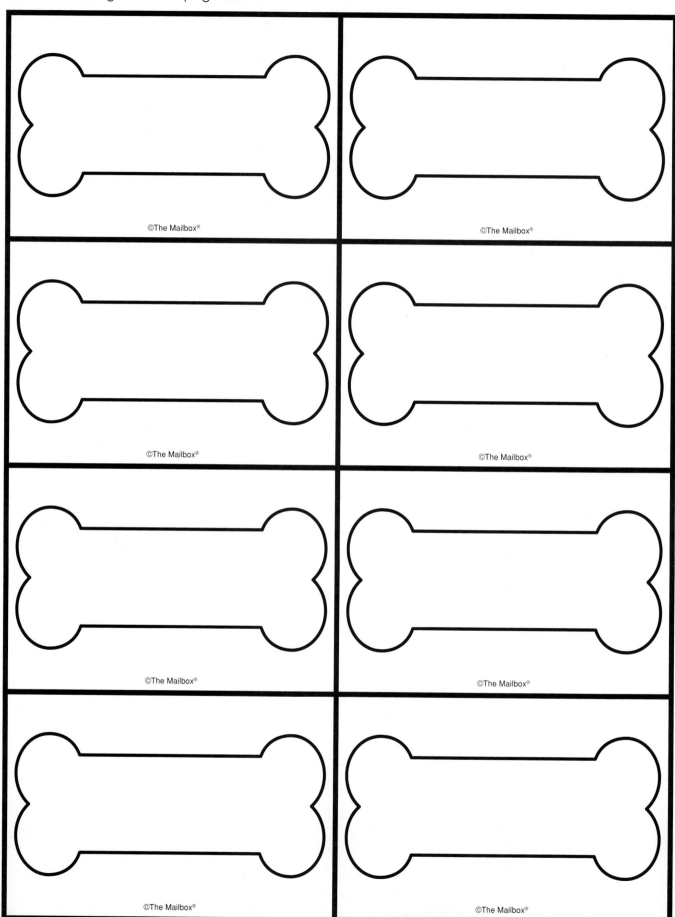

©The Mailbox®

©The Mailbox®

©The Mailbox®

©The Mailbox®

©The Mailbox®

©The Mailbox®

©The Mailbox®

©The Mailbox®

CENTER UNITS

Centers With

Polka Dots and Spots

You'll spot little ones having fun with this unique center theme!

Polka-Dot Letters

Literacy Center

R is for *red*! Write a large letter *R* on a piece of bulletin board paper, laminate it, and then attach it to a table. Provide small circular cookie cutters and red play dough. Emphasize to youngsters that *red* begins with the letter *R*. A student visits the center and pats a piece of play dough to make it flat. He uses the cookie cutter to cut polka dots from the play dough and then places them on the *R*. After each child has had an opportunity to visit the center, consider swapping the props for a letter *Y* and yellow play dough. ***Letter-sound association, reinforcing letter names***

Janet Boyce
Tomball, TX

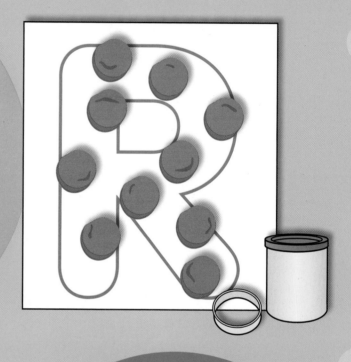

Dot, Dot, Dot!

Math Center

Place coffee filters, bingo daubers, and a large die at a table. Two youngsters visit the center, and each one takes a coffee filter. (You may wish to provide scrap paper for youngsters to place their filters on to protect the table.) One child rolls a die and counts the dots. Then she chooses a dauber and makes a corresponding set of dots on her filter. Her partner repeats the process. Students continue, choosing from the variety of daubers.

Beth Sharpe
The Malvern School
Medford, NJ

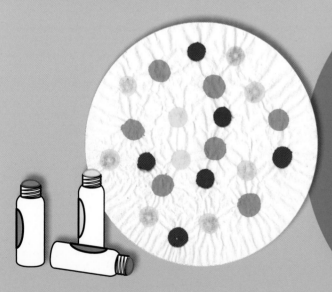

Balloons in the Sky

Art Center

Provide shallow pans of colorful paint, bottle caps (or corks), cotton balls, unwrapped blue crayons, glue, and white construction paper. A child takes a crayon and rubs it on a sheet of paper to make a blue sky. She dips the top of a cap into the paint and then makes prints on the paper. She continues with other caps and colors. Then she stretches out cotton balls and glues them to the paper so they resemble clouds. When the paint is dry, use a fine-tip permanent marker to draw a string from each balloon.

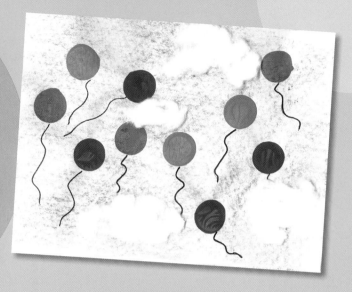

Sticky Spots

Fine-Motor Area

This quick and easy center will keep little fingers busy! Attach a sheet of chart paper to an easel and place a supply of dot stickers nearby. Youngsters simply remove stickers from the pages and attach them to the paper!

Suzanne Moore
Tucson, AZ

Dot Jump!

Gross-Motor Area

Cut large circles (dots) from sheets of craft foam and place them near an open area. A child picks up the circles and tosses them like Frisbee flying discs into the open area. Then he attempts to hop from dot to dot!

See page 192 for a spot-themed reproducible for your science center.

Ladybug

Leopard

Giraffe

Dalmatian

Note to the teacher: Give each child a copy of this page and explain that many creatures have spots. Help him identify the animals. Then have him dip a pencil eraser in paint and make spots on the creatures. If desired, have him transform the pictures into a booklet with a cover titled "What Has Spots?" *Investigating living things*

Crazy Mixed-Up Centers

What would happen if you took items from some centers and placed them in other centers? You would have some crazy mixed-up centers that encourage creative play!

ideas contributed by Roxanne LaBell Dearman
NC Intervention for the Deaf and Hard of Hearing, Charlotte, NC

Plastic food in your art center?

Remove plastic fruits and vegetables from your housekeeping area and place them at your art center. Also provide bowls and baskets for arranging the items. Print examples from the Internet of still life paintings that involve fruits and vegetables and display them in the area. Youngsters come to the center and paint or draw still life pictures as desired.

Paintbrushes in your block area?

Place the paintbrushes from your art center in your block center. Little ones visit the center and build various structures, such as homes, offices, or stores. Then they select a paintbrush and pretend to paint the outside of the buildings.

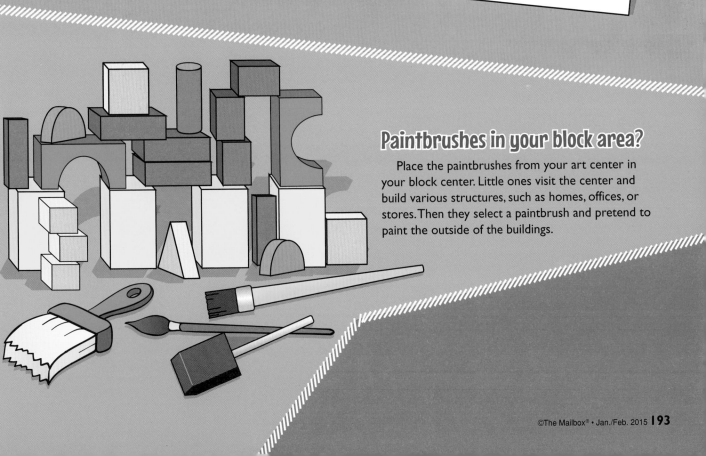

Puzzles in your sensory center?

Place sensory filler, such as rice, paper shreds, oatmeal, or cornmeal in your sensory tub or table. Then get a chunky wooden puzzle and bury the puzzle pieces in the filler. (For an extra challenge, bury the pieces from two puzzles.) A child digs through the filler and removes a puzzle piece. Then she sets it appropriately in the puzzle base. She continues until all the pieces have been found and placed.

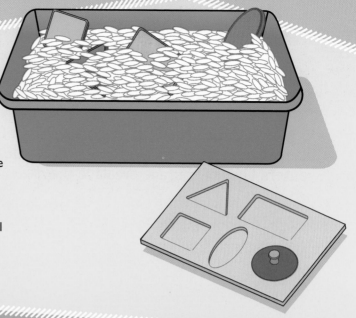

Blocks in your math center?

Put blocks in your math center along with rulers. Youngsters visit the center and build towers that are taller than 12 inches. As they build, they check their progress by holding the rulers next to their structures.

Play dough in your writing center?

Put play dough in your writing center, along with a rolling pin, chopsticks, craft sticks, and toothpicks. A child rolls out a piece of dough so it's flat and smooth. Then he chooses an item and uses it to "write" in the play dough. He continues the process with other items. Then he smooths the play dough with the rolling pin and repeats the activity.

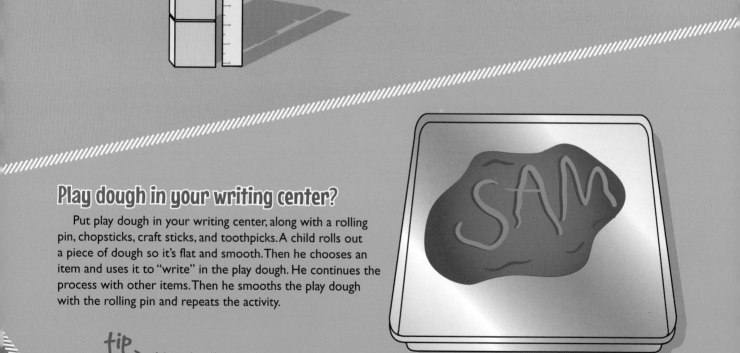

If desired, put letter cards at the center and prompt students to draw the letters in the play dough.

LITERACY UNITS

My Name Is Special!

Spotlight little ones' names with this collection of ideas just perfect for the beginning of the school year!

Highlighter Fun!
Recognizing one's name

You can keep attendance with this daily activity! Write students' names randomly on a sheet of paper and make several copies. Display one of the copies. Then call a youngster's name and give him a highlighter marker. Help the child find and then highlight his name. Continue with each remaining student. Repeat this activity each day. When you run out of name sheets, make a new batch with the names in different locations on the page.

Carole Watkins, Timothy Ball Elementary, Crown Point, IN

Lia   Nora
Sarah   Olive
Mia   Jared
O'Juan   Michael
Emma   David
Jacob

Large Letters
Reinforcing letter names, recognizing the first letter in one's name

Make a supersize letter cutout for each child's name. Write each student's name on the letter. Then laminate the letters, if desired. Attach the hook side of a Velcro fastener to each letter and attach the loop side to each child's picture. To begin, give each youngster his picture. Then hold up a letter. Ask, "Whose letter is this?" and prompt the children to attach their pictures.

Michele Rush, Rainy Dayz Preschool, Gig Harbor, WA

Alexander

Andy   Alan

Anna

tip When youngsters become comfortable with recognizing their own names and those of their classmates, consider making this a center! Simply display the letters. Then have youngsters visit the center and attach the photos.

Miracle

Miracle

The Name Helper
Matching letters in one's name, rhyming
Each morning, choose a youngster to be your Name Helper and write her name on a magnetic whiteboard. Below her name, attach a magnetic letter for each letter in her name, scrambling the letters. Have the child unscramble the letters. Then ask the remaining students what the letters spell. Finally, have little ones create nonsense words that rhyme with the child's name. Miracle, Biracle, Firacle!

Joan Arndt, Little Lambs Preschool, Fort Dodge, IA

Erase Your Letter!
Recognizing the first letter in one's name
This quick activity is a perfect time filler! Write the first letter in each child's name randomly on your board. Next, choose a child and have him come up to the board and erase his letter. Continue with each remaining child until all the letters are erased.

Mimi Philpott, Adams Traditional Beginnings, Phoenix, AZ

Whose Name?
Recognizing one's name
Youngsters will love this silly rhyme and activity! Write each child's name on a cutout copy of the apple pattern on page 198. Then place the apples in a gift bag. Lead students in performing the rhyme shown. Then pull out an apple and help the corresponding child recognize her name. Introduce the child to the class. Continue with the remaining apples.

Apple, "bapple,"   *Clap to the beat.*
Wiggle, jiggle—whee!   *Twist your torso.*
Whose name, whose name   *Clap to the beat.*
Do we see?

Apple Pattern

Use with "Whose Name?" on page 197.

TEC41074

5 Fall Writing Experiences!

Leaves, pumpkins, and all things fall! These writing activities are made for this splendid season.

1 That's My Leaf!
Investigating living things

Combine science skills and writing skills with this leaf recording sheet! Make a class supply of page 201. Gather a variety of fall leaves and place them in a container. Then have a child choose a leaf. With help, the youngster glues his leaf to the paper, circles the word to identify its size, colors the boxes to identify the different colors on the leaf, and then dictates information (or uses invented writing) to complete the sentence starter at the bottom.

Rebecca Bernard
Children's Creative Learning Center of Framingham
Framingham, MA

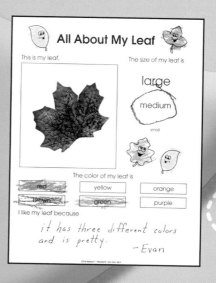

All About My Leaf

This is my leaf.

The size of my leaf is

large
medium
small

The color of my leaf is

red
yellow
orange
brown
green
purple

I like my leaf because

it has three different colors and is pretty.

— Evan

2 Dear Pumpkin
Communicating through writing

Read a variety of pumpkin-themed stories. (One of our favorites, *Pumpkin, Pumpkin* by Jeanne Titherington, is featured on page 157.) Next, hollow out a pumpkin, draw a face on it, and place it near your writing center. Provide a variety of paper and drawing utensils. Then encourage students to "write" letters and questions to the pumpkin or draw pictures for the pumpkin. When a youngster is finished with his work, have him place it in the pumpkin!

Expand It!

Developing details in writing

An inspirational seasonal picture is the key to this activity! Get an old calendar and remove the picture used for the month of October. Have a youngster join you and ask him to tell you what he sees in the picture. You might get a response like "I see a tree" or "I see leaves." Write his words on a sheet of paper. Then ask a question about the picture, such as "What colors are the leaves?" Edit the sentence to reflect his response and read it aloud. Continue with several other questions until a well-developed sentence is formed. Then post youngsters' writing around the original picture! Consider completing this activity each month with the appropriate calendar picture.

Carolynn Sidlauskas, Covert Elementary, Covert, MI

The really big tree has lots of orange and red leaves.

Sam

Write on It!

Developing fine-motor skills

Provide a pumpkin, washable markers, and damp rags. A youngster uses markers to write on the pumpkin. Then he removes the writing with a damp rag and begins again. If desired, provide a few letter or word cards for youngsters to use as a guide.

Cori Marinan, Howe School, Green Bay, WI

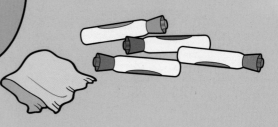

Art Journaling

Expressing oneself through art

Combine writing with this lovely leaf-themed art! First, have a child brush colorful paint on a leaf and then press the leaf on a sheet of paper. Have her do this a few more times. If desired, have her press rubber stamps in ink and then make prints on the page. After the project is dry, ask her to use a marker to write about how fall makes her feel. Or, if desired, have her dictate her thoughts.

Fall makes me happy

The leaves are pretty, and there are lots of squirrels.

~Sarah

All About My Leaf

This is my leaf.

The size of my leaf is

large

medium

small

The color of my leaf is

red	yellow	orange
brown	green	purple

I like my leaf because

Note to the teacher: Use with "That's My Leaf!" on page 199.

A SUPER Literacy Selection!

These anytime literacy activities are packed with creativity!

Clap and Toss
Counting syllables

This phonological awareness activity makes use of colorful pom-poms! Gather a container of pom-poms, an empty container, and several classroom objects. Hold up an object and have students say its name and clap its name. Then have a child toss one pom-pom into the container for each syllable in the word. Continue with each remaining object.

Karen Eiben, The Learning House Preschool, LaSalle, IL

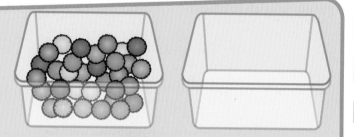

A Special Message
Tracking print from left to right, understanding that words have meaning

Decide on a special message relating to an upcoming event or holiday. Then type the message using a large point size. Print the message and cut out the separate words. Trace the word cards onto a sheet of poster board. Then place the first word in an envelope and put it in your classroom mailbox. Display the poster board. When youngsters arrive, exclaim with great excitement that the class has mail! Have a child open the envelope. Show youngsters the word and read it aloud. Then have a child attach it to the first space on the poster board. Continue in the same way, placing the words in the mailbox in order, one per day, until the message is finished!

Litsa Jackson, Covington Integrated Arts Academy, Covington, TN

Our	valentine	party
is	on	February
14!		

● See page 204 for a **writing activity**!

The Joke Bag
Speaking

Little ones will love this giggle-worthy activity! Decorate a bag as desired and title it "The Joke Bag." Include a parent note inside the bag explaining that the child and parent are to write a joke or a riddle on a slip of paper and put it in the bag. (You may wish to direct parents to the Internet, where they'll find lots of kid-appropriate jokes!) When the joke bag is returned to school, put on some funny accessories, such as glasses with a mustache or a goofy hat, and announce that it's joke time! Have the child tell his joke, with prompting as needed.

Debbie Pacetti, St. Angela Merici,
Fairview Park, OH

I Say, You Say
Rhyming

Recite the chant given, prompting youngsters to chime in with the rhyming word given in parentheses!

It's rhyming time; it's rhyming time.
Just chime on in to finish the rhyme!

I say, "I'm going on a hike."
You say, "I will ride my (bike)."

I say, "I am making a cake."
You say, "I am swimming in a (lake)."

I say, "I'd like to climb a tree."
You say, " 'Buzz, buzz,' says the (bee)."

I say, "I will take a train."
You say, "Let's fly in a (plane)."

I say, "Rhyming is such fun!"
You say, "Now this game is (done)."

Cindy Hoying, Centerville, OH

See page 205 for more rhyming practice!

Collect the Letters
Reinforcing letter names

Write the letter youngsters are currently studying on scraps of paper. Then hide the scraps around the room. Also write the letter on an index card and attach it to a plastic jar. When youngsters come across a letter during center time or free play, they say its name and put it in the jar. Consider doing this fun activity for each letter little ones study!

Dana Rangel, Saint John Center, Joliet, IL

What happens next?

Note to the teacher: Have a child look at a copy of this page. Then have her "write" or dictate to tell what happens next.

Rhyme Time!

Note to the teacher: Give each child a copy of this page and a bingo dauber. To reinforce the sound of rhyming words, have her tap each row of pictures with the bingo dauber as she says the picture names. For more advanced students, have each child name another word, real or nonsense, that rhymes with the picture names in each row.

Mixing Literacy with Art

Combine these two areas of study for delightfully educational masterpieces!

Make a Cover

Recalling plot and character details

Read aloud a picture book without showing youngsters the cover. When the read-aloud is finished, ask little ones to share what they think should be on the cover, encouraging them to recall characters, the setting, and the plot of the story. Next, give each child a sheet of paper and have her draw what she thinks the cover should look like. Finally, reveal the actual cover!

Deborah J. Ryan
Newberg, OR

Artsy Xs and Os

Reinforcing letter names

Gather a small group of youngsters and explain that when people write "XO" on a card or in a text, it means that they're giving that person hugs and kisses. Next, give each child a sheet of fingerpaint paper. On each paper, use a squeeze bottle of paint to draw a red *X* and a white *O*. Then have little ones fingerpaint the letters together and use a finger to write *X*s and *O*s in the pink paint!

Janet Boyce
Hinojosa Early Childhood and Pre-Kindergarten Center
Houston, TX

Red, Yellow, Purple
Letter-sound association

Prepare containers of red, yellow, and purple paint and put several brushes in each container. Gather a small group of youngsters. Have them identify each paint color and recognize that *red* begins with /r/, *yellow* begins with /y/, and *purple* begins with /p/. (For an easier version, only use two colors of paint.) Next, say, "/r/, /r/, /r/!" Help little ones identify that this is the beginning sound for *red*. Then prompt them to paint with red as they say, "/r/, /r/, *red*." Continue with each remaining sound until they have made a lovely piece of process art!

Line, Fine!
Rhyming

Gather a small group of youngsters and provide colorful markers and crayons. Give each child a sheet of paper. Then say, "Line, fine." Help little ones understand that the two words rhyme. Then have each child draw a line on his paper. Next, say, "Line, cat." These two words do not rhyme, so the youngsters do nothing. Continue in the same way until the papers are filled with colorful lines. Then prompt students to color the shapes created by intersecting lines.

Tap, Tap, Tap
Tapping and counting syllables

Place shallow pans of colorful paint at a table and gather a small group of youngsters. Give each little one a sheet of paper and an unsharpened pencil. Have each child dip the end of his pencil in a pan of paint. Then say a word. (For extra fun, have the word relate to a current classroom theme or holiday.) Then have each child repeat the word as he taps the paint-covered end of the pencil against the paper once for each syllable. Repeat the activity with another word. What a fun, expressive way to practice syllabication!

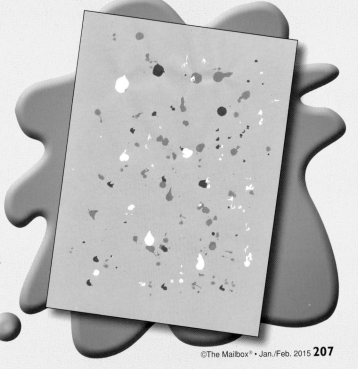

 Looking for a less-mess option? Simply use bingo daubers!

SPRING Into Literacy!

It's springtime! Celebrate this lovely season with a selection of skills on your favorite spring topics.

A Tisket, a Tasket

Identifying letters and sounds

Engage your active little ones with this whole-group game. In advance, obtain an Easter basket. Place a letter card in an envelope and place the envelope in the basket. To begin, seat students in a circle. Then give a volunteer the Easter basket. Lead students in singing the song shown while the child skips, marches, or gallops around the inside of the circle, dropping the envelope in front of a classmate when indicated. The classmate removes the letter from the envelope, identifies it and its sound (with help as needed), and then gives it to you. Replace the letter with a different one. Then have little ones play another round!

(sung to the tune of "A Tisket, a Tasket")

A tisket, a tasket,
A special Easter basket—
I wrote a letter for my friend,
And on the way, I dropped it.

Diane Wiley
Diane's Smartstart Preschool & Childcare
Meridian, ID

Caterpillar or Butterfly?

Beginning sounds /b/ and /k/

Cut out a copy of the caterpillar and butterfly cards on page 211 and attach them to the sides of a cube-shaped box to make a large die. Have a child roll the die. If the die shows a caterpillar, have little ones lie down and pretend to be caterpillars. Then ask a youngster to name another word that begins with /k/ like *caterpillar*. If the die shows a butterfly, have little ones stand and flap their arms as if their arms were wings. Then ask a child to name another word that begins with /b/ like *butterfly*. Play several rounds of the activity!

 See **page 213** for more terrific **butterfly stuff**!

Shake, Shake, Shake!

Counting syllables

Counting syllables is super fun with spring-themed percussion! Cut out a copy of the cards on 212. Place rice or beans in plastic eggs and then secure the eggs with tape. Give an egg to each child and place the cards facedown in your circle-time area. Have a youngster turn over one of the cards and name the picture. Emphasize that the picture shows something we see in the spring. Then have little ones say the picture name, shaking the egg once for each syllable. Have little ones name how many times they shook the egg. Then remove the card. Continue with the remaining cards.

For an extra challenge, have volunteers write the number of syllables on sticky notes and attach them to the pictures.

There's Something New!

Participating in a rhyming song

Guide youngsters in singing this super spring song!

(sung to the tune of "The Farmer in the Dell")

In spring, there's something new!
In spring, there's something new!
[See leaves and flowers too].
In spring, there's something new!

Continue with the following: *See chicks and ducklings too, see bees and tadpoles too, see worms and puddles too*

Cindy Hoying, Centerville, OH

Drip Drop R

Identifying letter **R** and its sound

Tint a cup of water blue and provide a sheet of paper labeled with a letter *R*. Have a child place the paper on a paper towel–lined tray. Then help her identify the letter *R* and its sound. Help her realize that *rain* begins with /r/. Have her use an eyedropper to drip blue water on the letter *R*, prompting her to say "/r/" for each drop.

adapted from an idea by Danielle Lockwood
Colchester, CT

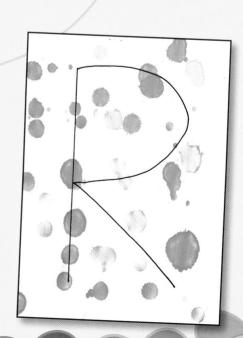

A Tulip Booklet
Print and book awareness

Combine literacy and science with this adorable spring booklet that's sure to be a family keepsake! Help a child follow the steps below to create each page of her booklet. When the pages are dry, bind them together with a cover labeled "Happy Birthday, Tulip!"

Steps:

Page 1: Use a brown crayon to draw a ground line. Press the edge of your fist in brown paint and then press it on the paper to make a print (tulip bulb). Label the bulb.

Page 2: Repeat steps for page 1 but omit the labeling. Then use a green crayon to make a shoot coming out of the bulb. Use a brown crayon to draw roots coming from the bulb. Label the shoot and roots.

Page 3: Repeat steps for pages 1 and 2, but omit the labeling. Next, press the edge of your hand in green paint and press it on the paper to make a stem. Make green thumbprints (leaves) on either side of the stem. Then make a colorful thumbprint (bud) at the top of the stem. Label the stem and bud.

Page 4: Repeat steps for pages 1–3 but, instead of making a thumbprint bud, make a handprint. Label the bloom.

Roxanne LaBell Dearman, NC Intervention for the Deaf and Hard of Hearing Charlotte, NC

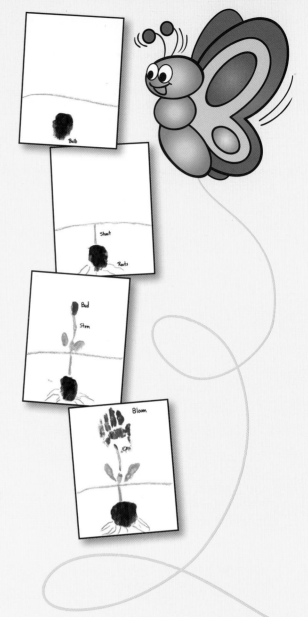

Here Is the Bug!
Participating in a rhyming fingerplay

Celebrate springtime critters with this adorable fingerplay! After several performances, have students notice that the words *tree, flee, free,* and *me* all rhyme. Encourage youngsters to name other words, real or nonsense, that rhyme with the these words.

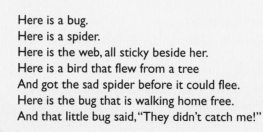

They didn't catch me!

Here is a bug.	*Hold up pointer finger on right hand.*
Here is a spider.	*Hold up left hand and wiggle fingers.*
Here is the web, all sticky beside her.	*Stop wiggling and splay fingers.*
Here is a bird that flew from a tree	*Swoop right hand and grab left.*
And got the sad spider before it could flee.	*Open and close hand like a beak.*
Here is the bug that is walking home free.	*Hold up pointer finger on right hand.*
And that little bug said, "They didn't catch me!"	*Wiggle finger.*

Cindy Hoying, Centerville, OH

©The Mailbox®

©The Mailbox®

©The Mailbox®

©The Mailbox®

©The Mailbox®

©The Mailbox®

Spring Picture Cards

Use with "Shake, Shake, Shake!" on page 209.

bird
©The Mailbox®

caterpillar
©The Mailbox®

flower
©The Mailbox®

leaves
©The Mailbox®

rain
©The Mailbox®

puddle
©The Mailbox®

rainbow
©The Mailbox®

butterfly
©The Mailbox®

tadpole
©The Mailbox®

Dot It!

Dot each letter on the 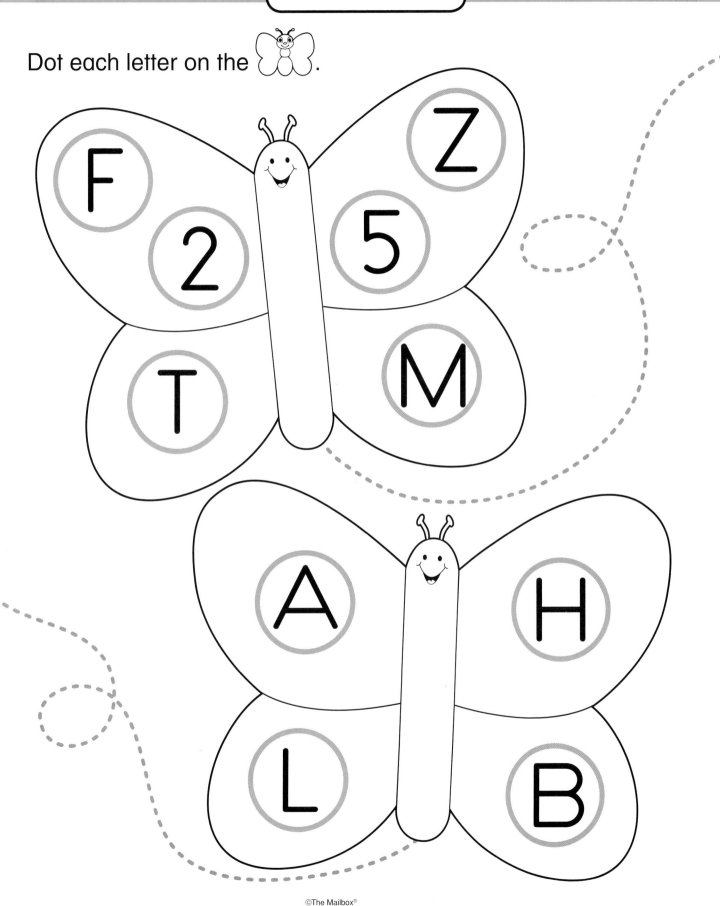 .

Note to the teacher: Have a student use a bingo dauber, marker, or crayon to mark each circle that shows a letter.

Time for Phonological Awareness

Little ones get a lot of phonological awareness practice with these zippy activities!

Concept of spoken word
5–10 minutes

Word Taps

hat

warm-up: Have students stand and follow your lead in tapping in sequence their toes, knees, hips, shoulders, and head. Repeat the tapping sequence a few times to confirm your students' understanding.

Activity: To begin, say five or fewer one-syllable concrete words. Each youngster taps a different body part in the practiced sequence for each word he hears. For example, when you say, "Hat, chair," a little one taps his toes and his knees; then he stops. Encourage students to say the words as they tap. Repeat several times, varying the number of words each time. When youngsters are successfully tapping out one-syllable words, include two-syllable concrete words. Then progress to sentences containing five or fewer words. "The puppy is so cute!" *(toes, knees, hips, shoulders, head)*

One-syllable concrete words:

box	cat	dog	fish	house	car	corn	rock	shoe
jeep	school	tire	barn	wheel	bag	card	drum	star

Two-syllable concrete words:

paper	puppy	tiger	soccer	turtle	cabin	honey	kitchen	building
castle	table	bunny	window	pizza	napkin	spider	monster	sandwich

Sentences:

I sat down.	She is funny.	Is it raining?
Tommy runs fast.	The cat ran home.	Did the train stop?
Get in the car.	Your slippers are blue.	Spot loves to play ball.

Fish Go Swish!

Warm-up: Remind students that two words that sound alike at the end, like *fish* and *swish,* are rhyming words. Ask if *sit* and *hit* rhyme. *(Yes.)* Then ask if *book* and *cat* rhyme. *(No.)* Invite a child to explain why *book* and *cat* do not rhyme.

Activity: Have each student use his hands to make a fish shape as shown. Show students how to swish their fish through the air. Invite students to practice the movement and then have them hold their fish still. Next, choose a pair of words from one of the lists below. Ask students to repeat the words and decide if they rhyme. Direct them to swish their fish if the words rhyme and to hold their fish still if they do not. Repeat with different word pairs.

Rhyming Word Pairs

sun	fun	bell	sell
gill	bill	him	rim
wet	pet	boss	toss
fin	win	cat	hat
lake	cake	man	pan
red	bed	jug	rug
lip	sip	fish	wish

Nonrhyming Word Pairs

dig	sock
nap	rim
dot	bag
sun	cat
bed	dog
lap	fan
cup	fox

Ladybug, Ladybug

In advance: Cut out a construction paper copy of a ladybug wristband (patterns on page 217) for each child and tape the short ends together. Slide a wristband onto each child's wrist.

Activity: Recite the rhyme. Then ask students to listen for the /l/ sound at the beginning of the word *lion*. When the sound is identified, prompt each student to raise his wristband hand and fly his ladybugs in a circle over his head. Repeat the activity, this time using the word *mix*. Explain that because the word *mix* does not begin with the /l/ sound, the students' ladybugs cannot take flight. Repeat.

Ladybug, ladybug,
Listen for a sound.
If you hear a /l/,
Then fly around!
[Lion].

 See **page 218** for more practice with **beginning sound /l/**.

Word List

lip	lost	lake	load
like	lamp	lap	line
look	land	latch	loop
little	leg	lick	log
lunch	low	let	lamb
love	lung	life	low
left	last	list	lump

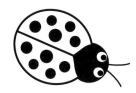

©The Mailbox®

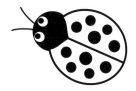

©The Mailbox®

©The Mailbox®

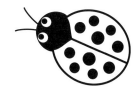

©The Mailbox®

©The Mailbox®

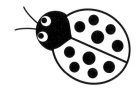

©The Mailbox®

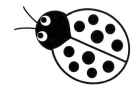

©The Mailbox®

Two of a Kind

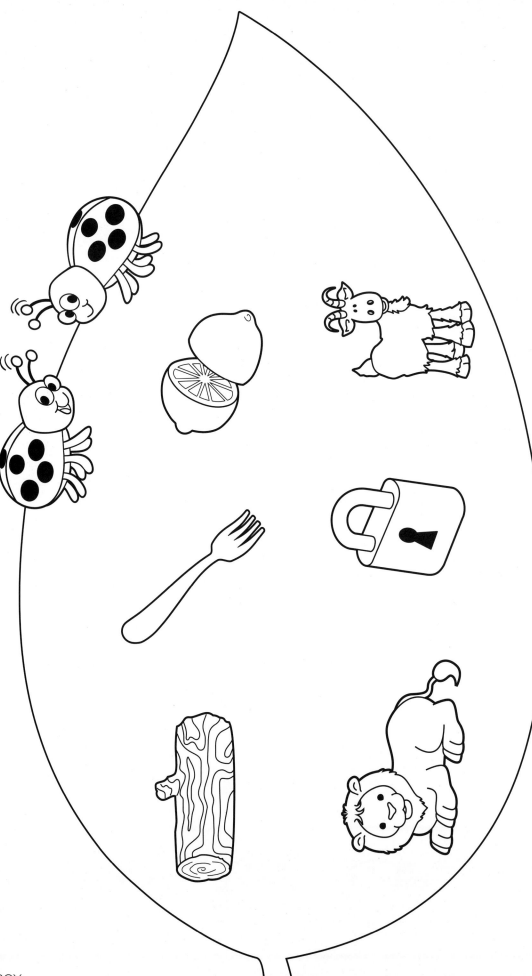

Color the pictures that **begin** with /l/.

For More Learning Ask the child to choose a picture that begins with /l/. Write the word; then have her circle the letter *l*.

MATH UNITS

Math With Classic Songs

These familiar songs are just perfect for encouraging preschool math skills!

Cindy Hoying, Centerville, OH

"This Old Man"

A Bone for the Dog

Counting to ten

The dog in this story sure is happy, because he gets a bone during every verse! Make ten simple bone cutouts (or use real bone-shaped treats). Get a stuffed toy dog. Lead students in singing the first verse of the song, prompting a child to give one bone to the dog when indicated. After the verse, have students confirm that the dog has one bone. Continue with each remaining verse until the dog has ten bones. Lucky dog!

What Did He Play?

Identifying numbers, rhyming

Place number cards from 1 to 5 (or 1 to 10 for advanced students) facedown on your floor. Then gather youngsters around the cards. Prompt a child to flip a number over and have youngsters name it. Then sing the corresponding verse of the song, prompting youngsters to supply the name of the number and the word that rhymes with it. Continue with the remaining cards.

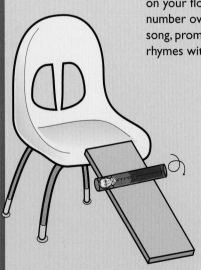

Rolling Home!

Estimating

Little ones will love this silly activity! Color and cut out a copy of the old man and house patterns on page 223 and attach the old man cutout to a cardboard tube, trimmed to size. (Hint: tape or glue the cutout so it is flush with the tube.) Lean a length of cardboard or a wooden board against a chair to make a ramp and place the house several feet from the bottom. Have students sing the song to refresh their memories. Then ask, "If the old man rolls down the ramp, do you think he will stop before he rolls home or will he roll past his home?" Have students share their thoughts. Then encourage a child to let the old man go at the top of the ramp. Encourage students to evaluate their predictions. This activity also makes a fun center!

"Baa, Baa, Black Sheep"

How Many Bags?
Reinforcing number names, counting

Cut out copies of the bag cards on page 224 and gather number cards 1 through 5. Write the first four lines of the song on sentence strips, leaving a blank space for the number. Place the "3" card in the space. Then lead students in singing the four lines. Next, have a child count out three bag cards and place them in the pocket chart. Confirm his work, remove the number and bag cards, and repeat the process with a new number card.

Big Sheep, Little Sheep
Sorting, patterning

Use blocks or toy fencing to create a fenced-in area on your floor. Place a supply of small and large black pom-poms (sheep) in the fenced-in area. Sing the song with youngsters. Then have them notice that some of the sheep are large and some are small. Have students help you sort the sheep into two groups: large sheep and small sheep. Point to the large sheep and have students say, "Baa!" in their biggest sheep voices. Then point to the small sheep and have students say, "Baa!" in their tiniest sheep voices. Help students create a line of sheep in an AB pattern. Finally, have them read the pattern aloud by saying, "Baa!" in the appropriate voices as you point to the sheep.

Wool for Everyone!
One-to-one correspondence

Gather a supply of large black pom-poms (wool). Then sing the slightly altered song below, giving one piece of wool to each child named. Continue in the same way, prompting volunteers to help you hand out the wool as you sing.

Baa, baa, black sheep, have you any wool?
Yes sir, yes sir, three bags full.
One for [child's name] and one for [child's name];
One for [child's name] and one for [child's name].
Baa, baa, black sheep, have you any wool?
Yes sir, yes sir, three bags full.

"Shoo Fly"

Where Is the Fly?

Identifying shapes

Color and cut out a copy of the fly pattern on page 224. Make several shape cutouts and place them on your floor. Secretly place the fly beneath a shape. Then exclaim with great drama that you see a fly buzzing around! Prompt students to sing "Shoo Fly." Inform students that they shooed the fly and it's hiding beneath a shape. Have a student name and then lift a shape to see if the fly is beneath it. If it is, rehide the fly and play another round of the game. If it isn't, call on another youngster to choose a shape.

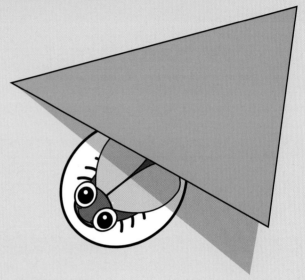

So Many Flies!

Counting sets

Draw from one to five simple flies on separate pieces of paper. Hold up one of the pages and have children count the number of flies. Then lead them in singing the adapted version of the song below, inserting the appropriate number. Continue with each remaining sheet of flies. For extra fun, have a youngster swat the flies with an unused flyswatter after each version of the song!

[Two] flies don't bother me.
[Two] flies don't bother me.
[Two] flies don't bother me
For I belong to somebody!

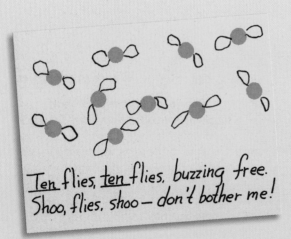

Ten flies, ten flies, buzzing free.
Shoo, flies, shoo—don't bother me!

Shoo!

Making a set, making a class book

Give each child a sheet of construction paper programmed as shown. Help a child choose a number. Then have her use a bingo dauber to make a corresponding number of prints on the page. Next, have her use a fine-tip black marker to make wings on each print so it resembles a fly. Write the number word in the text. Then bind youngsters' pages together with a cover titled "Shoo Flies!" Read the story aloud, prompting children to count each set of flies and recite the text with you.

Bag Cards

Use with "How Many Bags?" on page 221.

TEC41074

TEC41074

TEC41074

TEC41074

TEC41074

Fly Pattern

Use with "Where Is the Fly?" on page 222.

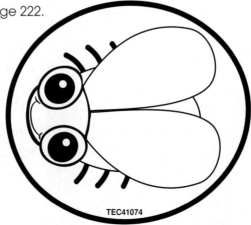

TEC41074

Thanksgiving Math!

Little ones will gobble up these engaging and educational math activities!

ideas contributed by Cindy Hoying
Centerville, OH

Sort the Feast!
Sorting, patterning

Little ones need to sort out this mixed-up Thanksgiving feast! Gather cotton balls (mashed potatoes), small yellow pom-poms (corn), and orange craft foam triangles (pumpkin pie slices) and place them in a tub. Have little ones help you sort the potatoes, corn, and pie slices into three piles. Then use the manipulatives to begin a pattern. Have youngsters continue the pattern and then read it aloud. Pie, corn, pie, corn!

Cranberry Shake
Counting, identifying colors

Get a bag of fresh cranberries and tape a sheet of paper to the bottom of a lidded plastic container. Have a child count out 15 cranberries and then place them in the container. (Depending on the child's counting skills, you may wish to use a smaller number.) Also help the youngster add several dollops of colorful paint, identifying each color as she does so. Help her attach the lid. Then prompt her to shake the container vigorously. After several moments, encourage her to open the container. Then help her remove the cranberries to reveal her artwork!

Sara Barbour
Apple Tree Christian Learning Center
Rockford, MI

Feathers, Feathers Everywhere!

Sorting by different attributes

Gather craft feathers in a variety of colors and sizes and place them on a blanket. Have each youngster hold on to the edge of the blanket. Then have little ones lift the blanket in the air and say, "Turkey feathers!" as the feathers fly around. Have students retrieve the feathers. Finally, help them sort the feathers by color and then by size.

Pilgrims on the Ship

Identifying numbers, counting

Gather a small group of little ones and give each child a copy of page 227 and a small cup of raisins (or cereal). Tell students that they're going to pretend the raisins are Pilgrims. Then have each child place the appropriate amount of Pilgrims on each *Mayflower*. Check youngsters' work. Then, if desired, allow little ones to have a raisin snack.

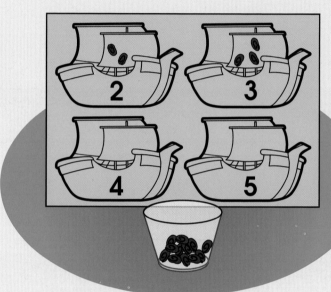

Gobble, Gobble!

Comparing numbers, understanding the concept of zero

Cover the six-dot sides of a pair of dice with masking tape. These sides will now represent zero. Fold a yellow strip of tagboard in half so it resembles a turkey beak. Gather two youngsters and give one child the beak. Have the remaining child roll the dice. Then encourage the first child to identify the number of dots on each die and snap his turkey beak above the die that shows the most dots. Have students switch roles for the next round.

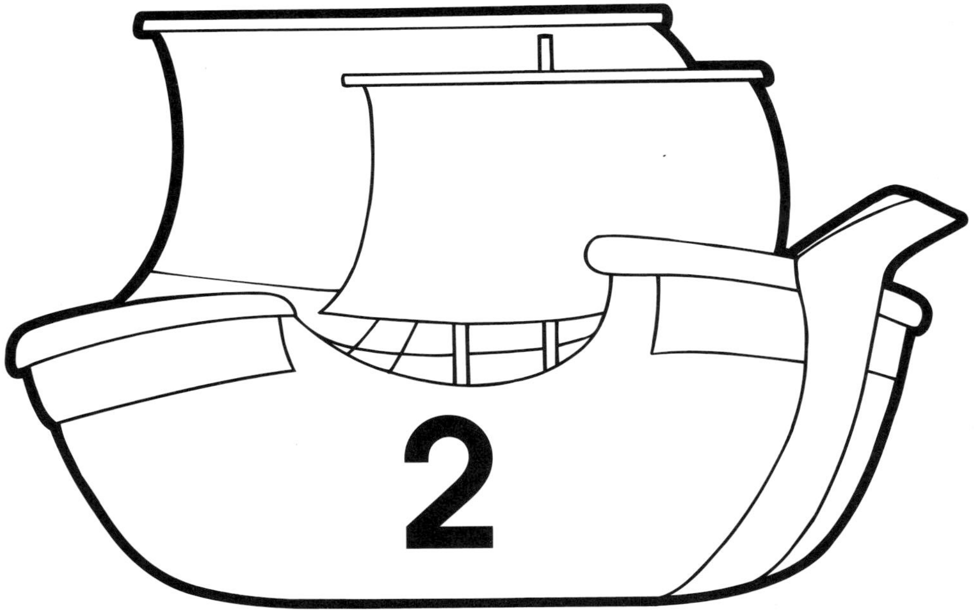

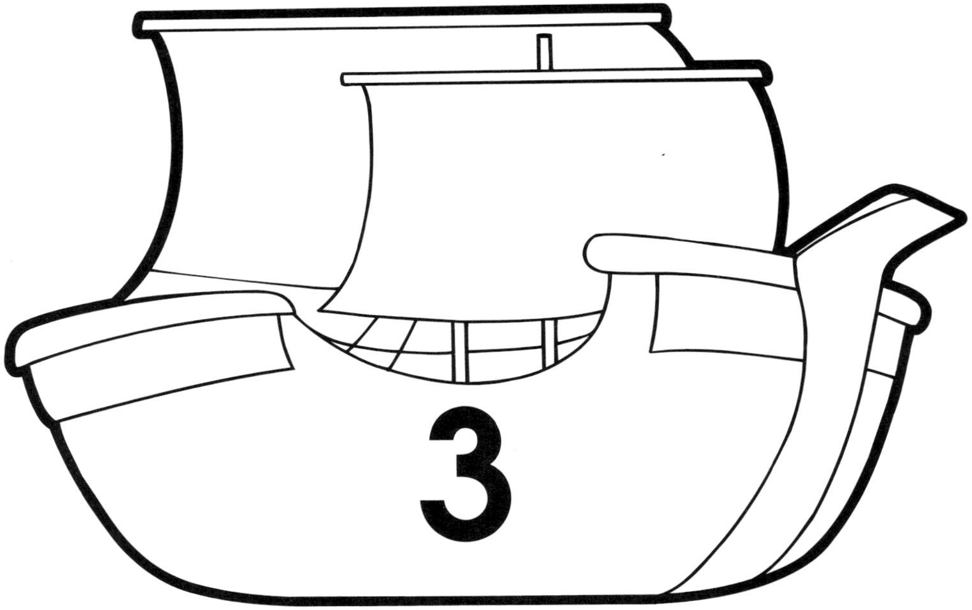

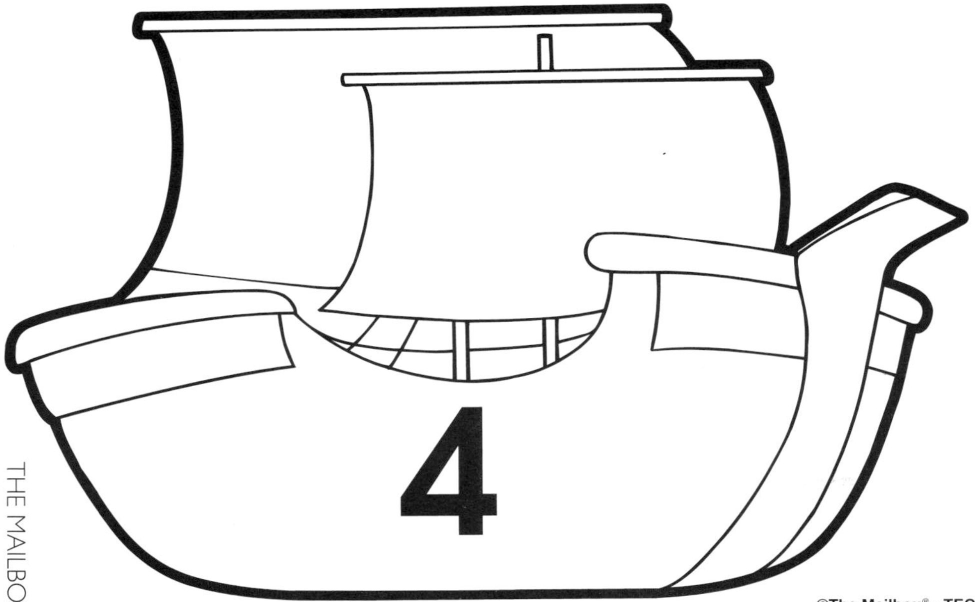

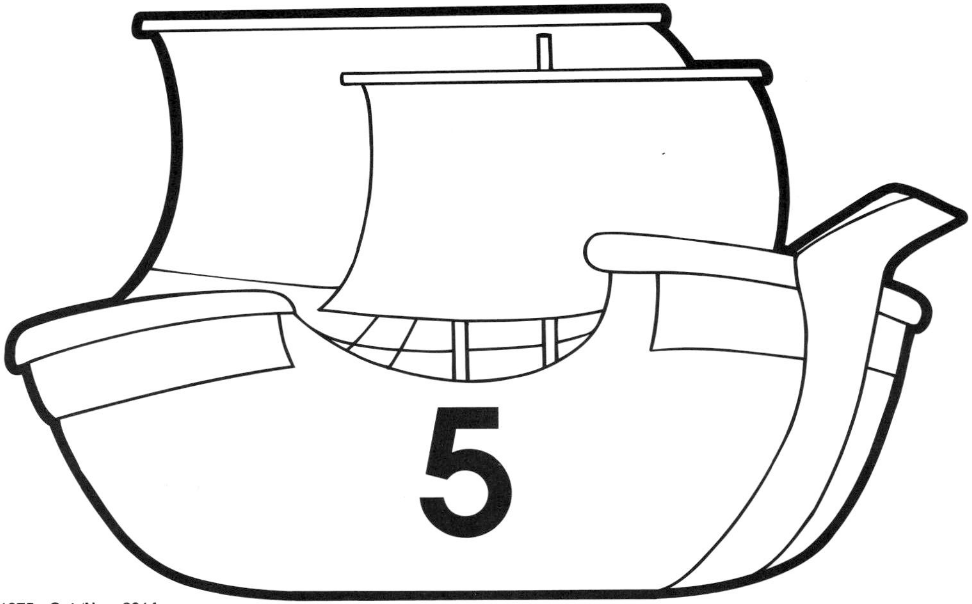

3

5

2

4

©The Mailbox® • TEC41075 • Oct./Nov. 2014

Note to the teacher: Use with "Pilgrims on the Ship" on page 226.

Turkey Booklet

Make a copy of pages 228–230 for each child. Help her follow the directions for the cover and each booklet page. Then help her cut out the pages, stack them in order behind the cover, and staple the project to make a booklet.

Cover and booklet page 1: Color the cover and page. Then tear five small scraps of black paper (seeds) and glue them to the page.

Turkey Dinner

by _____

I see five black seeds.

1

Booklet pages 2 and 3: Color the pages. Then dip a finger in red paint and make four red fingerprints (berries). Dip a cork in brown paint and make three prints (acorns). Use a brown fine-tip marker to add acorn cap details to each acorn.

I see four red berries.

2

I see three brown acorns.

3

Booklet pages 4 and 5: Color the pages, leaving the corncobs uncolored. Dip a finger in yellow paint and make prints (kernels) on the corncobs.

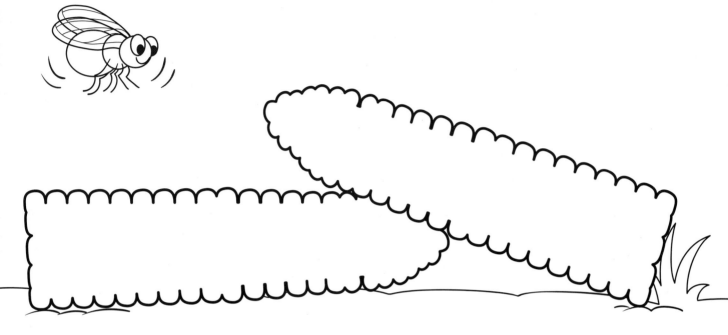

I see two yellow corncobs.

4

I see one full turkey!

5

Learning Numbers 1-10

Help little ones recognize, identify, and form numbers with these preschool-perfect number rhymes and activities!

inspired by number rhymes by Mary Ann Craven
Fallbrook United Methodist Preschool

#1

Youngsters learn to make the number 1 with this simple action song!

(sung to the tune of "Twinkle, Twinkle, Little Star")

Make a line, and then you're done.   *"Write" a 1 in the air.*
You've just made the number one.   *Clap to the beat.*
You've one nose and just one chin.   *Touch your nose and your chin.*
You've one belly and one grin.   *Pat your belly and point to your smile.*
Make a line, and then you're done.   *"Write" a 1 in the air.*
You've just made the number one.   *Clap to the beat.*

#2

Place separate sets of pom-poms in several containers, making sure that most of them have sets of two. Prompt little ones to "write" a number 2 in the air with their fingers as they say the rhyme **"Make an ear and then a shoe. That's the way you make a two."** Next, have a child open a container and count the pom-poms aloud. If there are two, have students repeat the rhyme while writing a 2 in the air. If not, have students stay still. Continue with each remaining container.

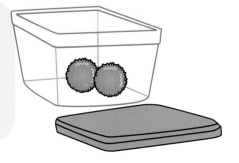

#3

Write the number 3 on a sheet of paper and make a copy for each child. To begin, have her draw a tree in each of the two spaces on the number 3. Then have her follow the number with her finger as she says, **"Around a tree and around a tree— you have made the number three!"**

Teach little ones the number 4 with this engaging action song.

(sung to the tune of "The Wheels on the Bus")

Go down and over and down some more.　　　"Write" a 4 in the air.
It's a four! It's a four!　　　Clap to the beat.
Go down and over and down some more.　　　"Write" a 4 in the air.
You've made a four!　　　Clap to the beat.

5

Draw a supersize number 5 on chart paper and then draw a cloud as shown. Have each child color and cut out a copy of a bird pattern on page 234. Then help her attach it to a craft stick. Make a bird stick puppet for yourself as well. Then trace the 5 with your stick puppet as you say, **"Fly through the sky and down you dive. Go around a cloud. It's number five!"** Next, repeat the process, prompting youngsters to recite the rhyme with you and "fly" their birds in the air to make a 5.

6

Give each child a sheet of paper labeled with a large number 6. Have her trace the number with her fingers and say its name. Next, have her press her finger on a yellow ink pad and make six fingerprints below the number. Use a fine-tip marker to transform the fingerprints into chicks. Then lead her in performing the action chant shown.

Down and around until it sticks.　　　Trace the 6 with your finger.
1, 2, 3, 4, 5, 6 chicks!　　　Touch each chick as you count.

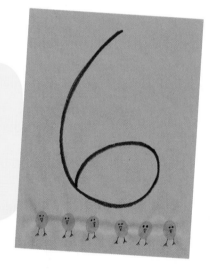

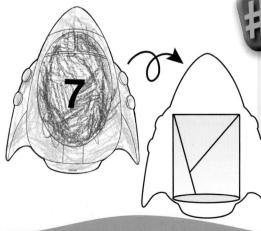

7

Seal an envelope for every two youngsters in your class. Then cut the envelopes in half. Have each child color a copy of the rocket pattern on page 234. Then help her cut it out and attach it to an envelope half to make an envelope puppet. Have each child slide her puppet onto her dominant hand. Then have her move her puppet through the air to make a number seven as you lead her in reciting the rhyme shown.

Zoom through the sky and down from heaven;
That is how you make a seven!

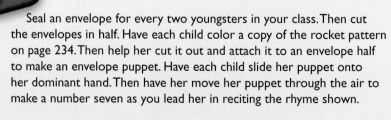

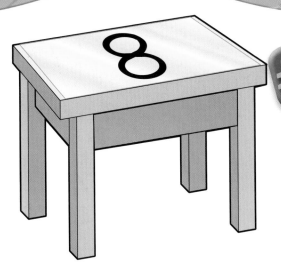

#8

Attach iridescent cellophane to a tabletop. Then use a permanent marker to draw a number 8 on the cellophane. Invite a child to the table. Then guide her to "skate" her fingers over the number while reciting **"Skate round and round, then through the gate. That's the way you make an eight!"** For extra fun, have her recite the rhyme and trace the number with an ice cube.

#9

Make a copy of page 235 for each child. Then gather a small group of youngsters and lead them in reciting the action rhyme shown. Next, give each child a copy of the page and have her trace the 9, say its name, and count the nine monkeys. Finally, have her color the page.

Around the head and down the spine.   *"Write" a 9 in the air.*
That's the way you make a nine!   *Clap to the beat.*
Nine little monkeys swinging on a vine.   *Pretend to hold a vine and swing.*
Nine little monkeys are mighty fine!   *Continue swinging.*

Cindy Hoying, Centerville, OH

#10

Gather several cards with a variety of pictures and symbols, including several cards that show the number 10. Place the cards facedown on the floor. First, guide students in reciting the action rhyme shown several times. Then have a child choose a card. If the card shows a ten, have all the youngsters repeat the action rhyme. If not, have her place the card aside. Continue with each card.

Down with a one, then round and round.   *"Write" a 10 in the air.*
A number ten is what you've found!   *Wiggle all ten fingers.*

Bird Patterns
Use with "#5" on page 232.

TEC41076

TEC41076

Rocket Ship Pattern
Use with "#7" on page 232.

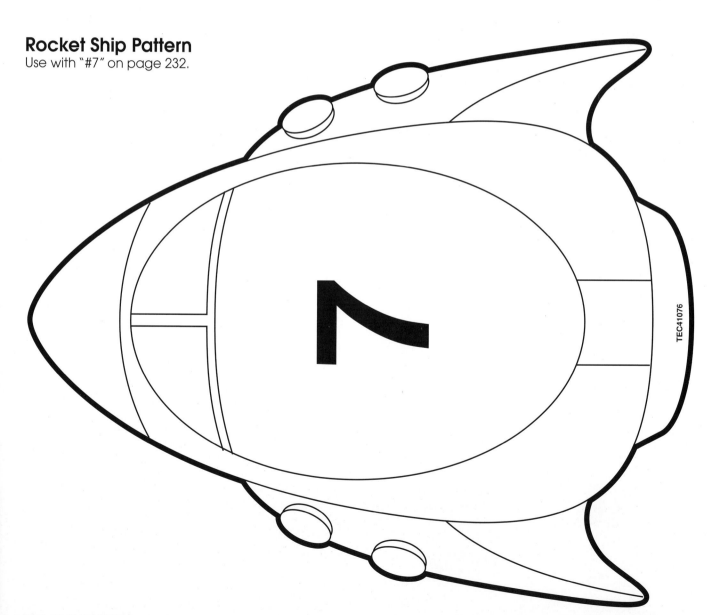

TEC41076

©The Mailbox® • TEC41076 • Dec. 2014

MATH
for Little Ones

Encourage enthusiasm for math with exciting activities that focus on preschool-perfect skills!

Name Math

One-to-one correspondence, comparing sets, counting

This activity appeals to little ones' love of their own names! Gather a small group of youngsters and give each child a name card labeled with her name. Next, have her count the letters in her name. Then have her place a connecting block or linking cube on each letter. Have her count the blocks and attach them together. Encourage students to compare their towers of blocks, prompting them to use words like *more, fewer,* and *equal.* For extra fun, have students connect all their blocks together and then count them.

When students are familiar with this activity, place the name cards and connecting blocks in your math center for independent fun and practice!

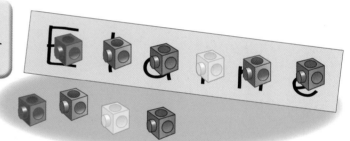

Heather Stinson
Clarke Schools for Hearing and Speech
Northampton, MA

What Time?

Introducing the concept of time

Get a play clock (or transform a poster board circle into a clock face using brads and construction paper hands). Explain some specific times during your day and show them on the clock. For example, you might say, "I wake up at 6:00 AM." or "I have dinner at 5:30 PM." Have students pantomime the events. Next, prompt students to name specific times they do certain things, like take a bath, go to bed, or watch their favorite television show. Show each time on the clock and have little ones pantomime the activity. What a simple way to introduce time!

Deborah J. Ryan, Newberg, OR

Folding Fun!

Manipulating shapes, reinforcing the characteristics of a triangle

Gather a small group of youngsters and give each child a square cloth napkin (or handkerchief). Help her fold the napkin from corner to corner to make a triangle. Then lead students in singing this song as they point to the sides and corners of the triangle.

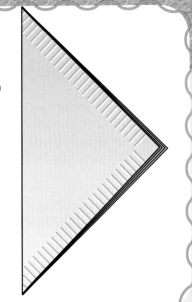

(sung to the tune of "Twinkle, Twinkle, Little Star")

> I'm a triangle; look at me.
> Count my sides—one, two, three.
> I have corners. Do you see?
> Count them now, and you'll find three.
> I'm a triangle; look at me.
> Sides and corners—one, two, three.

Marie E. Cecchini, West Dundee, IL
Roxanne LaBell Dearman, NC Intervention for the Deaf and Hard of Hearing, Charlotte, NC

Who Has a Friend?

One-to-one correspondence, introducing the concept of odd and even

Give students a snack of five crackers and then have students pair their crackers one to one. Point out that four of the crackers have friends, but the last one does not. Explain that this makes five an odd number. Repeat this activity at the next snacktime, giving students an even number of snacks. No snacktime? Choose your favorite manipulative or complete the activity with natural objects, like seashells or pinecones.

Laurie Eberli, Just for Kids Preschool, Everett, WA

Time to Tally

Understand that numbers represent quantities, tallying objects

Attach a sheet of paper to a clipboard and then take little ones outside for a walk. Choose a specific item or animal to look for. You might consider choosing birds, trucks, cars, or dogs. Have students point out whenever they see the focus item. Then mark a tally on your sheet. After several tallies have been marked, go back inside. Have students count aloud as you write the tally marks on a sheet of chart paper. Prompt a child to write the number next to the tally marks. Repeat this activity each day with a different item. Then compare the numbers on the chart paper. We saw more cars than trucks!

Elise George, St. Mary School, Riverside, IL

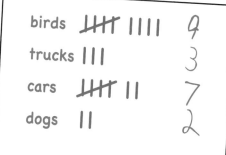

birds	‖‖‖ ‖‖‖	9
trucks	‖‖‖	3
cars	‖‖‖ ‖‖	7
dogs	‖‖	2

Pennies in My Bank

Reinforcing coin names, counting a set of ten and extra ones

A catchy and simple song makes this supervised center extra appealing! Set out a lidded plastic container labeled with the number 10 and a supply of pennies. Gather two youngsters at the center and give each child between 11 and 19 pennies. Help the youngster count the pennies and then arrange them into two piles to show one group of ten and the extra ones. Prompt her to place the group of ten pennies in the container and then secure the lid. Then lead youngsters in singing the song while she shakes the container. Repeat the process with the remaining youngster.

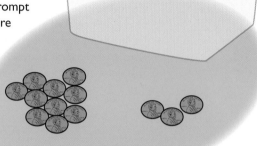

(sung to the tune of "The Farmer in the Dell")

Ten pennies in my bank,
Ten pennies in my bank,
Clink, clank, clink, clank, clink, clank,
Ten pennies in my bank!

Cindy Hoying, Centerville, OH

Make a Line

Using a five frame, naming "how many," reinforcing the term **equal**

Make a copy of a five frame on page 239 for each child and yourself and provide manipulatives, such as bear counters. Have students count the spaces in the five frame. Then place three bears on your five frame and recite the chant shown below. Prompt a youngster to count the number of bears in the line without touching them. Then have each child place the same number of bears on her five frame, from left to right. Ask, "How many more bears will I need to make five?" Help youngsters understand that two more bears are needed. Have little ones clear their five frames. Then repeat the activity with a different number of bears.

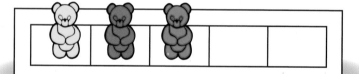

How many will it take to make a line
Equal to this one of mine?

Colleen Dabney, Williamsburg, VA

See page 240 for a **reproducible** that helps little ones understand the **relationship between numbers and quantities**.

Note to the teacher: Use with "Make a Line" on page 238.

Peas, Please!

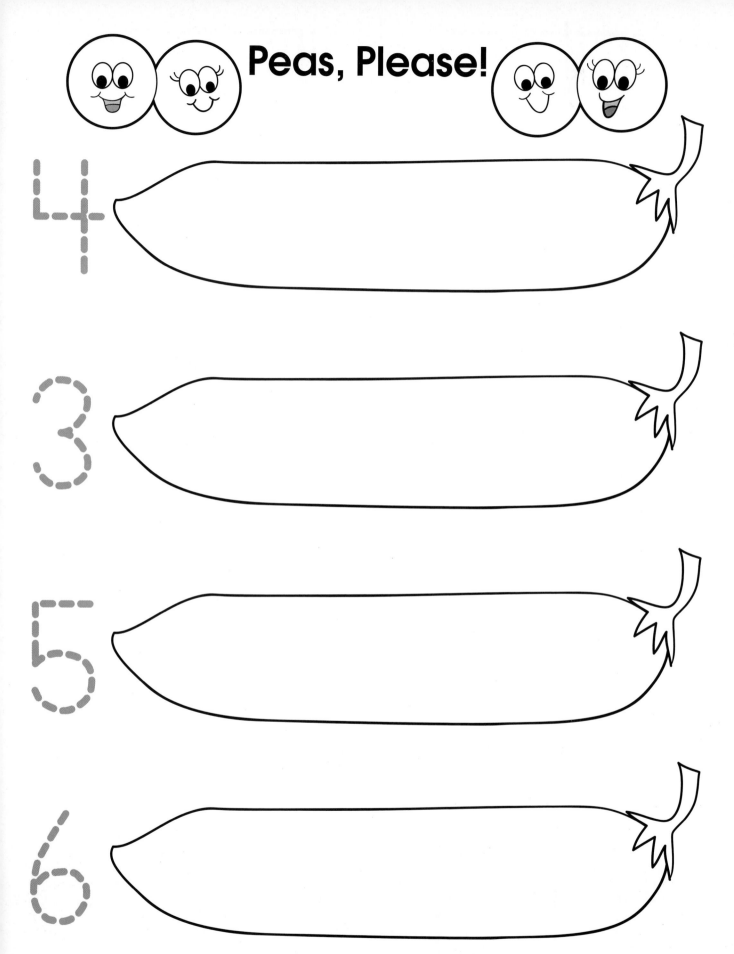

Note to the teacher: Give a child a copy of this page. Have her trace each number and then make an appropriate number of green fingerprints (peas) in each pod.

Draw a Picture, Solve a Problem

Your little artists give their math skills an excellent workout with these low-prep ideas!

How Many Birds?

Show little ones how to draw a simple bird similar to the ones shown. Give each child a sheet of blue paper. Have her draw a few clouds on the paper. Then say, "Three little birds were flying in the sky." Have each child draw three simple birds on her paper. Then say, "Three more birds joined them." Prompt each student to add three more birds to her page. Then prompt her to count all her birds and write the total number on the paper, with help as needed.

Finger Friends

Give each child a crayon and a half sheet of paper. Then explain to youngsters that they are going to draw finger friends. Help a child trace one of his fingers on his paper. Then have him draw a face on his tracing. Next, have him add two more finger friends to the paper. Finally, have him count how many finger friends are on the paper and then write the number, with help as needed.

Cindy Hoying
Centerville, OH

Cookie Cravings

Have each child draw five simple cookies on a sheet of paper. Say, "Oh no! A cookie-eating bird is swooping down to eat one of your cookies!" Have each child move a hand like a swooping bird and pretend that it ate one cookie. Have her cross out that cookie. Ask, "How many cookies do you have left?" Prompt little ones to count. Then repeat the process several times, sometimes having the bird "eat" more than one cookie, until all the cookies have been crossed out.

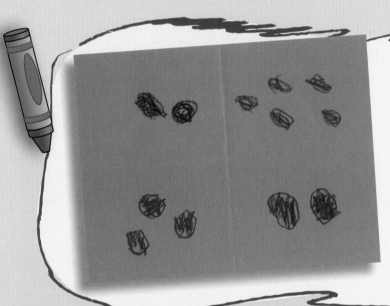

Round Food Fun!

Give each child a purple crayon and a sheet of paper that has been creased into fourths. Then have her pick a box on the paper. Say, "I ate one grape." Have her draw one grape in the box. Then say, "Then I ate one more grape." Have her draw one more grape in the box. Finally, have her count the total number of grapes you ate. Continue with the remaining boxes and different circular foods, such as blueberries, pepperoni rounds, and blackberries.

The Leprechaun's Gold

Little ones have to be very sneaky to get this leprechaun's gold. Give each child a copy of page 243. Have him color the picture and draw five gold coins in the pot. Next, whisper to little ones, "We will have to be very sneaky to get a piece of the leprechaun's gold." Have each student pretend to quietly snatch a piece of gold. Have him cross out that piece of gold. Then congratulate youngsters on fooling the leprechaun. Ask, "How many pieces of gold are left?" Have little ones count aloud to find the answer. Then continue having youngsters "remove" one or even two pieces of gold at a time until they have all the leprechaun's gold!

Note to the teacher: Use with "The Leprechaun's Gold" on page 242.

Play Dough MATH

What do you get when you combine play dough with math skills? Why, you get squishy, engaging math practice that gives fine-motor skills a workout!

idea contributed by Janet Boyce
Hinojosa Early Childhood and Pre-Kindergarten Center, Houston, TX

Making Snails

Comparing length and size

For this simple measurement activity, gather play dough and a plastic knife. Have a child roll play dough into a rope shape. Then encourage her to use the plastic knife to cut the rope into two or more sections. Next, have her line up the sections and compare their lengths, using words such as *longer, shorter, longest,* and *shortest.* Next, prompt her to roll each length of play dough into a snail shape and then compare their sizes. That snail is the biggest!

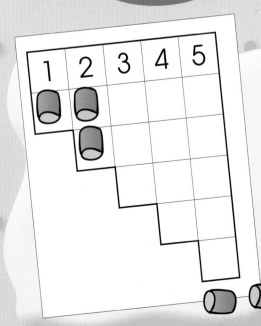

Candy Maker

Associating written numerals with quantities

Make a copy of the grid on page 246 and laminate it. Then place it on a table along with play dough and scissors. Have a youngster pretend to be a candy maker. Encourage him to roll out a rope of play dough and then cut it into small pieces (candies). Then have him put the appropriate number of candies beneath each numeral. Finally, have him name each numeral and count the corresponding set of candies aloud.

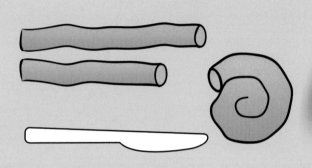

Number Squash

Forming numbers, identifying numbers, counting

Gather large number cards and place them near a mound of play dough. Provide a toy hammer. A child chooses a card, identifies the number, and traces it with his finger. Then he counts aloud while he hammers the play dough a corresponding number of times. He repeats the process with other number cards. What fun!

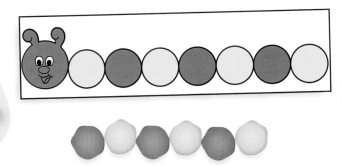

Caterpillar Patterns

Copying and extending patterns

Make a copy of the caterpillar strips on page 247 and cut them out. Then color the caterpillar to make a pattern using the colors of your play dough. Place the strips on a table along with the corresponding play dough. A child chooses a strip and reads the pattern aloud. Then she re-creates the caterpillar with balls of play dough, extending its length as desired.

Add Some Craft Sticks!

Forming shapes, counting, identifying numbers

Provide colorful play dough, craft sticks, shape cards, and number cards. Then see what your little ones create! They might use the craft sticks to make or draw shapes in the play dough, or they might identify numbers and count that many craft sticks to place in balls of play dough. You're sure to see lots of math skills develop!

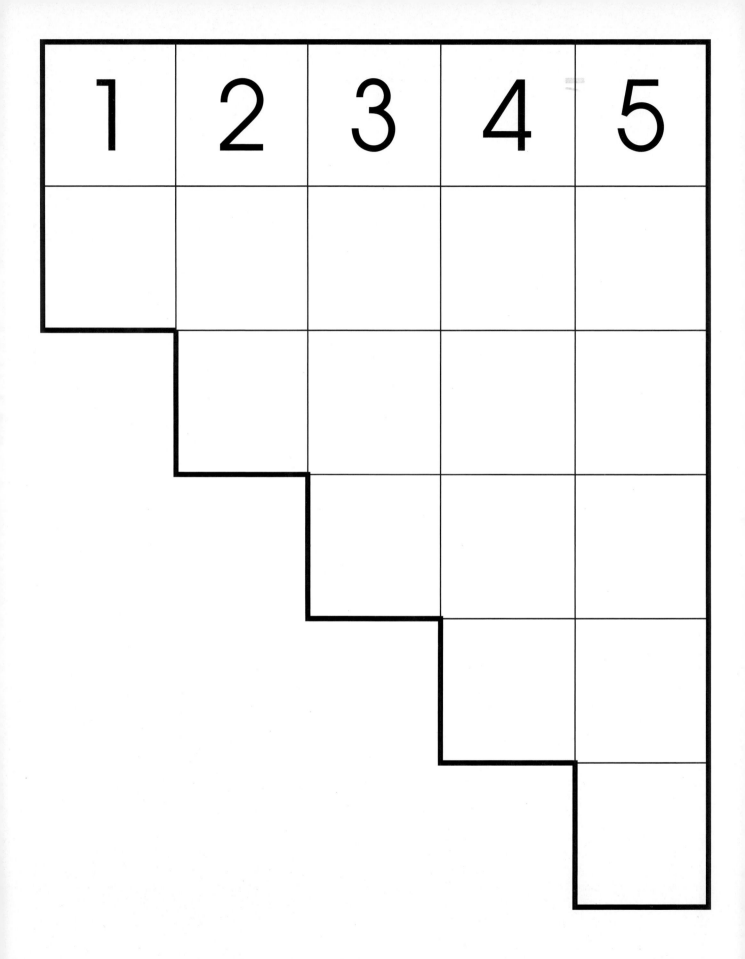

1	2	3	4	5

Note to the teacher: Use with "Candy Maker" on page 244.

©The Mailbox®

©The Mailbox®

©The Mailbox®

Five Frame Fun!

Introduce your little ones to working with a five frame with these fabulous activities!

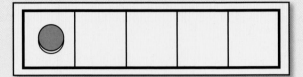

People on the Train

Give each child a five frame (see page 249) and five counters. Have students count the spaces in the five frame aloud. Then say, "There are five empty seats on the train. One person gets on the train." Have a child place a counter on the five frame. Ask her how many more people can fit on the train, prompting her to count the remaining spaces. Continue in the same way, adding "people" until all five seats are filled.

Doria Owen, William Paca Old Post Road Elementary, Abingdon, MD

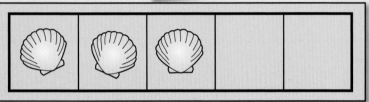

The Number Game

Gather number cards from 1 to 4 and place them facedown. Provide a pair of youngsters with a five frame (see page 249) and manipulatives. Have youngsters count the number of spaces aloud. Next, have a child draw a number card, name the number, and place that many manipulatives on the frame. Have his partner count the remaining spaces on the frame. Help students conclude that this is the number of items that need to be added to make five. Have students remove the manipulatives and prepare to play another round.

Five Dinosaurs

Draw a large five frame on your board (or on a sheet of chart paper). Make five cutout copies of the dinosaur card on page 249. Then attach a dinosaur to each space on the five frame. Lead students in singing the song shown, removing a dinosaur when appropriate. Whisper, "How many dinosaurs went away?" Have students count aloud as you point to the open space. Then whisper, "How many dinosaurs are still there?" Point to the spaces with dinosaurs as little ones count aloud. Repeat the process for four more verses until all the dinosaurs have gone away.

(sung to the tune of "Five Green and Speckled Frogs")

[Five] dinosaurs all green
Looking so fierce and mean,
Big stomping feet upon the ground—pound, pound!
One got so close to me,
I hid behind a tree.
It left before I could be found. Shhhh…

Cindy Hoying, Centerville, OH

Use with "Five Dinosaurs" on page 248.

©The Mailbox®

©The Mailbox®

Note to the teacher: Use with "People on the Train" and "The Number Game" on page 248.

Math in the Garden!

Cultivate math skills with this idea collection!

Center

Sowing Seeds

Plant the seeds of math knowledge with this center activity! In advance, make several copies of the math mat on page 251. Then cut out a colorful supply of the counters on page 252. Next, make a supply of "seed packets." To make a seed packet, glue a counter to an index card and then draw an appropriate number of seeds on the back. A child visits the center and chooses a mat and three packets. He counts the seeds on one packet and then "plants" that many vegetable or flower counters in a row. He continues with each remaining packet. **Counting sets, making matching sets**

Small-Group Activity

Plant and Pick

Gather number cards from 1 to 10. Place numbers 6–10 in a stack (for planting). Then place 0–5 in a separate stack (for picking). Give each child a garden mat (see page 251) and a supply of counters (see page 252). Each child in the group draws a card from the planting stack and then places that many counters on her mat. Then each child draws a card from the picking stack and "picks" that many counters from her garden. Next, prompt students to compare their mats to decide who has the most or fewest items left in their gardens. Then play another round! **Developing subtraction skills**

Math Story Problems

○ Plant seven heads of lettuce in your garden. A hungry bunny eats two of them. How many are left? **Counting, subtraction**

○ In the top row of your garden, plant five flowers. In the middle row, plant two flowers. In the bottom row, plant four flowers. Which row has the most? Which has the fewest? Are any of the rows equal? **Positional words, counting, comparing sets**

○ Use two colors of flowers to make a pattern in your garden. Plant two other rows to match. **Patterning**

○ Plant the following in a row: one head of lettuce, one tomato, and one green bean. Which one is first? Second? Third? **Ordinal numbers**

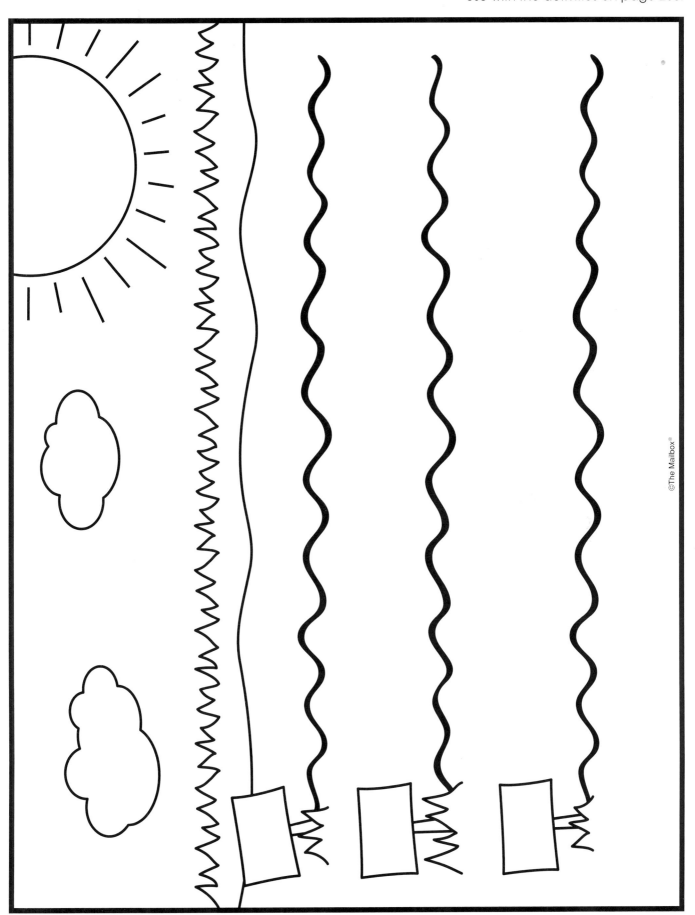

©The Mailbox®

Vegetable and Flower Counters

Use with the activities on page 250.

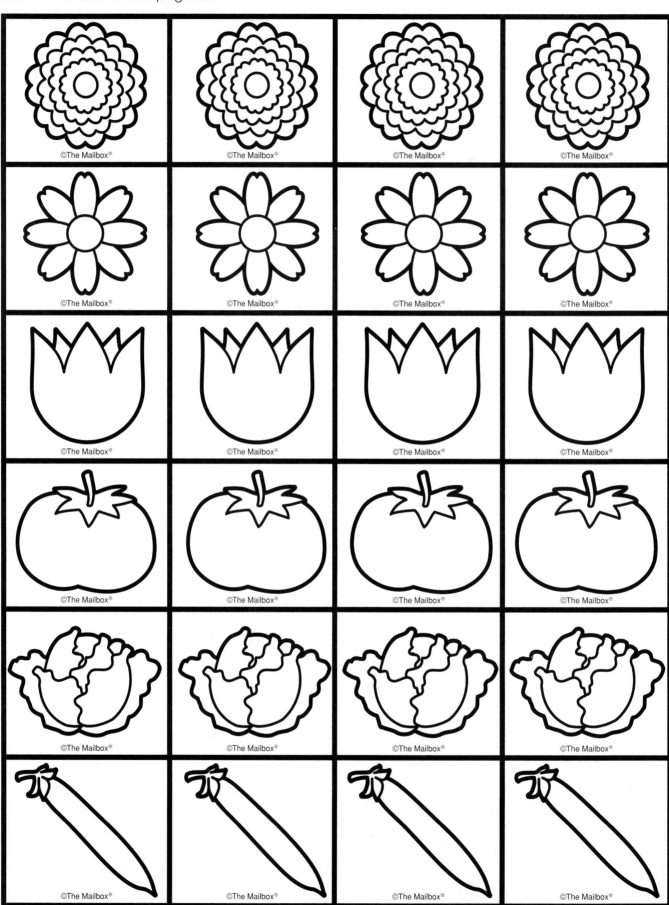

TEACHER RESOURCE UNITS

A Handy School-Year Calendar!

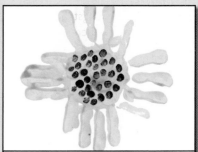

Have a child complete each project on a 9" x 12" sheet of construction paper. Then simply staple a calendar to the project. These projects can all be completed at once to make a full school-year calendar, or they can be sent home month to month!

concept contributed by Rachael K. McCain, Blanchard, LA

August

S	M	T	W	T	F	S
					1	2
3	4	5	6	7	8	9
10	11	12	13	14	15	16
17	18	19	20	21	22	23
24	25	26	27	28	29	30
31						

September:
This handprint art looks like a crayon box! Paint a child's hand with the colors shown. Then have her press her hand on a sheet of green construction paper. When the paint is dry, use a fine-tip marker to add the words shown.

October:
A jack-o'-lantern is the perfect project for the October calendar. Paint a youngster's palm orange. Then have her press it on the paper. Next, have her attach a green paper stem and black paper facial details. If desired, have her use a green marker to draw a vine. Boo!

November:
Instead of doing a handprint turkey, try making this cornucopia! Have a little one press his hand in brown paint and then make a print on the paper. Add cornucopia details with a black marker. Then have him press a finger in purple paint to make a cluster of grapes. Finally, have him press a cork in orange paint to make oranges and red paint to make apples.

December:
Have a child use a green fine-tip marker to make a swirling line on the paper. Then have her press her pinkie finger in green paint and make small dots along the line. Next, encourage her to press her thumb in colorful paint and make a print next to each green dot. What a cute string of lights!

January:
Use fingerprints to make some lovely New Year's fireworks! Help each student paint her fingers with red, white, and blue paint. Next, have her make prints on a sheet of black paper, as shown, so the prints resemble fireworks. Have her sprinkle glitter on the paint. Then use a white pen to write "Happy New Year!"

February: Youngsters put a handful of love into this project! Swirl pink and red paint in a pan. Then have a child press his hands in the paint and make prints on the paper so the prints resemble a heart. If desired, have him sprinkle heart confetti on the wet paint.

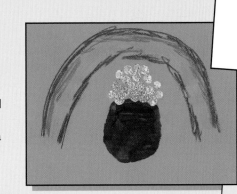

March: To make this lucky pot of gold, paint a child's palm black and have him make a print on the paper. Then encourage him to make yellow fingerprints above the pot of gold and to sprinkle gold glitter on the prints. If desired, when the paint is dry, have him draw a rainbow on the page.

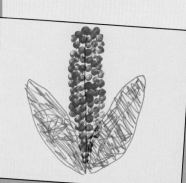

April: Draw a green line on the paper. Then make purple fingerprints near the line. Finally, draw leaves at the bottom. What a lovely hyacinth!

May: This simple nest filled with eggs is perfect for May! Have a child use a paintbrush to paint a simple branch on the paper. Then paint his palm brown and have him press it on the branch (nest). Next, have him make blue thumbprint eggs. If desired, use fine-tip markers to add details.

June: Have a child paint his hand with colorful paint and make a print (fish) on the paper. Next, help him make fingerprint bubbles. When the paint is dry, use a marker to add an eye to finish the fish.

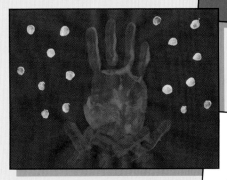

July: To make a campfire with fireflies, have a child press an entire finger in brown paint and make several prints (logs) on a sheet of black paper. Next, paint his hand with red and orange paint. Then have him make a print above the logs (fire). Finally, help him make yellow fingerprint fireflies on the page.

August: This splendid sunflower is made from handprints. Have a child dip his hand in yellow paint and make four handprints on the paper, overlapping the palm print each time. Add brown fingerprint seeds.

Get Out the GLUE!

When it comes to using glue, practice—and a few very fun and cute tips—makes perfect!

Glue Stick Moderation

Little ones love to twist the glue stick so that a large portion is exposed, but often this results in broken glue sticks. To demonstrate how far to turn a glue stick, show students how to twist it so the glue is barely peeking over the top. Tell students that this is peekaboo glue and that all of their glue sticks should be playing peekaboo when it's time to glue. *Hana Zuber, New England Hebrew Academy, Brookline, MA*

Click It!

To keep glue sticks from drying out, remind little ones to click the top in place with a fun rhyme! Hold a glue stick in one hand and its top in the other. Then say the rhyme shown, clicking the top on the glue stick on the word *click*.

When you're finished with the stick,
Please make sure you make it click.

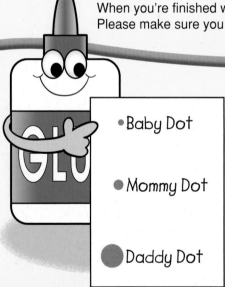

- Baby Dot
- Mommy Dot
- Daddy Dot

The Dot Family

Before you bring out glue bottles for the first time, tell students this adorable story! Draw a small, a medium, and a large dot on a sheet of chart paper. Then introduce them as the Dot family. Explain that the Dot family helps you know how much glue to use. Sometimes, you use Baby Dot—she's a teeny-tiny dot. Sometimes, you use Mommy Dot—she's a little bit bigger than Baby Dot. Every once in a while, it's important to use Daddy Dot, who's a bit bigger than Mommy Dot. Next, give each child a copy of page 257 and have her use a glue bottle to squeeze the appropriately sized dots of glue on the page. How cute! *Bernette V. Alegre, Virginia Beach, VA; Jody Romig, Newburgh United Methodist Preschool, Newburgh, IN*

Glue Worms

Here's a fun reproducible that gives students a workout with liquid glue! Tint a bottle of glue with green food coloring. Then gather a few youngsters and give each child a copy of page 258. Have her color the page as desired. Then encourage her to trace each apple worm with the glue.

Munch, Munch, Munch!

The Dot Family

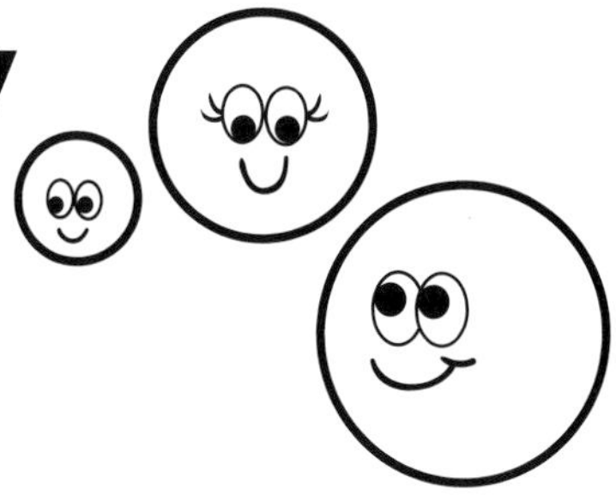

Baby Dot

· · · ·

· · · ·

Mommy Dot

● ● ● ●

Daddy Dot

⬤ ⬤

Munch, Munch, Munch!

©The Mailbox® • TEC41074 • Aug./Sept. 2014

Note to the teacher: Use with "Glue Worms" on page 256.

Good-For-You Snacktime

Your little ones will love these fun and healthy snacktime options!

Cucumber Sandwiches

Provide thin cucumber slices, squares of cheese, and turkey lunch meat squares. Give each child six cucumber slices, three squares of cheese, and three squares of meat. A child places a slice of meat and cheese on a cucumber slice. Then he places another cucumber slice on top to make a sandwich. He continues to make two more sandwiches with his remaining items. If desired, give each child a small amount of light ranch dressing to dip his sandwiches in.

Chimpanzee Food

The method of eating this snack is half the fun! Explain that chimpanzees poke long sticks or grass into holes to gather bugs to eat. (If desired, do a YouTube search for "termite fishing" to show youngsters a video of a chimpanzee in action!) Next, give each child several small pretzel sticks, a few raisins, and a dollop of light whipped cream cheese. Have her get a bit of cream cheese on one end of her stick and press it onto a raisin (bug). Then prompt her to use her tool to eat the bug and then eat the pretzel stick as well! *Katie Dimitrijevich, YMCA Preschool, Beaver Dam, WI*

Crunchy Frozen Bananas

Get firm, ripe bananas, flavored lowfat yogurt, and any desired low-sugar cereal. Empty the yogurt into a pie pan (or other flat container). Pour the cereal into another pie pan and crush if desired. Place waxed paper on a cookie sheet. Peel the bananas, cut them in half, and then push a craft stick into each half. Have a child hold a banana by the stick and then roll it in the yogurt. (You may need to help by spooning yogurt over the banana.) Then have him roll it in the cereal and place it on the waxed paper. Freeze the bananas. Then serve these tasty and healthy pops! *Jodi L. Slaton, Springfield Urban League Head Start, Springfield, IL*

Classroom Management: 2 Timely Topics

It's the beginning of the school year, and you just might have these two topics on your mind!

Center-Time Management

Dramatic Play

- Program a different basket cutout (see page 261) with each center name. Then attach the baskets to sheets of construction paper. Laminate the paper and attach the hook side of Velcro fasteners above each basket to correspond with the number of children allowed at the center. Then display each basket near its center. Program apple cutouts (see page 261) with each child's name and attach the loop side of a Velcro fastener to the back of each apple. A child attaches his apple above a basket to choose his center! *Suzi Hart, New Life Day Care Center, Tonawanda, NY*

- Reinforce how many youngsters are allowed at a center with fun rhymes, such as "One and two, me and you," "One, two, three—we all agree," or "One, two, three, four—then no more." *Dana Rangel, St. John Center, Joliet, IL*

- Attach a picture of each center to a sheet of poster board. Then use hot glue to attach a colorful bottle cap or milk cap next to each center option to create a mission control board! When assigning a youngster to a center (or when the child is choosing where to go), have him go to the mission control board and push the corresponding "button" before going to the center. *Nancy Foss, Wee Care Preschool, Galion, OH*

Attention Grabbers!

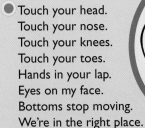

- Touch your head.
  Touch your nose.
  Touch your knees.
  Touch your toes.
  Hands in your lap.
  Eyes on my face.
  Bottoms stop moving.
  We're in the right place.

Marci Gibison
Ephrata Church of the Brethren Children's Center
Ephrata, PA

- One, two, three—eyes on me!
  Four, five, six—lips are zipped!
  Seven, eight, nine—it's learning time!

Toni Adams
Heart of Holmen Day Care
Holmen, WI

- Raise your hands in the air.
  Wave them around like you just don't care.
  Wave them fast!
  Wave them slow!
  Wave them high.
  Wave them low.
  Clap them; clap them.
  Give a snap!
  Fold them nicely in your lap.

adapted from an idea by Ranelle Cole
MSSU Child Development Center
Joplin, MO

TEC41074

TEC41074

TEC41074

Simple Assessment

Assess your little ones' basic skills with these simple and creative options! Then place the results in a portfolio to keep track of youngsters' progress.

Monthly Math

Assess **one-to-one correspondence and counting abilities** with monthly themed assessments! For the month of October, give each child a web cutout and bug stickers. Have her count to five as she attaches bug stickers to the spiderweb. Write any notes on the back of the project and place it in her portfolio. Later in the year, have students count to ten for the assessments.

Other monthly options: November—paper-punched leaves on a tree drawing; December—star stickers on black paper; January—snowflake stickers on blue paper; February—heart stickers on a heart cutout; March—gold circle cutouts on a black pot cutout; April—jelly bean stickers on a basket cutout; May—flower stickers on green construction paper

Sue Fleischmann, Sussex, WI

One-Paper Assessment

You can assess several skills with this one paper! Make a copy of page 263 for each child. Fold each paper where indicated. Have each child write her name on the flap. Next, have her show the proper way to use a gluestick as she glues the flap down. Then observe her as she holds scissors and cuts along each line up to the dot. What a simple way to assess **name-writing, gluing, and scissor skills!**

Trudy Naddy, Olive Ranch School, Granite Bay, CA

Fill the Folder

This assessment collection also makes a great keepsake! Get a class supply of paper folders with fasteners and program each folder with a different child's name. In each folder, attach a sheet protector for each month in the school year. Each month, have each student do a **person drawing** and samples of her **handwriting, cutting, and coloring**. Place the items in a page protector and then use a permanent marker to label the protector with the date. Continue for each remaining month.

Tracy Henderson, Brook Hollow Weekday Program, Nashville, TN

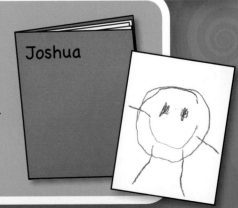

fold line

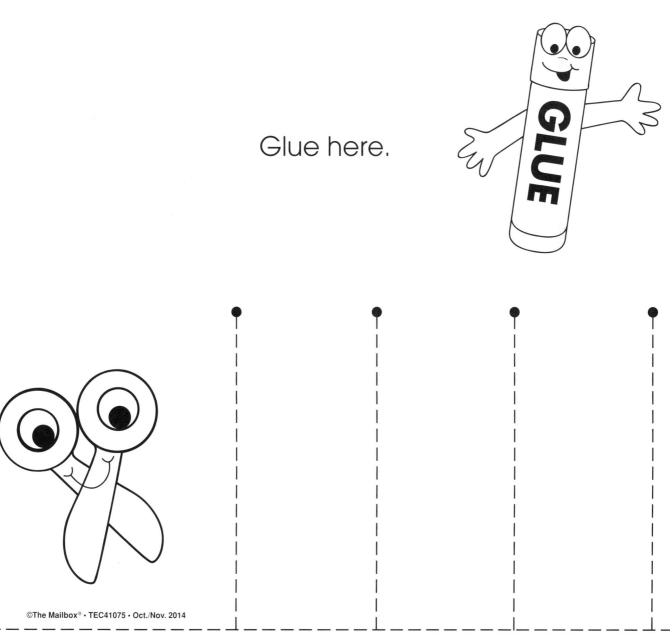

Glue here.

6 Tips for a Smooth Day!

Check out these simple tips and tricks that are sure to make your day run smoother!

1 **Mess-Free Projects** Before youngsters take part in a messy project, cover your tables with large garbage bags and tape them in place. When the project is finished, you can easily remove the bags and toss them or save them for another messy-project day! *Shirley Iacobucci, For Kids' Sake Preschool and Daycare, Boardman, OH*

2 **Quiet Hall Walking** Have little ones line up. Then tell youngsters, with great dramatic flair, that if they're really quiet while walking in the hall, no one will even know that they're there. Students will love tiptoeing down the hall pretending they are invisible! *Ronna Adkins, First Baptist Church Day School, Pikeville, KY*

3 **Taking Turns Talking** Place a plastic hoop (magic circle) in the center of your circle time area. When a child has something to say, have her stand or sit in the magic circle. Only the person in the circle is allowed to talk. *Carole Watkins, Timothy Ball Elementary, Crown Point, IN*

Using Listening Ears

To get little ones' attention during circle time, say the beginning of a common phrase that names two things that go together, such as "macaroni and...." Youngsters respond with the word *cheese!* Continue with other suggestions (see those shown) until youngsters are focused and ready to listen. *Emily Porter, Scott County Schools, Georgetown, KY*

Suggestions:
salt and...*(pepper)*
up and...*(down)*
peanut butter and...*(jelly)*
hot and...*(cold)*
king and...*(queen)*
boys and...*(girls)*
shoes and...*(socks)*
cats and...*(dogs)*

Cleaning the Room

Each day, assign a child to be the cleanup inspector. At the end of center time, have the cleanup inspector walk around the room to make sure that her classmates are putting the toys away correctly. What a great way to motivate children to do a good job cleaning the room! *Michelle Gwinn, Wood County Schools, Parkersburg, WV*

Filling Time Between Activities

If you need to fill moments before the next activity, hold up a letter card and help students name the letter and its sound. Then lead them in singing the song shown, inserting the name and sound of the letter and performing the actions. Continue with other letter cards. What a fun way to fill time with literacy and gross-motor skills! *Susan Foulks, University City United Methodist Church Weekday School, Charlotte, NC*

(sung to the tune of "If You're Happy and You Know It")

If you're a [D] and you know it, make the sound—[/d/, /d/]!
If you're a [D] and you know it, make the sound—[/d/, /d/]!
Clap your hands, turn around,
Reach down low, and touch the ground.
If you're a [D] and you know it, make the sound—[/d/, /d/]!

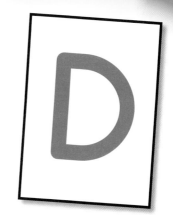

Fun and Festive SNACKTIME!

Searching for healthful snacks for little ones to make during December? Look no further!

● **Cottage Cheese Snowmen**

To make one of these simple snacks, have a child place a large dollop of cottage cheese on a plate. Then have her use the back of a spoon to smooth it to form a circle. Next, have her place blueberries on the cottage cheese to make eyes and a mouth. Finally, help her put a dollop of peach, apricot, or orange preserves on the cottage cheese so it resembles a nose.

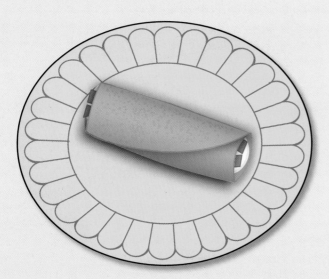

● **Christmas Roll-Ups**

Give a child half of a spinach tortilla and help her spread whipped cream cheese on it. Next, have her sprinkle chopped tomatoes or red peppers on the cream cheese. Then help her roll the tortilla. What a tasty red and green treat!

● **Trees and Crackers**

Have each child unwrap a triangle of Laughing Cow cheese. Have her push half of a small pretzel (tree trunk) into the cheese. Then encourage her to use a small paintbrush to paint the cheese with slightly diluted green food coloring. Finally, encourage her to place a star-shaped cheese cutout above the tree. Give each child several crackers and a butter knife and encourage her to spread her holiday tree onto crackers. Yum!

How do I help children develop patience?

● Teach students the chant shown. Encourage each student to recite the chant whenever he needs to wait for his turn.

> **Waiting is so hard to do.**
> **I need patience to get through.**
> **This is something I must learn:**
> **To wait until it is my turn.**

● Provide a timer for a child who struggles with patience. Set the timer at the beginning of the activity to show how long it will be until the next activity. This visual tool helps the child know how much longer she has to wait and will eliminate interruptions.

● Teach numeration as you promote patience. To help children wait for your individual attention, label five index cards, each with a different number from one to five. Put the cards in order; then store them in a student accessible location. When a child needs your help, have him take a number. Announce numbers to indicate whose turn it is to have your attention.

● Have students brainstorm a list of things they can do whenever they need to wait. The list could include activities such as practicing counting, quietly talking to a neighbor, or playing I Spy or another quiet game. Whenever students need to wait, they will already know what they can do to keep themselves occupied.

Potato Possibilities!

What can you do with potatoes in the classroom? Lots!

ideas contributed by Amber Dingman, Sterling, MI, and
Cheryl Karp, Hewlett East Rockaway Jewish Centre Nursery School, East Rockaway, NY

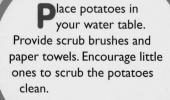

Provide several different types of potatoes (red, baking, sweet, fingerling) and place them at a table. Allow youngsters to sort them into groups by different attributes.

Place potatoes in your water table. Provide scrub brushes and paper towels. Encourage little ones to scrub the potatoes clean.

Encourage little ones to push blunt-end toothpicks into a large potato to strengthen little fingers.

Give each child a "potato baby" to take care of. Have him discuss the characteristics of his potato. Then encourage him to compare his potato to his classmates' potatoes. Have little ones measure their potatoes with linking cubes or string and compare the lengths to other items in the classroom. When spring arrives, have little ones plant their potatoes. Then, in fall, harvest the potatoes and donate them to a soup kitchen.

Place cooled boiled potatoes at a center along with plastic knives, plastic plates, and a large bowl. Youngsters cut the potatoes into small pieces and place them in the bowl. Use the potatoes to make a healthy vinegar and oil–based potato salad for snacktime. An online search will turn up plenty of recipes!

THEMATIC UNITS

A NURSERY RHYME WELCOME!

Welcome little ones to school with decorations and activities based on nursery rhyme favorites!

Ready Your Room!

Attendance Display— "Hey, Diddle, Diddle"

Cut out and personalize a copy of the cow pattern (see page 273) for each student. Then attach self-adhesive Velcro fasteners to the cows. Also cut a yellow crescent moon and glue it to black poster board. If desired, add fun glitter details to the moon. Then attach self-adhesive Velcro fasteners above the moon. Display the poster board and scatter the cows on the floor (or on a table). A child finds his cow and attaches it to the poster board so it's "jumping" over the moon. When you gather for circle time, lead students in reciting "Hey, Diddle, Diddle." Then point to each cow and have the corresponding youngster stand and give his best jump!

Birthday Display— "Patty-Cake, Patty-Cake"

Gather baking props, such as a mixing bowl and spoon, a metal cake pan, and a bag of flour. Take a photo of each child holding his choice of props. Then cut out the photos and attach a simple chef's hat cutout to each one. Have youngsters help you decorate 12 cake cutouts (enlarge a copy of the pattern on page 273). Label each with a different month and attach the cakes to your display along with youngsters' photos. Finally, add the altered nursery rhyme shown!

Patty-cake, patty-cake, baker's man
Bake me a cake as fast as you can.
Roll it and prick it and say, "Yippee!"
Let's celebrate birthdays for you and me!

Job Display— "Humpty Dumpty"

For this simple job chart, write job titles on small sheets of red construction paper. If desired, give each sheet some brick detailing. Then display the sheets in your room. Cut out a personalized copy of the Humpty Dumpty pattern on page 274 for each child. To assign jobs, place a Humpty Dumpty on each wall!

Sara

Line Leader

Continue the nursery rhyme theme in your room by using the patterns in this unit for cubby tags and nametags!

Peep's Sheep
Circle Time: Get-acquainted activity

Cut out and personalize a copy of the sheep pattern on page 274 for each child. Gather youngsters and say the chant shown, holding up a sheep when indicated. Help students identify the sheep's name. Then find someone in the class with that name. Have students clap for the found sheep and their new friend. Then continue with each remaining sheep, prompting students to join you in saying the chant when they are comfortable with the words.

Little Bo Peep, we found your sheep,
And each one has a name!
What is the name of this sheep,
And whose name is the same?

Finding Balance
Circle Time: Gross-motor skills

In advance, attach a length of tape to your floor. Lead students in reciting "Humpty Dumpty." Then discuss that Humpty Dumpty must have had a difficult time balancing on the wall. Ask students if they have ever balanced on anything and if it was difficult. Prompt students to balance on one foot. Then have them balance on their other foot. Next, have students walk along the tape line very carefully, pretending that they are walking along Humpty's wall.

Keely Saunders
Bonney Lake Early Childhood Educational Assistance Program
Bonney Lake, WA

Make a Booklet!
Center: Sequencing, expressing oneself through art

Make a copy of the sequencing cards on page 275 for each child. Have each child color the cards and then help her cut them out. Recite "Hey, Diddle, Diddle" and have her put the cards in the correct order. Then have her glue each card to a different dessert-size paper plate. Stack the plates and hole-punch them. Then tie them together with ribbon or bind them with a small metal ring. Little ones will love to take this home to share with their parents!

Spiders Aren't Scary!
Circle Time: Dramatizing a rhyme

You'll hear lots of giggles with this reenactment of "Little Miss Muffet"! Attach a string to a large plastic spider. Get a stool and a plastic bowl and spoon. Then sit on the stool with the bowl and spoon and give the spider to a volunteer. Pretend to be Little Miss Muffet as you lead students in reciting the rhyme. Prompt the child to hold the spider by the string and put it near you when appropriate. Then give a yelp and "run away" with great dramatic flair! Play several rounds, prompting youngsters to be Miss Muffet as well as the spider.

Patricia Barbara
Clark Elementary
Charlottesville, VA

Put Him Together
Center: Fine-motor skills

For this "Humpty Dumpty" activity, youngsters *can* put Humpty together again! Make a colorful egg cutout for each child. Place torn pieces of white paper (eggshells) in a container. Provide scrap construction paper and a circle punch for youngsters to use to make eyes. Gather a few students at a center and give each child an egg cutout. Present the eggshells and encourage the child to put Humpty Dumpty back together by gluing the shells to the egg. Finally, have him punch two circle shapes, draw pupils on the circles, and then attach them to the egg. Humpty feels a lot better now!

Bonnie Brandt
Beginnings Learning Center
Santa Monica, CA

What's in the Cake?
Circle Time: Speaking

Get a mixing bowl, a spoon, a cake pan, and a tambourine (or other rhythm instrument). Tap a steady beat on the tambourine while you lead students in reciting "Patty-Cake, Patty-Cake." Then ask a child to name something she would put in the cake. Have her pretend to add the item to the bowl and then stir. Recite the rhyme again and then ask another child to add to the batter. Continue for several rounds and then "pour" the batter into the pan for "baking." **Extend this activity by placing the items in your housekeeping center for independent fun!**

Cow Pattern

Use with "Attendance Display—'Hey, Diddle, Diddle'" on page 270.

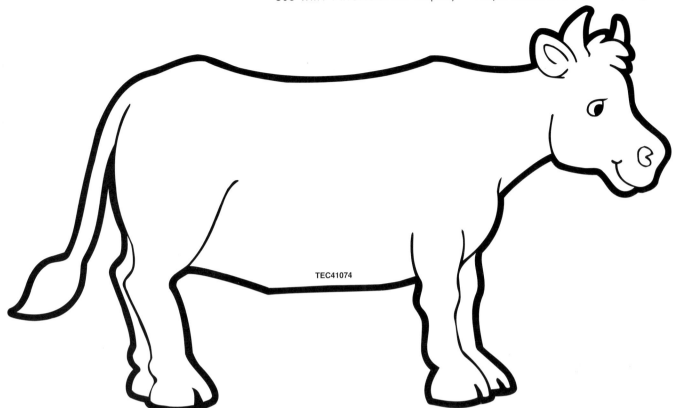

TEC41074

Cake Pattern

Use with "Birthday Display—'Patty-Cake, Patty-Cake'" on page 270.

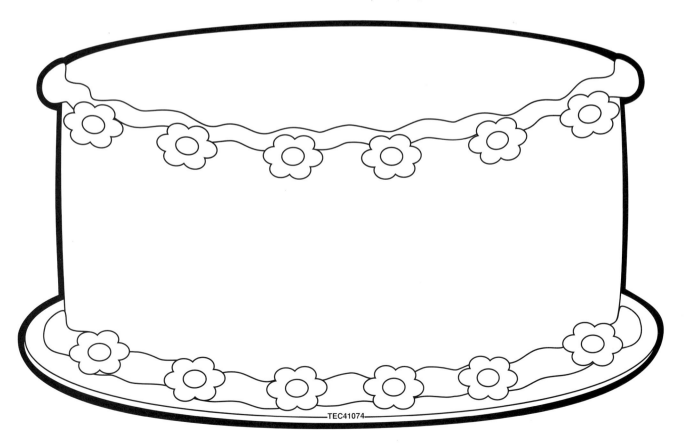

TEC41074

Humpty Dumpty Pattern

Use with "Job Display—'Humpty Dumpty'" on page 270.

TEC41074

Sheep Pattern

Use with "Peep's Sheep" on page 271.

TEC41074

TEC41074

TEC41074

TEC41074

TEC41074

LET'S EXPLORE OUTER SPACE

Outer space is such a fascinating place! Introduce your little ones to this theme with a selection of super activities.

A PAPER TOWEL MOON

Writing

This simple method creates a project with a remarkably realistic lunar surface! Cut a circle from a white paper towel for each child. Then have a child dampen a paper towel cutout in a bowl of diluted white glue. Next, help her spread the paper towel on a sheet of black paper. Encourage her to press her fingers in light gray paint and then "dance" them across the cutout to make crater-like prints. Finally, have the child tell what she knows about the moon. Use a white crayon or gel pen to write her words below the moon.

Fun Variations!

- Cut the paper towels so they resemble different moon phases.
- Add yellow paint to the diluted glue so the moon resembles cheese.
- Glue a die-cut cow above the moon.
- Layer torn paper towel or small paper towel circles on the wet project for more texture.

Paula Bateman
Hunter's Glen Childhood Learning Center
Plano, TX

The moon is in the sky. It is white and has bumps.

-Sari

COLLECT THE ROCKS

Developing fine-motor skills, engaging in imaginary play

Spray-paint medium-size rocks silver. Then place the resulting "space rocks" in your sand table along with glow-in-the-dark stars or craft foam star cutouts. Provide clipboards with paper, writing utensils, magnifying glasses, tongs, and a bucket. Have your little space travelers use the magnifying glasses to observe the rocks, "write" notes on the paper, and then use the tongs to place the rocks in the bucket.

Sarah Helms, Newhope Preschool, Mansfield, OH

THE SKY AT NIGHT

Participating in a song

Lead little ones in singing this jolly song about the night sky! If desired, have students make special "space shakers" to use for accompaniment. Give each child a small empty water bottle. Have him add colorful aquarium gravel (space pebbles) to the bottle and glitter (space dust). Secure the lid with tape. Then have little ones shake their space shakers as they sing the song!

(sung to the tune of "Up on the Housetop")

At night, I look up in the sky—
So many things catch my eye.
I see the moon, and I see stars
And planets like Jupiter and Mars.
Look, look, look—what a sight!
Look, look, look—stars so bright!
At night, I look up in the sky—
So many things catch my eye!

Suzanne Moore
Tucson, AZ

ASTRONAUTS ON THE MOON!

Developing presubtraction skills

Cut out copies of the astronaut suit patterns on page 279. Then cut out student head shot photos and glue each one to a different suit cutout. (Or have youngsters draw faces on the cutouts.) Transform each cutout into a stick puppet. Place gray play dough on a tabletop in a mound (the moon's surface). Then tell two youngsters a story about astronauts and have them use the puppets to show the events. For example, say, "Five astronauts are walking on the moon." (A child chooses five of the stick puppets and pushes them into the moon's surface.) Then say, "One astronaut is tired and decides to go back to the ship." (A child removes one astronaut.) Then have youngsters count the remaining astronauts to determine how many astronauts are still on the moon.

For extra fun, make a simple alien stick puppet. Every few turns, bring out the alien and say, "Oh no! It's an alien! Everyone go back to the ship!" Have youngsters remove all the astronauts from the moon and then help them realize that there are zero astronauts left!

SHEEP BLAST OFF!
Rhyming
Attach star stickers to a large piece of black paper (outer space) and gather white pom-poms (sheep). Read aloud *Sheep Blast Off!* by Nancy Shaw. In this rhyming story, the sheep from the series that includes *Sheep in a Jeep* board a spaceship that lands in their field. Fortunately, an alien is still aboard, because the sheep have a difficult time controlling the ship. The alien puts the sheep to sleep and then takes them safely back to the field. After the story, place the black paper on the floor. Say the word *sheep* and a second word that may or may not rhyme. If it rhymes, have a child choose a sheep (pom-pom) and place it in outer space. Continue with other rhyming and nonrhyming word pairs.

MAKING CRATERS!
Exploring the sense of touch
Provide play dough and a variety of items that make circular impressions, such as cardboard tubes and plastic lids and containers. Have a child pat out a chunk of play dough (or provide a rolling pin for her to roll the dough). Then have her press the items in the dough to make a variety of craters. Prompt her to run her hand over the dough to feel the impressions. Then have her roll the dough again and repeat the activity.

STARS AND PLANETS!
Expressing oneself through art
Have a child dab a clean toothbrush in white paint and then help her run her thumb over the bristles to spatter the paint on a sheet of black paper. After a desired effect is achieved, have students make colorful cork prints (planets) on the page. To complete this outer space process art, encourage the youngster to sprinkle glitter on the planets.

 tip For extra lovely art, have a child attach star stickers when the paint is dry!

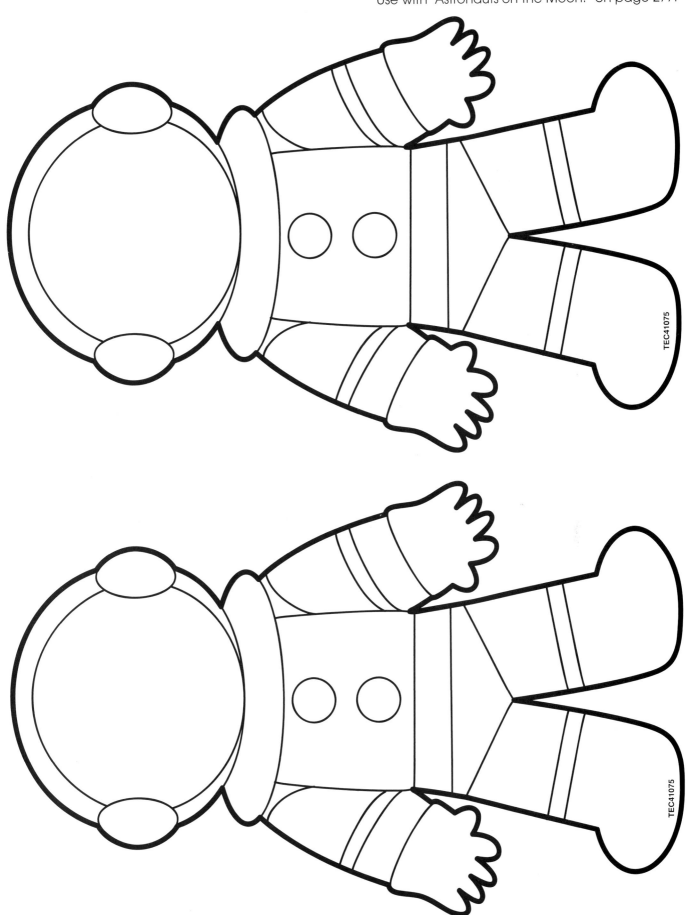

TEC41075

TEC41075

Sheep, Geese, Cows, and Pigs: Down on the Farm!

Sheep Asleep
Developing presubtraction skills

Choose five youngsters (sheep) and have them lie down and pretend to sleep. Lead the remaining students in singing the song shown, prompting one of the sheep to wake up and wander back to sit with his classmates. Encourage students in counting the remaining sheep. Then sing the song again, reducing the number by one. Continue until there is one sheep left. Then sing a final verse, altering the words as needed.

(sung to the tune of "Five Little Speckled Frogs")

[Five] little fluffy sheep
Lie down to go to sleep.
They dream of happy fluffy things—baa, baa!
One sheep wakes up and then
Wanders out of the pen.
Now there are just [four] fluffy sheep—baa, baa!

Add to the fun with these adorable headbands! To make one, decorate a black head cutout with eye and nostril details. Then attach the head to a paper headband along with ear cutouts. Glue on cotton balls as shown. This idea is brought to you by Joan Schmittel of Warrenton, Missouri!

Found on the Farm?
Investigating living things, sorting

Cut out a copy of the cards on page 283. Then place the cards facedown on the floor and gather students around them. Have a child flip a card. Help her identify the animal. Then lead students in reciting the chant shown. Have little ones decide whether the animal belongs on the farm or not. Then set the card aside. Repeat the activity with each remaining card, prompting youngsters to sort the cards into two piles as they go.

E, I, E, I, E, I, O!
Should it stay, or should it go?

Where Is Goose?

Responding to a story through art

Read aloud *Barnyard Banter* by Denise Fleming. In this story, noisy farm animals are all doing what they should be doing, but where is Goose? Goose flits through each spread chasing a butterfly. After the read-aloud, have students complete this adorable art project that answers the question "Where is Goose?" Make a class supply of simple goose cutouts. Tape each goose to a sheet of fingerpaint (or construction) paper. Have a child fingerpaint the page, painting over the goose. Then have the child say, "Where is Goose?" and remove the cutout to reveal the white goose shape underneath!

Lois Wachtel, Boca Raton, FL

Pig Tails

What can you do with rotini noodles? Try these two neat options!

- Cook the noodles in water tinted with red food coloring. The noodles will turn pink and look like little pig tails! Serve them with a little butter and garlic salt. **Snack**
- Place uncooked noodles in a resealable plastic bag along with a little rubbing alcohol and red (or pink) food coloring. Seal the bag and shake it. Then dry the dyed pasta on a paper towel. Use these little pig tails as counting manipulatives and for collage art projects. **Counting, arts and crafts**

Hayley Hanson, Little Acorns Child Care, Long Lake, MN

Who's in the Barn?

Dictating information to be written down

Who's in the barn? Youngsters decide with this project! Have each child color four jumbo craft sticks with a red crayon. Then help her glue them to a sheet of paper so they resemble a barn. Next, encourage her to draw farm-related pictures—such as farm animals, a tractor, and a farmer—in the barn. Prompt the child to talk about her picture. Then write her words below the drawing.

Roxanne LaBell Dearman
NC Intervention for the Deaf and Hard of Hearing
Charlotte, NC

Thank You!

Moo! Thank You!

Participating in a song

Lead youngsters in singing this adorable farm song filled with very polite animals! If desired, get a cutout for each animal and display it when little ones sing the corresponding verse!

(sung to the tune of "The Farmer in the Dell")

A farmer feeds the [cows],
And they say, "[Moo]! Thank you!"
There are so many chores to do.
Cock-a-doodle-doo!

Continue with the following:
pigs; Oink
sheep; Baa
geese; Honk
horses; Neigh

Cindy Hoying, Centerville, OH

Cow Spots

One-to-one correspondence, making a set

Give a child a copy of page 284 and provide a black ink pad (or a shallow pan of black paint). Write a number in the space on the sheet. Then help her identify the number. Encourage her to make a corresponding set of fingerprints (spots) on the cow, making sure she says the number each time she presses her finger onto the page. When she's finished, help her recount the spots.

adapted from an idea by Jean Ladden
Warminster, PA

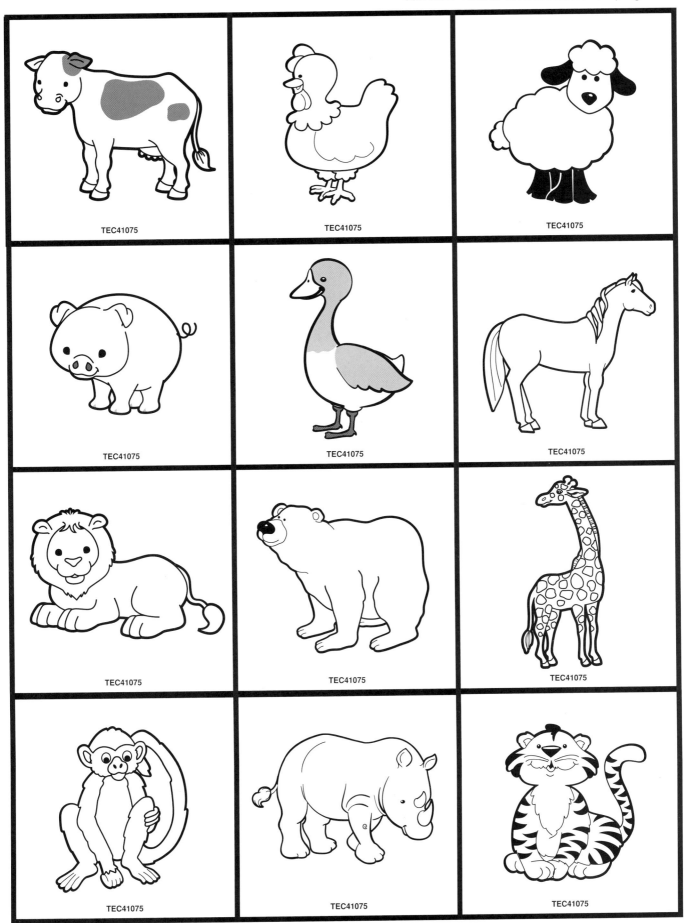

TEC41075

TEC41075

TEC41075

TEC41075

TEC41075

TEC41075

TEC41075

TEC41075

TEC41075

TEC41075

TEC41075

TEC41075

Note to the teacher: Use with "Cow Spots" on page 282.

Let's Learn About
Community Helpers!

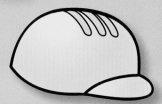

Little ones will love these unique activities about a variety of helpers around your community!

Delivery Driver Drama

Role-playing, gross-motor skills

Transform your sensory table into a dramatic-play center with a gross-motor twist! Empty your sensory table and place two chairs at the short end of the table. Now you have a pretend delivery truck! Seal boxes with packaging tape and place them in the table. Provide a clipboard with paper, a pen, and a set of keys. Youngsters are ready to deliver packages and keep track of their customers!

Roxanne LaBell Dearman
NC Intervention for the
    Deaf and Hard of Hearing
Charlotte, NC

Helper Hats!

Developing fine-motor skills

This display is an adorable addition to your community helpers unit! Print and cut out a large head-shot photo of each child. Also provide a variety of community helper hat patterns. (An Internet image search will turn up plenty of options.) Have a child choose a desired hat. Then help him cut it out and glue it to his trimmed head shot. Display these projects with the title "Helper Hats." What a cute display!

Sarah A. Gilmore
Springview Academy
Mt. Pleasant, SC

Beautician School

Role-playing

To create these fun hair-cutting props, cut lengths of yarn and then glue them inside small cardboard tubes as shown. Then draw faces on the tubes. Place the props at a center along with scissors and a trash can. Youngsters visit the center and trim the hair with small snips. You may also want to provide small paintbrushes for pretend nail painting!

Marla Householder
Jewish Community Council Preschool
Corpus Christi, TX

What Do They Say?

Participating in a song

Lead little ones in a sing-along to learn about a variety of community helpers!

(sung to the tune of "The Farmer in the Dell")

What does the [doctor] say
When [he's] at work each day?
[Open wide; let's look inside]!
[He] says it every day.

Continue with the following:
barber; Snip your hair just here and there
pilot; Skies are clear; let's give a cheer
firefighter; The fire's out without a doubt
baker; I'll make some cake and bread to bake

Suzanne Moore
Tucson, AZ

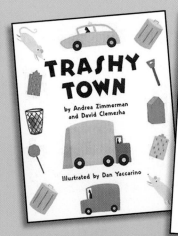

It's Trash Day!

Developing fine-motor skills

Read aloud *Trashy Town* by Andrea Zimmerman. In this story, Mr. Gilly, a trash collector, drives around the town gathering trash from the buildings in the community. Soon, Trashy Town is a tidy town! After the read-aloud, ask youngsters why they think it is important to have trash collectors. Then give each child a copy of page 287 and provide scraps of paper from your recycle bin. Prompt him to color the page. Then have him tear and crumple small pieces of paper and glue them to the garbage truck!

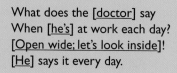

It's Trash Day!

Note to the teacher: Use with "It's Trash Day!" on page 286.

From Here to There!
Transportation

Car, boat, plane, or train—
focus on types of transportation
with these activities!

Take Me There
Participating in a song

Lead little ones in singing this song to get them thinking about different types of transportation!

(sung to the tune of "Clementine")

Transportation, transportation
Takes me where I want to go
In a car or in a plane or in a boat that I can row.
Transportation, transportation
Helps me get from here to there.
Go by land or go by water or by flying through the air.

Suzanne Moore, Tucson, AZ

Make a Match
Matching letters, matching uppercase to lowercase letters

Make a copy of page 291 and color it as desired. Then make a supply of three-inch circles (wheels). Label pairs of wheels with matching letters. **For youngsters that need an extra challenge**, label pairs with corresponding uppercase and lowercase letters. Then place the paper at a center and scatter the circles faceup. A child chooses a wheel, finds the match, and then places the circles on the bicycle. He continues with each remaining pair of matching wheels.

Chalene McGrath, Discovery Elementary, Brigham City, UT

Keep On Truckin'!
Reading environmental print

Have a child use construction paper shapes to put together a truck craft similar to the one shown. Label the truck "[Child's name]'s Trucking Company." Then have each youngster bring a piece of environmental print to school and attach it to her truck. Display the trucks with the title "Trucks on the Move!" Help students "read" the environmental print in the display.

Deborah Dry, Methodist Children's Center, Cary, NC

Red Light, Green Light Redo!
Gross-motor skills

Have little ones sit in a circle. Then prompt a child to stand and walk around the circle, saying "red light" each time he touches a classmate's shoulder. After several taps, he says, "Green light!" The child tapped stands up and names a form of transportation, such as a car, an airplane, or a boat. Then both children move around the circle pretending to be that form of transportation until they return to their seats and sit down. Continue for several rounds.

Marisol Rodriguez, Holy Innocents Center, Hammond, IN

It's on the Map
Developing fine-motor skills, engaging in pretend play

Attach a laminated road map to the bottom of your empty sand table (or to a table in your room). Then provide a variety of transportation-related toys, such as cars, trucks, planes, and helicopters. Encourage little ones to use the toys to engage in free play.

Angela Lenker
Montgomery Early Learning Center/Head Start
Pottstown, PA

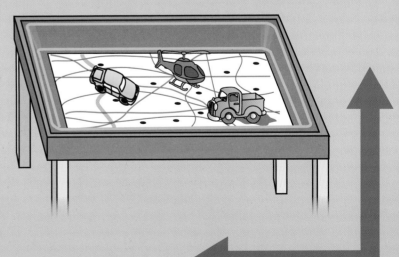

It's Adventure Time!

You're sure to hear lots of giggles with this action song that highlights some nonstandard forms of transportation!

(sung to the tune of "If You're Happy and You Know It")

Oh, let's go on an adventure [on a boat].   *Pretend to paddle throughout the song.*
Oh, let's go on an adventure [on a boat].
[On a boat], we'll take a ride.
We will travel far and wide.
Oh, let's go on an adventure [on a boat]!

Continue with the following:
in a car (Pretend to drive.)
on a bike (Pretend to hold handlebars and peddle.)
on a motorcycle (Pretend to rev the engine.)
on a camel (Bounce up and down enthusiastically.)
on an airplane (Hold out arms and pretend to fly.)
on a helicopter (Twirl arms above head like rotors.)
on an elephant (Slowly stomp and lean from side to side.)

adapted from an idea by Robin McClay
Jefferson City, MO

1234—Hawaii
5412—Alaska
3245—Japan
4123—Madagascar

Flight Numbers
Identifying numbers

In advance, write pretend flight numbers and interesting destinations on a sheet of chart paper. Ask youngsters if they've ever flown before and encourage students to share their experiences. Next, explain that flights have different numbers to help tell them apart. Focus youngsters' attention on the first flight number on the chart. Then have them help you identify the numbers. Next, announce that flight's destination. Have children pretend to pack things they would need for that location. Then encourage them to fly around the room. Repeat the process for each remaining flight listed.

Note to the teacher: Use with "Make a Match" on page 288.

Terrific Teeth

Make dental health a priority for little ones with these excellent activities that reinforce a variety of important skills!

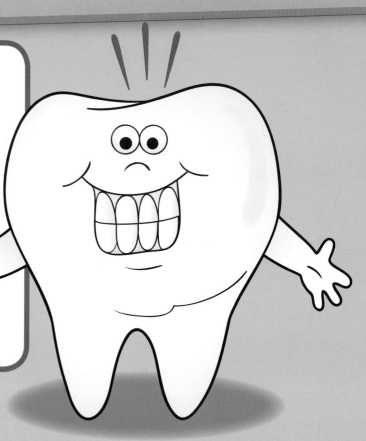

Smile!
Speaking

A smile is the best welcome of all! Explain to youngsters that it's important to smile when you're meeting someone new or greeting a friend. Ask students how they feel when someone smiles at them. After they share their thoughts, discuss how a smile is much more pleasant if the smiler has clean teeth and fresh breath. Ask little ones to share what they can do to have the best smile possible, such as brushing their teeth and eating healthy foods. Then have youngsters pass around a hand mirror and practice their best smiles!

Amy Bruening
Webster Elementary
Yankton, SD

From Dirty to Clean
Writing

Laminate a supersize tooth cutout and place it in a center along with washable markers. Allow youngsters to use the markers to practice writing on the tooth. After the tooth is covered with a lot of writing, exclaim, "This tooth is dirty and needs brushing!" Then allow youngsters to dip toothbrushes in water and "scrub" the stains away. Remove the remaining residue with a paper towel. Then encourage another group of youngsters to write on the tooth.

Karissa Rytting, Tadpole Preschool, Monument, CO

Brush Every Day

Participating in a song, gross-motor skills

Lead students in performing this action song that encourages healthy habits!

(sung to the tune of "Row, Row, Row Your Boat")

Brush, brush, brush your teeth.
Brush them every day!
Move your brush [up and down].
Scrub the plaque away!

Move finger (toothbrush) up and down.

Continue with the following:
side to side (Move finger from side to side.)
all around (Move finger all around.)

Jill Davis
Kendall-Whittier Elementary
Tulsa, OK

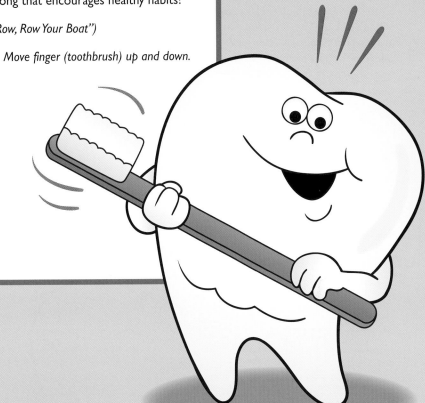

It's the Tooth Fairy!

Counting, participating in a group game

To prepare for this small-group game, cut out a few copies of the mouth pattern on page 295. Provide white linking cubes or unit blocks (teeth). Also get a paper crown, a bag of pennies, and a die. Gather four youngsters at a table. Designate one child to be the tooth fairy and have him wear the crown. Give him the bag of pennies. Give each remaining youngster a mouth and have her put four teeth on her mouth. To begin, a child pretends to lose a tooth and gives one to the tooth fairy. Next, the child rolls the die and counts the dots. Then, the tooth fairy counts out the same number of pennies shown on the die and gives them to the child. The game continues in the same way until all the teeth have been given to the tooth fairy. Then youngsters count their pennies and decide who has the most!

Susan Swiderek, All Saints Catholic School, Canton, MI

No More Plaque!
Developing healthy habits

Tint corn syrup yellow and then brush it onto linking blocks so it resembles plaque on a tooth. Allow the corn syrup to dry. Then place the blocks at a center along with toothpaste, toothbrushes, a tub of water, and a towel. To begin, discuss with youngsters that eating food and not brushing your teeth can cause a layer of sticky plaque. This plaque can cause cavities. Then allow little ones to visit the center, apply toothpaste to a toothbrush, and brush the plaque from the teeth. They use the water to rinse the teeth and then dry them on the towel.

Debby Bogorad, Loch Sheldrake, NY

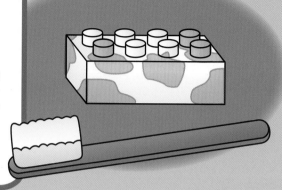

Healthy and Unhealthy Teeth

Happy Teeth, Sad Teeth
Graphing

Cut out copies of the tooth cards on page 296 so there is one card per child. Then place the cards in a bag. Place a blank graph on the floor or attach one to your wall. Program the graph with the title and labels shown. Have a child choose a card from the bag and identify whether it's a happy tooth (healthy) or a sad tooth (unhealthy). Then have her place it appropriately on the graph.

Stephanie Schmidt
Lester B. Pearson Public School
Waterloo, Ontario, Canada

Big on Brushing!
Developing fine-motor skills

These fun supersize toothbrushes look great on a wall display with tooth cutouts! To make one, glue a 3" x 18" strip of construction paper to a 6" x 9" construction paper rectangle. Then glue pieces of a white crepe paper streamer to the rectangle so they resemble bristles. This fun and easy craft is complete!

Jennie Jensen, Clarence, IA

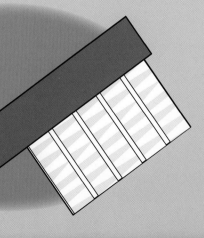

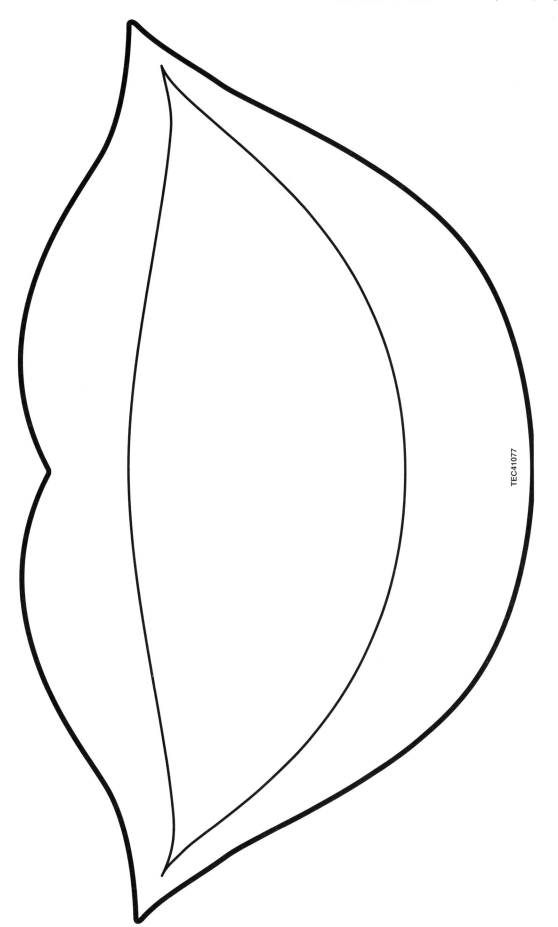

TEC41077

Tooth Cards

Use with "Happy Teeth, Sad Teeth" on page 294 .

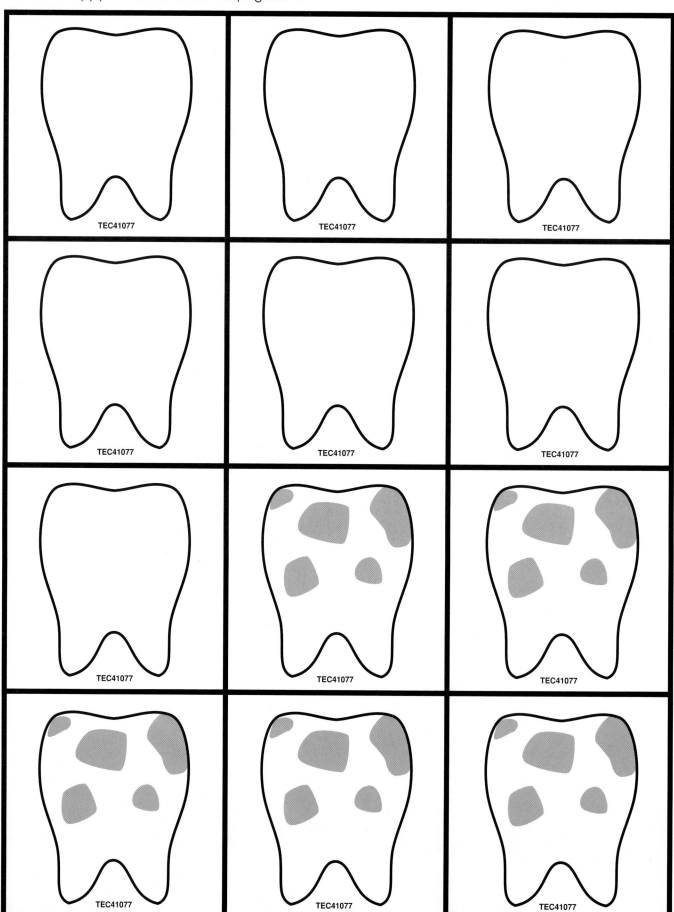

Going to the GROCERY STORE!

Little ones will relish these sweet grocery store activities!

A Meaty Center

Developing fine-motor skills, role-playing

Youngsters pretend to work at the grocery store meat department with this engaging center! Get foam trays (ask a local grocery store to donate unused ones or wash ones used for fruit or vegetables). Place the trays at a table along with red and brown play dough, resealable plastic bags, plastic knives, a hamburger press, and other things little ones can use to "prepare meat." If desired, also provide aprons. Little ones visit the center and pretend to work in the grocery store meat department.

Keely Saunders
Bonney Lake Early Childhood Educational Assistance Program
Bonney Lake, WA

Smallest to Largest!

Ordering by size

Gather several grocery store items that represent different sizes. Then choose three of the items and gather youngsters around. Help little ones identify the smallest item, the item that is slightly larger, and the largest item. Prompt a child to place the objects in order from left to right. Then ask little ones questions about the items, such as "Which one is the biggest?" and "Which one is the smallest?" Point to two of the items and have little ones decide which one is smaller and which one is larger. Repeat the process with other sets of grocery store items.

Jeanne-Marie Peterson, Charlottesville, VA

What's For Dinner?

Participating in a song, building vocabulary

Cut food pictures from a grocery store circular and place them in a gift bag. Then have a child draw one of the foods from the bag and identify it. Next, lead students in singing the song shown, including the name of the food item when indicated.

(sung to the tune of "O Christmas Tree")

Oh grocery store, oh grocery store,
What shall I buy for dinner?
Oh grocery store, oh grocery store,
What shall I buy for dinner?
I think I'll get some [name of food]!
Oh yes, I'd like some [name of food]!
Oh grocery store, oh grocery store,
What shall I buy for dinner?

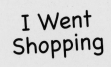

I Went Shopping

Print and book awareness, dictating information to be written down

These little booklets are a grocery store–themed twist on the text to the classic story *Brown Bear, Brown Bear, What Do You See?* by Bill Martin Jr. and Eric Carle. Have parents send in clean food wrappers, bags, and box panels. Make a simple six-page booklet for each child. (For a sturdy option, use tagboard.) Program the front of each booklet as shown. To begin, have each youngster cut out and glue a text card (see page 300) to each page. Next, have her choose five food wrappers and glue one below each text card. Finally, help her name each food item and come up with a descriptive word. Write her words on each text card as shown. Then help her read her story out loud!

LaToya Johnson, Lord and Johnson Home Daycare
Baytown, TX

Cereal Sugar Count

Identifying numbers, counting

Have parents send in cereal boxes. Then highlight the sugar content in the nutritional information on each box. Place the boxes at a center along with a supply of white pom-poms. A child identifies the number. Then he counts out a matching number of pom-poms and places them in the box. Be sure to emphasize to youngsters that it's important to watch how much sugar we eat because too much is bad for our health.

Cindy Hoying, Centerville, OH

HONEY BEES! Cereal

Healthy Options!

Participating in a song, developing healthy habits

Lead little ones in performing the song shown. Then prompt them to name healthy foods and unhealthy foods they've seen at the grocery store.

(sung to the tune of "If You're Happy and You Know It")

Healthy foods work to make our bodies strong!
Healthy foods work to make our bodies strong!
Fruits and veggies, meats, and cheese—
Yes, we would like some of these!
Healthy foods work to make our bodies strong!

Make muscles with your arms.
Make muscles with your arms.
Clap to the beat.
Rub tummy.
Make muscles with your arms.

Tami Crocker, Peter Pan Preschool, Palm Beach Gardens, FL

Check Us Out!

Following directions, developing fine-motor skills

These projects look great on a display! Take a photo of each child posed as if she is pushing a shopping cart. Then have her color and cut out a copy of a grocery cart pattern on page 301. Next, help her glue food wrappers and box panels (or grocery store circular pictures) to the back of the cart so the images peek over the top. Then have the child attach the photo and cart to a sheet of construction paper. For a display, simply attach the photos and carts to a bulletin board or wall with the title "Check Us Out!"

Jill Howard, First Foot Forward, Staten Island, NY

For a special touch, cut out a supersize cash register from bulletin board paper. Add it to the display along with a length of adding machine paper. Cute!

Text Cards

Use with "I Went Shopping" on page 298.

I went shopping.

What did I see?

I saw _____,

As _____ as can be!

TEC41077

I went shopping.

What did I see?

I saw _____,

As _____ as can be!

TEC41077

I went shopping.

What did I see?

I saw _____,

As _____ as can be!

TEC41077

I went shopping.

What did I see?

I saw _____,

As _____ as can be!

TEC41077

I went shopping.

What did I see?

I saw _____,

As _____ as can be!

TEC41077

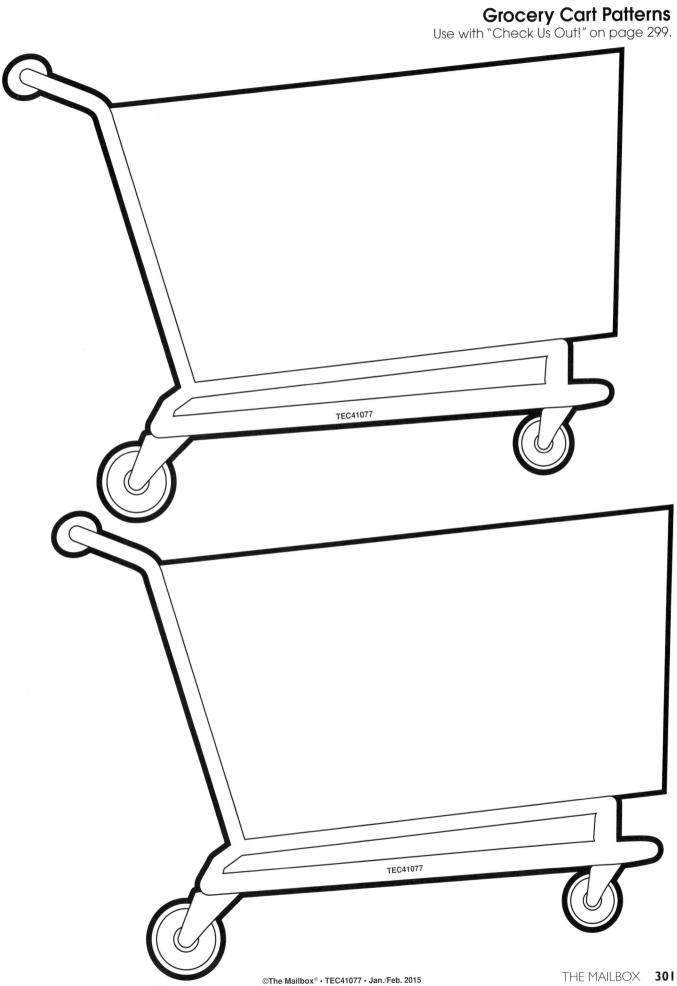

TEC41077

TEC41077

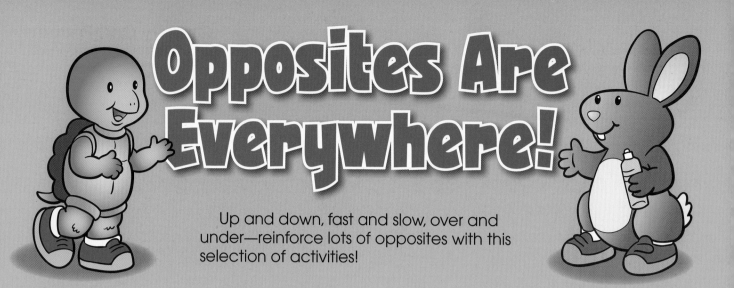

Opposites Are Everywhere!

Up and down, fast and slow, over and under—reinforce lots of opposites with this selection of activities!

Let's Look Around!

Participating in a group activity

Introduce opposites to little ones with this simple idea! Get two props from your classroom, such as two identical blocks. Ask, "Are these two blocks the same?" When little ones respond that they are indeed exactly the same, ask them how they know this. Next, introduce the term *opposites*. Tell youngsters that opposites are exactly different from each other. Then have little ones take an opposites tour of the room, having volunteers turn the light off and on, open and shut cabinets, jump up and down on the carpet, and pull a chair out and push it in. In each example, help students name the opposites.

Donna Olp, St. Gregory the Great Preschool, South Euclid, OH
Susan Neaveill, Champaign, IL

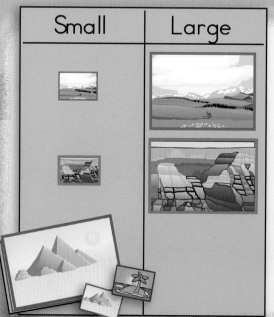

Large and Small

Sorting, comparing size

Gather old calendars and remove the large pictures. Then cut out the small pictures provided on the back of the calendar. Make a simple chart from bulletin board paper like the one shown. Place the chart on your floor. Then stack the large pictures and scatter the small ones nearby. To begin, prompt little ones to name the opposite of large (*small*). Then hold up one of the large pictures. Say, "This picture is large!" Place the large picture on the chart. Then ask, "Who can find the matching small picture?" Have a volunteer find the matching picture and place it on the chart. Have the volunteer pat each picture and say, "Small, large!" appropriately. Continue with each remaining picture pairing.

Robin Saxe, Kiddie Campus, Utica, NY

The Over-Under Game

Gross-motor skills

Help little ones name the opposite of over *(under)*. Then invite them to play this engaging game! Depending on your class size, have little ones stand back-to-front in one or two lines. (Make sure there is room between each child and his classmates.) Give the leader of each line a ball. Then have him pass the ball over his head to the next child in line, prompting each child to say "over" appropriately. Have students continue until the ball has gone all the way down the line and back. Then repeat the process, having youngsters pass the ball under their legs.

Jennifer Langford, Valley View Baptist Preschool, Tuscaloosa, AL

So Many Opposites

Participating in a song

Lead little ones in performing this active opposites song. Then help them name and demonstrate different opposites, such as left and right, in and out, on and off, and hard and soft.

(sung to the tune of "This Old Man")

High and low,
Fast and slow,
Up and down,
And smile and frown—
These are opposites.
Now, let's all name a few.
I like opposites, don't you?

Reach up high; touch the floor.
Jog in place quickly; walk slowly.
Point up; point down.
Smile; frown.

Suzanne Moore, Tucson, AZ

Fast and Slow

Exploring the tempo of music

Give opposites practice a musical twist with this project. Give each child a sheet of paper that has been divided in half and labeled as shown. Then introduce students to the opposites fast and slow. Next, play a recording of fast music. As it plays, prompt students to draw on the side of the paper labeled "Fast." Repeat the process with a slow selection of music and the remaining paper half.

Roxanne LaBell Dearman
NC Intervention for the Deaf and Hard of Hearing
Charlotte, NC

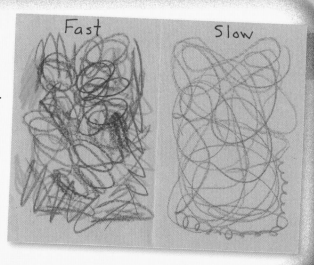

Splish, Splash, Ribbit! Down by the Pond

These pleasing pond ideas and activities are perfect for a preschool springtime!

Flashy Minnows!

Investigating living things, developing fine-motor skills

These glittery little minnows don't result in messy fingers! Provide cotton swabs, gray paint, silver glitter, blue construction paper, and a box or container to catch the glitter. Before beginning this project, show youngsters photos of minnows (an Internet search will turn up plenty of options). Explain that minnows are common in ponds and have students notice how the minnows have shiny scales. Next, have each little one use a cotton swab to paint short lines (minnow bodies) on the page. Next, have her use the cotton swab to give the minnows little tail fins. Finally, have her place the project in the box and sprinkle glitter on the wet paint. Have her tap any excess glitter from the project into the box.

Janet Boyce
Hinojosa Early Childhood and Pre-Kindergarten Center
Houston, TX

Splash!

Splash!

Developing subtraction skills, responding to a read-aloud

Read aloud *Turtle Splash! Countdown at the Pond* by Cathryn Falwell. In this story, turtles sunning on a log get startled by various pond inhabitants and, one at a time, splash into the pond. During a second reading of the story, give each child a copy of page 307 and a green crayon. As each turtle is startled, have youngsters enthusiastically say, "Splash!" and cross out a turtle on the page. Have youngsters notice how many turtles are left on the page before continuing the read-aloud. At the end of the story, all the turtles are in the water!

Quack, Quack, Ribbit!

Gross-motor skills

Give youngsters a workout with some animal imitation! Take youngsters to an open area and have them stand in a row facing you. Stand several yards away from your class and turn your back. Then say, "Quack, quack!" On this cue, youngsters start waddling toward you. Next, say, "Ribbit, ribbit!" Little ones change from waddling to hopping. Every few seconds, turn around quickly, prompting little ones to freeze. Continue the game until a child reaches you. Then play again with two different pond critters, such as a dragonfly (flapping arms) and a turtle (slow crawling).

Kristalyn Gleason, Albuquerque, NM

Finding Food

Needs of living things, fine-motor skills

Little ones explore duck eating habits at this center! Partially fill your water table (or a plastic tub) and then add plastic bugs and green Easter grass (water plants). Cut several pieces of orange craft foam in the shape shown. Then fold the cutouts so they resemble duck bills. A child holds a duck bill between his fingers and thumb and uses it to snatch up various bugs and plants from the water!

Janet Boyce
Hinojosa Early Childhood and Pre-Kindergarten Center
Houston, TX

Are You Swimming?

Participating in a song, identifying pond dwellers

Cut out a copy of the pond dweller cards on page 308. Then place them in the middle of your circle time area on a blue pond cutout. Encourage a child to choose two of the cards and name them. Then guide little ones in singing the song shown, inserting the names of the two critters from the cards. Have the child then flip the cards over. Continue with remaining pairs of pond dwellers.

(sung to the tune of "Are You Sleeping?")

Are you swimming, are you swimming
In the pond, in the pond?
"Yes, I am," says [frog].
"Yes, I am," says [beaver],
"All day long, all day long!"

Suzanne Moore
Tucson, AZ

Hungry Frogs!

Sorting uppercase and lowercase letters, identifying letters

This literacy activity can be played indoors or outdoors! Get two pails and decorate them with eye cutouts and long felt tongues so they resemble frogs. Draw uppercase and lowercase letters on the pails as shown. Gather milk caps (or bottle caps) and use a permanent marker to draw a supersimple fly on the top and an uppercase or a lowercase letter on the inside. Place the caps in a container a few feet away from the pails. A child chooses a cap and identifies the letter (with help if needed). Then he "feeds" a frog by tossing the cap in the appropriate pail.

Cheryl Eklund
Mount Horeb, WI

Oh, Mosquito

Participating in a song

Lead little ones in singing this rib-tickling song, prompting them to quickly extend and retract an arm—as if it were a frog's tongue—when they say "zap!" Then, for extra giggly fun, have youngsters sing the song frog-style, replacing all the words with the word *ribbit*. Next, have them sing it mosquito-style, singing the song using a whining hum. What fun!

(sung to the tune of "Clementine")

Oh mosquito, oh mosquito,
Please be careful; have a care.
You are flying by a bullfrog.
He could eat you. Please, beware!

He is green, and he is bumpy,
And he has a tongue that's long.
Oh mosquito, oh mosquito,
There's a ZAP! And now you're gone!

adapted from an idea by Cindy Hoying
Centerville, OH

Design a Cattail

Problem solving, visual skills

Place long strips of blue paper at a center along with brown and green paint and creative materials to use for painting, such as pipe cleaners, cotton balls, cotton swabs, and sticks. Provide a real cattail or pictures of cattails. Have youngsters study the cattail and then use the items to paint representations of it on the blue strips. When the paint is dry, mount these artsy cattails on a pond mural or use them to decorate the spring attendance display on page 75!

Splash!

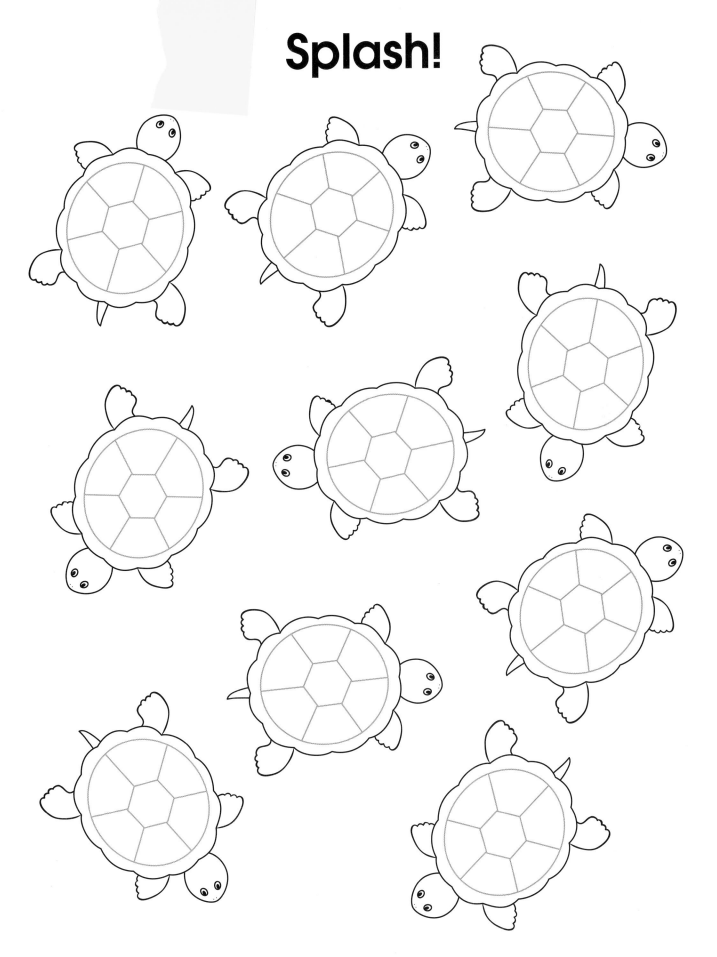

©The Mailbox®

Pond Dweller Cards
Use with "Are You Swimming?" on pag

frog

©The Mailbox®

duck

©The Mailbox®

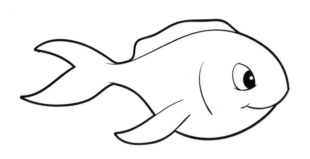

fish

©The Mailbox®

newt

©The Mailbox®

turtle

©The Mailbox®

beaver

©The Mailbox®

Hello, Summer!

Greet summer with activities
that are sure to make a splash.

At the Beach
Participating in a song

Have students close their eyes and imagine that they are at the beach. Invite them to share things that they might see or do while there. Then lead them in performing the song below!

(sung to the tune of "The Wheels on the Bus")

[The waves at the beach go in and out], *Children lean forward and then backward.*
[In and out, in and out].
[The waves at the beach go in and out].
That's how they go.

Continue with the following:

The fish at the beach go here and there   *(Put hands together; move them from side to side.)*
The dolphins at the beach go right on past   *(Move hand like a jumping dolphin.)*
My toes in the sand go squish, squish, squish   *(Twist in place.)*
The shovels at the beach go dig, dig, dig   *(Pretend to dig.)*

Cindy Hoying, Centerville, OH

Up and Down the Tree
Dramatizing a story, reinforcing letter names

In advance, prepare a jumbo coconut tree cutout and laminate it for durability. Place the tree, play dough, and letter-shaped cookie cutters at a center. After reading *Chicka Chicka Boom Boom* by Bill Martin Jr. and John Archambault, youngsters visit the center and cut letters from the play dough. Then they re-create the story by having the letters climb up the tree and then fall down.

Susan Norton
Busy Bee Preschool
Thatcher, AZ

Sunny Patterns
Patterning

Cut a large circle (sun) from yellow poster board and draw a fun face on it. Attach red, yellow, and orange strips of card stock (rays) to clothespins. Place the sun in the center of your circle time area and set the rays nearby. Clip a few rays to the sun to start a pattern. Then invite a child to continue the pattern by adding a ray to the sun. Continue around the circle until each child has added a ray.

Jen Rhine, St. Paul's Christian Preschool
Mountville, PA

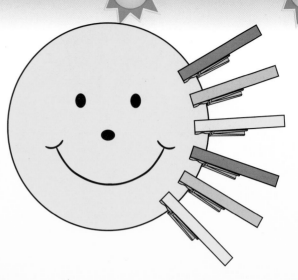

Antsy for Summer
Fine-motor skills

Provide cutout copies of the ant patterns on page 312, black tissue paper squares, thin black paper strips (legs), and paper eyes. A child crumples tissue paper squares and glues them to an ant. Then she glues legs and eyes to the ant. Attach these simple projects to a display as shown!

Jennifer Gemar
Tripp-Delmont School District
Tripp, SD

We're Getting ANTSY for Summer!

Boat Races
Exploring motion

Float small plastic boats in your water table and provide turkey basters. A center visitor fills a turkey baster with water, aims it at a boat, and then squeezes it to propel the boat around the water!

Margaret Cromwell
Grace Episcopal Preschool
Georgetown, TX

Watermelon Spin
Letter identification

Place a watermelon in the center of your circle time area. Also include a facedown stack of letter cards that includes several *W*s. Spin the watermelon. Invite the child who is facing the stem end of the watermelon to take a card. Direct him to show the card to his classmates and then name the letter. If the card has a *W*, say, "Watermelon wiggle!" Then prompt him to stand up and wiggle. Next, have him place the card aside and spin the watermelon to choose the next child.

Doris Sligh
YMCA Child Development Center at Colonial Williamsburg
Williamsburg, VA

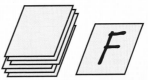

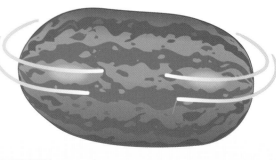

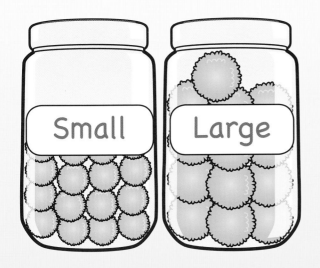

Catching Fireflies
Sorting and counting

Hide small and large yellow pom-poms (fireflies) around the room so there is one for each child. Set two clear plastic jars labeled as shown near your circle time area. Invite each youngster to "catch" a firefly and place it in the correct jar. After all the fireflies have been caught, ask students which jar they think has more fireflies. Then lead youngsters in counting the fireflies in each jar to check their guesses. Remind little ones that real fireflies should always be released after observation.

Roxanne LaBell Dearman
NC Intervention for the Deaf and Hard of Hearing
Charlotte, NC

Going Camping
Participating in a song

Show students a backpack and ask them to help you decide what to pack for a camping trip. Invite volunteers to name things you should pack. Then lead youngsters in singing several verses of the song, using students' suggestions and the ones listed below.

(sung to the tune of "Clementine")

Going camping, going camping,
Going camping by the lake.
I will bring along my [flashlight].
That is something I will take.

Suggested items: *pillow, sleeping bag, fishing pole, water bottle, hiking boots, bug spray, bicycle, swimsuit, marshmallows, sunscreen, binoculars*

Cindy Hoying
Centerville, OH

Ant Patterns

Use with "Antsy for Summer" on page 310.

©The Mailbox®

©The Mailbox®

INDEX